ACADEMIA LUNARE

Spec Fic for Newbies

A Beginner's Guide to Writing Subgenres of Science Fiction, Fantasy, and Horror

Tiffani Angus and Val Nolan

Academia Lunare
LUNA PRESS PUBLISHING

Cover Image © Francesca Barbini 2023

Text © Tiffani Angus and Val Nolan 2023

First published by Luna Press Publishing, Edinburgh, 2023

The right of Tiffani Angus and Val Nolan to be identified as the Authors of the Work has been asserted by each of them in accordance with the Copyright, Designs and Patents Act 1988.

Spec Fic for Newbies © 2022. All rights reserved. No part of this publication may be reproduced, stored in a retrieval system, or transmitted in any form or by any means, electronic, mechanical, photocopy, recording or otherwise, without prior written permission of the copyright owners. Nor can it be circulated in any form of binding or cover other than that in which it is published and without similar condition including this condition being imposed on a subsequent purchaser.

An earlier version of 'Spaceships' was published as 'Starship Stories' in *Sci-Fi: A Companion*, ed. Jack Fennell (Peter Lang, 2019). Material reproduced here with permission.

www.lunapresspublishing.com

ISBN-13: 978-1-915556-12-7

This book is dedicated to all our students:
past, present, and future.

Contents

INTRODUCTION — 1

CHAPTER ONE - SCIENCE FICTION — 5
SPACESHIPS — 8
ALIENS — 15
BIG DUMB OBJECTS — 23
ROBOTS, ANDROIDS,
AND ARTIFICIAL INTELLIGENCE — 30
MILITARY SF — 38
UTOPIA — 45
DYSTOPIA — 53
APOCALYPTIC FICTION — 61
CYBERPUNK — 68
SOLARPUNK — 76

CHAPTER TWO - FANTASY — 84
FOLKTALES AND FAIRY TALES — 87
WITCHES — 94
HIGH FANTASY — 101
SWORD AND SORCERY — 110
GRIMDARK — 117
HISTORICAL FANTASY — 123
STEAMPUNK — 130
URBAN FANTASY — 136
PARANORMAL ROMANCE — 143
TIME TRAVEL — 150

CHAPTER THREE - HORROR	157
GOTHIC HORROR	160
SUPERNATURAL HORROR	167
VAMPIRES	174
PSYCHOLOGICAL HORROR	182
BODY HORROR	189
ZOMBIES	196
SUBURBAN HORROR	203
TECHNO HORROR	209
SPLATTERPUNK	216
COSMIC HORROR	223
CONCLUDING THOUGHTS	231
AUTHORS' BIOGRAPHIES	232
REFERENCES	233

INTRODUCTION

A Few Words by Way of Greeting

This is not a rule book. That's because there is no *one* way to write Science Fiction, Fantasy, and Horror. Hopefully this is more of a conversation.

Between us, we've had 20 years of these conversations with students, with professional writers, and with each other. We've helped students explore the history and meanings of these genres, and we've helped a lot of people write a lot of stories in the process. We've seen the mistakes; we've seen them in the classroom, and we've made them ourselves. In response, we've devised strategies to help novice writers surmount the challenges of distinguishing and writing these genres for the first time.

The material in this book is based on our own teaching and writing practices, and draws from our own work with Undergraduate, Masters, and PhD students, many of whom have gone on to publish and even win awards for their fiction. The idea is to give anyone who wants it a sense of what it's like to write SFF/H. To that end, we operate here with the same principle that underlies our teaching: we're not interested in telling you what you can't do. We're not interested in giving you a catechism of dos-and-don'ts. This book isn't intended as a summary of doctrine or canon. It's more a buffet of *why-not-try-this* or *have-you-thought-about-that*. Because we want you to try new things and have a go at writing fiction in these hugely exciting fields. Most of all, this isn't a book about gatekeeping. It's a book about throwing the gates wide open for novice SFF/H writers and handing them a set of keys—though not the *only* keys—to unlock their creative projects.

So, *are* you a writer? Sometimes people hesitate to call themselves that unless they have… <checks notes> …a contract with a major publisher or a hundred published stories or a fountain pen carved out of a unicorn's horn or something.

A better question is do you *want* to be a writer? If so, congratulations! Consider yourself dubbed "Writer".

We wrote this book for you.

How to use *Spec Fic for Newbies*

There's a lot of writing advice out there in the world, so much so that it can almost be overwhelming. Certainly, it can be contradictory and confusing, especially when people try to cover all of Science Fiction or Fantasy or Horror in a single class of a general-purpose Creative Writing course! No, we prefer to put the time in. We've had the opportunity and privilege to design and teach many dedicated modules about these subjects. In the process we've found that what benefits students is focussing on one idea—one subgenre—at a time. This helps novice writers gain competency step by step, feel in control of their writing, and genuinely learn something about their chosen field(s).

Thus, we've structured *Spec Fic for Newbies* as though it's a series of classes we're teaching (and, in many cases, this material echoes our lecture notes!). Each chapter—Science Fiction, Fantasy, and Horror—contains ten sections, each one of which in turn focuses on a specific subgenre or recognisable genre trope (Solarpunk, say, or Zombies). For each we provide the following: a short history of that subject; either a spotter's guide to its different manifestations (such as different kinds of supernatural creatures or different types of Big Dumb Objects) or a spotlight on a certain writing element/technique, and sometimes both; a brief look at why it's cool to write that subgenre (please forgive our enthusiasms); a list of things to consider or watch out for; and two activities to get you started on your way. The idea is to give you a taster, a quick way into a variety of subjects under the umbrella of Speculative Fiction. They may not all be for you, and they don't have to be, but hopefully you'll give them a go.

Throughout this book you'll also find suggested stories, novels, comics, television, films, and even non-fiction sources that you can engage with if you wish to see published or produced examples of what we're talking about or if you simply want to know more about a subject. While we offer many examples, it's however very likely that your favourite novel or television show or movie isn't mentioned here (we know, we know; how can you *possibly* take us seriously when we don't forensically dissect the narrative mechanics of *Fireball XL-5* or whatever?!). This is just the nature of the beast. Would that this were a TARDIS and could contain infinities! Any one of our chosen subgenres could be the subject of a book like this.

Of course, something to keep in mind when approaching the writing, reading, and criticism of SFF/H is that these labels are mostly marketing designations for the publishing industry. They exist so that their sales offices know where to place a book in a bookshop. Calling something "Fantasy" or "Horror" is a way of helping readers find what they want to read next. Indeed, critic Farah Mendlesohn claims that the term "genre" when applied to SFF/H is a bit of a misnomer because these genres, especially Science Fiction and Fantasy, don't follow formulas in the same way that Romance or Crime Fiction do.[1] For example, you can usually guess that, at the end of a

---

1. Mendlesohn, 2003, pp. 1–2.

Romance novel, the couple will get together, and at the end of a Crime novel the criminal will be caught. But can you so easily predict what happens at the end of a SF story? Or a Fantasy story? Or Horror? As a reader you should be scratching your head, trying to figure out how to answer that question because you really can't! As a writer, too, you should be thinking of yourself less as checking off boxes and more as joining in that conversation we mentioned earlier, adding your take on a subgenre or trope or premise to the overall context of that element. This doesn't mean you have to go back and read piles of "classic" SF or Fantasy (honestly, nobody has time for that!). But it's a good idea to know what's going on in the genre now so that you can be part of what's happening! Always remember, the most important part of writing is *reading*.

Another idea threaded throughout this book is the importance of considering the story you're trying to tell beneath all the fun SFF/H elements of explosions and tentacles and robots. This is the theme, or, at its most basic, this what your story is *actually about*. (Consider this your first Element Spotlight!) Theme isn't "the moral of the story", though they can be related. It isn't teaching a lesson (trust us as lecturers: no one wants to be lectured to!). No, it's about one of the core strengths of Science Fiction, Fantasy, and Horror as narrative forms: it's about conveying a truth that you as a human want to share with other humans. Think back to when you were a new reader; your teachers likely taught you that themes were one-word deals like "love", "war", "grief", or "friendship". That's a good start, but now it's time in your evolution as a writer to stretch your wings and start thinking about how you can take that single word and expand it to a phrase or even a sentence. The more you can develop and focus your theme, the better you'll be able to write a successful story that resonates with readers. Novice writers often believe that the more general they make their theme (or their setting or character) then then more people will be able to identify with it. In actuality, the opposite is true. The more *specific* you make your fiction—even if it's about aliens or monsters—then the more convincing your readers will find it and the more they will trust you. Sometimes it takes a few drafts to discover your theme; believe us, we've been there! But if you're nearing what you think is your final draft and can't yet say aloud your more-than-one-word theme, you won't be connecting to your own writing as deeply as you might hope to. And even though SFF/H is full of cool stuff such as time travel and ghosts and magic, it's also about deeper meaning, which is something we hope you'll discover in this book.

Because even though Science Fiction is usually about the future and often (but not always!) set on planets other than Earth, and Fantasy is about magical realms or a tweaked present or past Earth, and Horror overlaps with each, they're all really about the here and now. All good fiction, regardless of genre, is about the time and place in which it is written. The classic example here is the original *Star Trek* series (1966–'69). Sure, on the surface it's about Captain Kirk making out with green aliens but, in another way, it's actually about race relations in 1960s America, it's about the impact of the Vietnam War, and it's about the struggles of being different. It uses SFF/H writing as a means of smuggling serious discussion of serious topics past those vested interests who would rather we not examine the problems plaguing our societies. The best SFF/H writing today does the same. It approaches big serious ideas such as the climate crisis or racial inequality or gender identity or the spectre of fascism from the side rather than head on.

Because what you're writing are never *just* stories about robots or elves or faraway magical lands. Don't ever let anyone tell you that.

What you are writing are stories about us. About now. About you and how you see the world.

Just remember, there are no rules.

CHAPTER ONE

SCIENCE FICTION

What is Science Fiction?

Whole books have been written in an attempt to answer just that question (indeed, whole *careers* have been spent arguing about whether it's "Science Fiction", "Sci-Fi", or "SF"!). When we think of SF though, we probably think of a handful of typical tropes: a rocket ship, an astronaut of some description, an alien (that somehow speaks English), or a robot (that somehow doesn't). We probably imagine a story set on a distant planet or in a far future defined by flying cars and easy interstellar travel. All of which is Science Fiction, but is hardly *all* Science Fiction and, for that matter, is rarely what Science Fiction is really *about*.

Like Fantasy and Horror, Science Fiction is often looked down on by the literary establishment. It's dismissed as juvenile. Or worse, it's regarded as some kind of ephemeral pursuit, which is a shame because the people who write it off as silly are depriving themselves of some of the most exciting, insightful, and inventive fiction there is! "But," people say, "isn't 90% of Science Fiction just crud?!". Such a statement was once put to author Theodore Sturgeon who, after considering the matter, replied that "ninety-percent of *everything* is crud!".[1] This is now known as Sturgeon's Law, and it can be applied to any number of fields, not just stories about megastructures on the edge of black holes, but also to realist literature!

But that, of course, still doesn't tell us what Science Fiction is.

Go search for a definition and you will find many—it must have this, it must have that—but they all tend to be reductive in one way or another. They tend to be limiting and exclude from the outset. A better and more inclusive way of looking at Science Fiction, be it set five minutes in the future or five millennia in the future, is to think about the *effect* it has on the reader or viewer. One of our favourite ways of thinking about this is the idea of cognitive estrangement as put forward by the critic Darko Suvin. This says that Science Fiction has an intellectual component (that'd be the "cognitive" part), meaning it engages our minds and, crucially, it serves to

---

1. Doyle, Shapiro, and Mieder, 2012, pp. 76–77.

make things *strange* (that'd be the "estrangement" part). What things, you ask? Well, anything, really! Anything can be made strange if you put it in a new setting that forces the reader to see it, *to really see it* anew. This can be as simple as a mode of transport or communication, or as complex as gender norms or racism or the economic basis of capitalism. By removing these things from our real-world context, the Science Fiction writer (you!) has the opportunity to examine them from a variety of perspectives, to explore different approaches, and even to challenge ingrained injustices.

So, if you were to hold us at blaster point and demand that we define the genre, we'd have to say that Science Fiction is the literature of *now*! By which we mean that Science Fiction is almost always about the time in which it is written (or about something happening in the author's life). It's a way of conceptualising and expressing big ideas that aren't easily captured. It's a way of exploring how things we typically take as normal are in fact deeply, *deeply* weird social constructions (Money?! Hereditary monarchy?!) that we all go along with; by setting these things on, say, Planet Zog, Science Fiction makes the weirdness of accepted norms plain to see!

That said, writers often have lots of preconceptions about the genre. The major one we've encountered is that people sometimes worry that they need to understand science. The truth of the matter is that you don't. Does it help? Sure, especially in terms of language and description, but it's often enough for fiction to be science *flavoured* as well as internally consistent. Another question that comes up again and again concerns the differences between Science Fiction and Fantasy. A recent social media spat revolved around this topic (we can say "recent" regardless of when you're reading this because the debate *keeps* happening!), and the seriousness with which people responded to the issue is a measure of its importance: "If it's a f*cked up sphere that's Science Fiction and if it's a f*cked up orb that's Fantasy"[2]; "If there's a robot or space ship, it's Science Fiction. If there's a MAGIC robot or space ship, it's Fantasy"[3]; "If Henry Cavill is wearing latex, it's Science Fiction. If Henry Cavill is wearing leather, it's Fantasy"[4]; or, one of our favourites, "You just have to look at the snout. SF has a narrow snout; Fantasy is broad and wide. You can also check the teeth: if they're interlocking, it's probably Fantasy".[5]

In actuality, and as we stress elsewhere in this book, these genres, along with Horror and, indeed, realist Literary Fiction, are just different modes of storytelling with different palettes of tropes, different sets of expectations, and slightly different—though often overlapping—readerships. None of

---

2. @OfSymbols, 2022, n.p.
3. @EvanNichols, 2022, n.p.
4. @last_fandaniel, 2022, n.p.
5. @ErinLSnyder, 2022, n.p.

them are inherently better or worse than any other. In fact, the boundaries between them, insofar as they exist, are porous and largely artificial (consider how the *Star Wars* franchise happily combines lightspeed engines and turbolasers with characters who are essentially wizards and ghosts!). In this way, it's probably healthiest to think of the differences between the genres as the following: "Science fiction is when a story and its audience benefits from it being discoverable by people looking for a story filed under the label of Science Fiction. Fantasy is the same thing but filed under Fantasy".[6]

What this means for you as a writer is that you should write *your* story.

Because, at the end of the day, Science Fiction is whatever you want it to be.

---

6. @AlexandraErin, 2022, n.p.

SPACESHIPS

A technological rather than supernatural imagining of the fantastic voyages underpinning pre-industrial stories such as those of the Argonauts, Odysseus, Sinbad, or Brendan the Navigator, spaceships are perhaps the most recognisable symbol of Science Fiction as a genre. So, climb aboard, set your controls for the heart of the Sun (or maybe not!), and let's fly!

A Short History of Spaceships

Overtaking the projectile capsules of Jules Verne's *De la Terre à la Lune* (1865), the spacecraft as interplanetary and later interstellar conveyance initially blasts forth in David Lindsay's Modernist journey to another star aboard a crystal torpedo in his highly regarded, but nowadays little read, *A Voyage to Arcturus* (1920). Though Lindsay "conflates science with magic and myths", he builds upon the scientific romances of Verne, H.G. Wells, and the other pre-Einsteinians to clear the air of mediaeval sky ships and prepare for the launch of the recognisable modern form of spacecraft in the pulp stories of the 1920s and '30s.[1]

The first appearance of a familiar interstellar spacecraft is usually dated to Raymond Quiex's 1926 story 'The War in Space' in which a diabolical scientist travels aboard a starship in search of a supreme power. This is standard enough fare for an era when writers rarely displayed interest in the experiential aspects of star travel and "just wanted to put their protagonists in new exotic locations" as quickly as possible.[2] More influential than Quiex—though still caught between "scientific plausibility" and "the desire of writers to get their protagonists among the stars"[3]—was E.E. "Doc" Smith's *The Skylark of Space*, serialised in *Amazing Stories* in 1928. Smith presents his craft as a *machine*, a product of the industrial age and technical imagination rather than the prevalent "magic carpet" version of starflight that would still flit in and out of magazines for years to come (think Leslie Stone's 'Across the Void', 1931).[4] Smith, though still handwaving (meaning not directly addressing or just making things up for authorial ease) the challenges of interstellar distances, places much emphasis on things such as the design of gyroscopic stabilisers, the internal arrangement of his craft, and the practice of celestial navigation. While creating a stereotype that later comes, arguably in retrograde fashion, to define the topical and rhetorical

---

1. Rabkin, 1977, p. 149.
2. James, 1999, p. 257.
3. James, 1999, p. 257.
4. Owl Lady, 2016, n.p.

focus of "hard" SF, *Skylark* offers a versatile and infinitely customisable architecture (even in Smith's own revisions) around which later writers could construct their own spacecraft through ever-evolving stylistic and formal variations.

The years after World War II saw aviation and nascent aerospace accoutrements such as wings and rockets taking centre stage. Captained by the likes of Arthur C. Clarke (the Earth-fleeing fleet of 'Rescue Party', 1946), Robert A. Heinlein (the spherical "Torchships" of juvenile novels such as *Time for the Stars*, 1956), as well as Samuel R. Delany (the proto-**Cyberpunk** interstellar craft of his prescient *Nova*, 1968), the starship developed across the following decades from an expedient protagonist-delivery system into an integral platform for SF storytelling in and of itself. This long voyage towards depth and technical realism—or at least consistent scientific fantasy proffered by authors with increasing knowledge of engineering, mathematics, and physics—culminated in the starship's post-World War II achievement of mainstream prominence. Such recognition occurred via both page (for example Brian Aldiss's *Non-Stop*, 1958, published as *Starship* in the United States; or Heinlein's acclaimed if politically divisive *Starship Troopers*, 1959), as well as on screen (consider the USS *Enterprise* of *Star Trek*, 1966-'69—"Not just a spaceship [...] but a starship. A very special vessel and crew"[5]—or the vessels of the *Star Wars* saga, which began in 1977).

For the most part, these starcrafts remained under the control of their crews. Yet the evolution of interstellar vessels into characters in their own right would come with Anne McCaffrey's *The Ship Who Sang* (1969) wherein physically disabled children are given the option to become "shell people", surgically modified in self-contained life-support systems to serve as a starship's "brains". Later variants on this idea include the literal embodiment of a starship inside a human head in Ann Leckie's Ancillary Justice series (2013-'15). Fully artificial consciousnesses, meanwhile, are epitomised by the near-godlike starship "Minds" of Iain M. Banks's Culture novels (1987-2012), who are largely benevolent but idiosyncratic characters defined by a combination of rationality, righteousness, and a tendency towards irreverent humour. Moving further away again from the masculine pulp-fiction ideal of dry, precise physics, and more towards character-based fiction, a new generation of authors are providing fresh riffs on the established starship leitmotifs of space opera, **Military SF**, and coming-of-age narratives. These include not just Leckie, but Becky Chambers's *A Long Way to a Small, Angry Planet* (2014), the volatile and complex universe of Yoon Ha Lee's *Ninefox Gambit* (2016), and the **Body Horror** of the decaying worldships (crossing over with **Big Dumb Objects**) of Kameron Hurley's *The Stars*

---

5. Roddenberry and Coon, 1968.

are Legion (2017). Beneath this work lies an even more vibrant and diverse ecosystem of online spaceship fiction (including *Clarkesworld, Strange Horizons, Lightspeed, Tor.com, Uncanny*, and many others), which in scope rivals—and in terms of literary merit easily exceeds—that of the pulps almost a century before.

A Spotter's Guide: Permission to Come Aboard

Philosopher Timothy Morton in his book *Spacecraft* (2022) usefully identifies eight archetypical space vehicles: arks, juggernauts, frigates, fighters (*pew-pew!*), explorers, yachts, what he calls the "*machina cum dea*" (a spacecraft so advanced that it might as well be magic), as well as coracles (or single-person, metaphorically "spiritual" space vehicles).[6] Yet for writers, a more practical way of thinking about spacecraft is to divide them into four broad categories of increasing energy consumption:

- **The sleeper ship:** Carrying passengers and crew in some form of suspended animation, these are popular in film and television (think the *Alien* franchise, 1979 onwards), as they allow storylines to begin as late as possible and so harken back to the pulp notion of the starship as conveyance. That said, many authors are savvy to the dangers of "leaving several centuries of travelling exclusively to automated processes"[7], which, presumably, is why stories set aboard these craft so often revolve around technical failure (see the cryogenic casualties of K.A. Applegate's *Remnants*, 2001). This implied rejection of the pulp's "Gosh, wow!" mechanistic faith becomes overt in the sleeper ship's closest competitor, what Stephen Baxter literally called an *Ark* (2009), and in which the critic Fredric Jameson saw "nothing but a pretext for the spectacle of the artificial formation of a culture within [a] closed situation": that being the generational spacecraft.[8]
- **The generational spacecraft:** These are crewed by generation after generation of people born and trained on board who may not actually ever see their destination (Molly Gloss's *The Dazzle of Day*, 1988, or Ursula K. Le Guin's novella *Paradises Lost*, 2002). Don Wilcox's 'The Voyage That Lasted 600 years' (1940) is the first story to commit entirely to the generation-ship concept, structured as a series of vignettes following a "Keeper of Traditions" who wakes from hibernation every century and witnesses increasingly traumatic upheaval among the ship's inhabitants. Heinlein defines

---

6. Morton, 2022, p. 20.
7. Caroti, 2011, p. 18.
8. Jameson, 1973, p. 57.

the generation-ship story's most recognisable pattern in *Orphans of the Sky* (1941; 1963) in which the descendants of an original crew on a centuries-long interstellar journey have forgotten that they're on a starship. Yet it's in Kim Stanley Robinson's *Aurora* (2015) that the generation-ship story achieves both its peak and its nadir. A typical generation-ship coming-of-age tale wrapped around a clear-eyed if pessimistic view of the difficulties presented by closed-cycle life-support systems, human biology, and the ethical issues of condemning unborn generations to lifetimes in space, *Aurora* serves as a metafictional rebellion against those who set the trope's initial course. Deemed by critic Adam Roberts to be "the best example of its sub-genre yet written", the novel is uniquely sceptical of the entire interstellar enterprise.[9]

- **The relativistic starship:** Craft travelling at a significant percentage of, but still below, lightspeed can take advantage of time dilation so that long trips will seem much shorter to the passengers. Poul Anderson's arresting thought experiment *Tau Zero* (1970) is the quintessential story of a relativistic starship: during an interstellar voyage to a nearby star, the starship *Leonora Christine*'s engines are damaged and, unable to decelerate, the ship carries its desperate crew closer and closer to lightspeed (the tau zero of the title). In the process, the disparity between subjective time for those on board and external time becomes impossibly great. More recently, kilometres-long relativistic starships known as "Lighthuggers" have been integral to Alastair Reynolds's Revelation Space novels (2000–'21); in his carefully constructed plots the effects of time dilation serve to slowly draw together spatially and temporally distant storylines across hundreds of pages.
- **Faster-than-light craft:** Dominating mass-media storytelling such as *Star Trek*, *Star Wars*, and so on, faster-than-light craft transcend our current understanding of physics, to the extent that critic Edward James deems them "closer to fantasy than to science".[10] Such craft allow the writer to bypass the inconvenience of Einstein's universal speed limit by using some form of space warping (generally attributed to John W. Campbell's *Islands of Space*, 1931; 1957), generating or navigating wormholes, or by travelling through higher or lower dimensions of "hyperspace" (again Campbell, *The Mightiest Machine*, 1934–'35; 1947).[11] Representative examples include the "jumps" of Isaac Asimov's Foundation series (1940s and '50s) and *Battlestar Galactica* (2004–'09); the inertialess drive of Smith's Lensman series (various dates due

---

9. Roberts, 2015, n.p.
10. James, 1999, p. 256.
11. James, 1999, p. 259.

to rewrites, 1937–'54) and its descendants in the work of Heinlein and Larry Niven, along with the "jumpgates" used to access hyperspace in television's *Babylon 5* (1993–'98) and, with variations, in the work of Banks (*The Algebraist*, 2004), Leckie, and the later seasons of *Stargate SG-1* (1997–2007).

Things That are Cool About Spaceships

Spaceships do more than simply link planetary systems or stellar clusters; they ply richly imagined routes between subgenres and even across the barriers between mediums. From stories inspired by historical and contemporary maritime adventures to those grounded in astrophysical accuracy, from fiction to television to comic books to videogames, from widescreen space opera to nuanced character studies, spaceships are instruments of peace and of war, of exploration and of commerce (both legal and otherwise), and, ultimately, vessels for human stories. More than that, however, spacecraft are vehicles for SF's own transformative journey over the last century and a half; they are propelled less by antimatter or improbability than by the unstoppable engine of our imaginations.

A Beginner's Guide to Boldly Going

- **Plot your course:** Ask yourself what kind of story you want to tell. Is it about the journey or the destination? If you're more interested in the interpersonal dynamics of a crew over a long span of time, then you're better off if your vessel takes its time (or, if it's a fast ship, finds itself constrained by technical or environmental factors, as in various *Star Trek* episodes). By contrast, if the role of a spaceship in your story is to connect an interstellar empire, then you're better off going fast! Thinking about this is useful as oftentimes our craft's speed will have a tangible impact on the structure of our story. For example, something like a cryogenic sleeper or gene-seed ship—the latter carrying frozen embryos instead of adults—"changes the story pattern by eliminating the social aspects" inherent in the generation-starship narrative.[12] Equally, a story employing a relativistic starship offers writers the challenges and opportunities of depicting time dilation, while a faster-than-light craft, in eschewing realistic limitations entirely, "shrinks the galaxy and allows the writer to imagine galactic conflict to be not unlike global conflict on Earth".[13]
- **Hire a crew:** A ship is only as interesting as its crew (don't tell the spaceship Minds of Banks's Culture book that we said that!). Does

---

12. Caroti, 2011, p. 17.
13. James, 1999, p. 264.

your spacecraft have a military hierarchy or a civilian leadership? Are your protagonists scientists, soldiers, civilians, or some combination? Perhaps they are pirates or prisoners or runaways. Maybe your ship is totally automated and discovered by a lone protagonist. In the same way that workplace culture is defined by our managers' leadership style and our colleagues' banter, a spacecraft's style is often defined by the kind of people aboard it. So, get cracking on that water-replicator chat!

- **Consistency, consistency, consistency!:** If your spacecraft is powered by gerbils running on a five-dimensional wheel, that's absolutely fine … as long as you don't turn around later and say, "Actually, it was antimatter all along!". This is to say that as long as your writing tends towards narrative consistency then your spaceship's scientific credibility can be based more on imagination. Keeping to the rules you set out in your story will help earn your reader's trust, but it can also serve as a kind of creative constraint, forcing you and your characters to solve problems without resorting to *deus ex machinas* cosplaying as technobabble.

- **Old clunker? No, a classic!:** While we're on the topic of realism… Are there space vessels and technologies of different levels in your story? Both the *Millennium Falcon* and the Death Star exist in the *Star Wars* universe but are vastly different narrative platforms. One's a scrappy smuggling ship rebuilt and modified by generations of questionable operators; the other is a state-level undertaking requiring literally galactic-level economics and project management! Even alluding to the presence of other tech levels within your story ("Hey, what's that other ship we can see across the space dock?") can add realism to your SF. Equally, don't be afraid to try something innovative. A reliance on easy tropes of faster-than-light travel—the idea of nonchalantly cruising to another star system at the press of a button—can lead to artistic lifelessness or, worse, fossilised canonicity (even *Star Trek*'s warp drive can become old hat!). Remember, there's no one way to tell a good story involving a spaceship or starship.

ACTIVITIES

Design your spaceship: Straightforward approaches to this includes simply sketching it, building it out of Lego if available, or even modelling it out of playdough. This will allow you to get a sense of your spaceship's physical arrangement, which in turn will help you understand how your characters are going to inhabit it and, hopefully, will even serve to generate story ideas. Start by considering the purpose of your ship—for example, is it a combat vessel or a luxury liner?—and then ask yourself practical questions: how large does it need to be; what kind of crew complement is it going to require; what kind of propulsion system is best suited (does it travel within a solar system or across a galaxy?); is it technological or biological in nature; what kind of mass is it going to have; and so on. Keep in mind that the real-world notion of form following function doesn't necessarily hold true in fiction! Sure, if we want to fly close to real-life physics then we'll need to acknowledge constraints such as excess heat, radiation shielding, and the balance between payload weight and power consumption, but if you want to take a lighter touch you can handwave physical constraints with convincing (meaning consistently!) depicted magic tech such as matter manipulation, effector fields, artificial gravity, or inertia dampers.

Interstellar traffic jam: Novelist Frederik Pohl once said that "a good science fiction story should be able to predict not the automobile but the traffic jam".[14] A good spaceship story is no different! Consider the "collapsars" of Joe Haldeman's *The Forever War* (1974) that enable ships to cover thousands of light-years in a split second, but that result in enormous relativistic time effects that leave them hundreds of years out of step when they return to Earth. So where are the consequences going to arise from the existence of interplanetary or interstellar travel in *your* stories? What happens when a gigantic cargo vessel gets lodged in a significant wormhole like a container ship in the Suez Canal, or when alien hackers scramble your network of hyperspace beacons? Remember: your characters may be embarked on a long journey, but something going wrong is a shortcut to drama!

---

14. Lamhourne, Shallis, and Shortland, 1990, p. 27.

ALIENS

Science Fiction has been fixated on alien intelligence for hundreds of years, from contact narratives externalising the anxieties of colonialism and imperialism, to interventions both violent and benign, to advanced beings who might not even notice our existence. From the allegorical to the incomprehensible, fictional aliens and alien cultures draw on a potent mix of biology, environment, and authorial intention. So, tell us… do you want to believe?

A Short History of Aliens

When we say "aliens" in a SF context, we usually refer to intelligent beings from another world or star system (hence why "extraterrestrial" is such a useful synonym), but they can equally emerge from higher or lower dimensions. They're embodiments of "difference" or of "the other" that often cause the reader or viewer to question their prejudices or preconceptions. They arrive in our social, political, or planetary realm by accident or design. They're here to offer us assistance or, perhaps, to seek it out. They're "the creation of a need", of a human desire to "designate something that is genuinely outside" ourselves, "something that is truly [nonhuman], that has no initial relation to [human] except for the fact that it has no relation".[1] *The Encyclopedia of Science Fiction* deems even the possibility of alien life an "existential provocation".[2]

Yet in many ways these aliens have always been among us. They've been "god, spirits, angels, and demons".[3] The Pythagoreans toyed with the notion of aliens in antiquity while, in the ninth and tenth centuries, moon dwellers and what we would now categorise as extraterrestrials cropped up in Japanese folklore and collections of Middle Eastern tales such as *One Thousand and One Nights*. Throughout the Renaissance and the Scientific Revolution, thinkers and astronomers such as Copernicus and Galileo challenged European notions of human centrality in the cosmos. Bruno the Nolan (by some dubious accounts, an ancestor of one of your authors here!) was burned at the stake in 1600 for his belief in a plurality of inhabited worlds. Meanwhile Johannes Kepler's fantastical *Somnium* (1634) portrayed demonic lunar beings, and Margret Cavendish's *The Description of a New World, Called the Blazing World* (1666) "uses an alien world in order to

---

1. Slusser and Rabkin, 1987, p. 6.
2. Killheffer, Stableford, and Langford, 2022, n.p.
3. Roush, 2020, p. 15.

outline her notion of the ideal society".[4] More chilling notions of the alien "other" were frighteningly realised during the Age of Exploration and the Atlantic Slave Trade that followed. Indigenous cultures in the Americas were devastated by European colonisation, and European slavers arriving in ships along the West African coast were the real-life embodiment of hostile alien invaders, visitors from a technologically advanced civilisation conducting violent abductions. In such a way, our own history provides a model for disastrous "First Contact" stories, what critic Andy Sawyer calls "the perennial tale of conceptual breakthrough in which humanity's place in the universe is irretrievably altered".[5]

Searches for such a breakthrough, and meditations on its potential consequences, predominate from the nineteenth century onwards. "Genuinely alien lifeforms" began to appear in literature in France in the 1860s (see Camille Flammarion's nonfiction *Les mondes imaginaires et les mondes réels* [1864; translated as *Real and Imaginary Worlds*] and his novel *Lumen*, 1887).[6] In the 1870s, astronomer Giovanni Schiaparelli observed a network of lines on the surface of Mars that he called "canali" in Italian. He intended to describe them as "channels", but the term was mistranslated into English as "canals" leading to a frenzy of speculation about life on the Red Planet that generated many classic tales of extraterrestrial life such as *The War of the Worlds* by H.G. Wells (1898). Fiction in the early twentieth century still portrayed aliens either as analogues of mythological figures—such as the vampiric Medusa or metaphorical minotaur that inspired Catherine Lucille Moore's best-known stories including 'Shambleau' (1933) and 'Black Thirst' (1934)—or, more commonly, through the colonial lens of white men (Tarzan creator Edgar Rice Burroughs's Barsoom stories (1912–1943), in which the former Confederate army captain John Carter is transported to an exoticised Mars). Yet more inventive lifeforms and richly imagined biospheres began to appear throughout the late 1930s and '40s, with work increasingly rooted less in Fantasy and more in evolutionary biology, as writers slowly sought to introduce more complex alien characters and strains of thought. As with stories about **Starships**, the result was a transition from gee-whiz stock imagery towards deeper interrogations of metaphorical and narrative possibilities. Though "Cold War panics about visitations by hostile aliens" predictably dominated SF and films from the 1950s and '60s,[7] the likes of Arthur C. Clarke in 'The Sentinel' (1951) and Stanisław Lem (in *Solaris*, 1961, and *His Master's Voice*, 1968) began to "use the alien-

---

4. Asselin, 2019, p. 74.
5. Sawyer, 2011, p. 108.
6. Killheffer, Stableford, and Langford, 2022, n.p.
7. Neal, 2014, p. 63.

encounter to probe the limits of human knowledge and understanding",[8] while Ursula K. Le Guin's Hainish sequence (1960s–'70s) offers "extended meditations upon the encounter with the alien" that "tend to center upon setting aside ego and materialist interests for the more utopian dynamic of communication, sharing, and empathy".[9] Later again, popular films such as *Close Encounters of the Third Kind* (dir. Steven Spielberg, 1977) drew direct inspiration from the real-world Search for Extraterrestrial Intelligence (SETI) programme, while the influential *Alien* (dir. Ridley Scott, 1979) turned the horror of colonial, biological, and economic violation back upon avatars of extractive western practices through the stunning Xenomorph performance by Nigerian visual artist Bolaji Badejo. Similar reflections on aliens as breaches of human bodily integrity, often with a psycho-sexual undertone, filtered through a resurgence of the "Supernatural Kidnap Narrative" in the UFO/abduction stories of the 1980s and '90s.[10] Whitley Strieber's *Communion: A True Story* (1987), for example, purported to be an account of the author's own terrifying alien encounters, one that went on to influence the racial purity panic of mainstream properties such as *The X-Files* (1993–2002).[11] Though a more nuanced version of that era's preoccupation with human/alien hybridisation underpins Octavia E. Butler's *Lilith's Brood* series (1987–'89).

Move away from the Anglo-American/European context, however, and we see how the alien or the other is framed differently by other cultures. For instance, political, organisational, and social responses to the existence of extraterrestrials predominate in Chinese author Cixin Liu's Three Body Problem trilogy (2006–'10). Meanwhile, as author and critic Miriam C. Spiers argues, many Indigenous American literary traditions portray the narrative of the monstrous other through a lens of "kinship" rather than conquest and annihilation.[12] In other cases, contemporary alien stories offer fertile ground for the interrogation of "racial and gender anxieties".[13] *District 9* (dir. Neill Blomkamp, 2009) tells a story of xenophobia and segregation directly inspired by South Africa's real life District Six, an area of Cape Town from which 60,000 inhabitants were forcibly relocated during the 1970s by the apartheid regime. Nonetheless, the film suffers from "problematic racial constructions,"[14] vilifying Nigerians in particular "even as it preaches empathy for the Other".[15] A powerful riposte to this is found in

---

8. Malmgren, 1993, p. 16.
9. Johnstone, 2019, p. 158.
10. Bullard, 1989), pp. 147–170.
11. Newman and Baumeister, 1996, pp. 99–126.
12. Spiers, 2021, p. 11.
13. Sawyer, 2011, p. 108.
14. Brooks, 2016, n.p.
15. Miller, 2014, n.p.

Nnedi Okorafor's enthralling *Lagoon* (2014). Set in Lagos, Africa's largest city, Okorafor's novel is a first-contact story directly inspired by the author's frustration and "righteous anger" with Blomkamp's film.[16] Okorafor, who pointedly mentions that the arrival of extraterrestrials is not the first invasion of Nigeria, gleefully blurs genre boundaries between alien arrival stories, West African folklore, socio-political critique, and eco-fiction (see also Tade Thompson's *Rosewater*, 2016).[17] In that way, the best contemporary fiction featuring extraterrestrials acknowledges stories about aliens for what they have always been: stories about how we see ourselves.

A Spotter's Guide: Who's Who?

The spectrum of alienness is vast, ranging from beings virtually identical to humans, to the bumpy foreheads that dominate on television, to blobs, reptiles, insectoids, post-organic synthetic life, and even sentient stars (as in Olaf Stapledon's *Star Maker*, 1937). Are there any limits? Most certainly not! But there are some alien archetypes that serve as useful starting points for any novice writer. And remember, it's always possible to mix-and-match!

- **The ancients:** These are also known as The First Ones (often includes aliens offering A Helping Hand). They are impossibly old beings—sometimes extinct species or forerunner races who've transcended the material plane—whose influence is often perceived rather than encountered directly. Story and character motivations commonly take the shape of their abandoned artifacts (see **Big Dumb Objects**), their databases of scientific knowledge, or their pseudo-spiritual teachings (The Ancients of *Stargate SG-1* did a good trade in all of these!). They assist in our characters' quests for ultimate wisdom about the universe, in many ways the keenest desire of the SF writer and reader. Of course, there is some overlap here with…
- **The enigmas:** This type includes Non-Corporeal Entities and Introvert Species. A good example of such enigmatic aliens is found in *Arrival* (dir. Denis Villeneuve, 2016) based on Ted Chiang's novella *Story of Your Life*, 1998). These can be both enjoyable and challenging to write as they lure readers into probing "the limitations of being human".[18] They suggest "the possibility of transcending those limits" while, simultaneously, tempting the writer to ruin the effect by explaining just too much about these beings' origin and motivation.[19]

---

16. Brooks, 2016, n.p.
17. Okorafor, 2014.
18. Malmgren, 1993, p. 17.
19. Malmgren, 1993, p. 17.

- **The allies:** These are peer and near-peer species to humanity. Predominating in mass-media storytelling (think *Star Trek*'s Vulcans), ally species are a staple of modern SF. This is, perhaps as academic Gary Westfahl put it, because humans "crave companionship in a vast, cold universe and aliens may represent hopeful, compensatory images of the strange friends we have been unable to find".[20] Ally species offer writers a shorthand for galactic cosmopolitanism and diversity via vibrant scenes of cantinas and spaceports (and now you have a Mos Eisley Cantina music earworm!). But be warned: the closer you move to the harder end of the SF spectrum, the more "alien" your aliens are likely to become.
- **The adversaries:** Often militarily in opposition to humanity but occasionally in philosophical or religious conflict, adversary aliens offer a mirror image to the allies and to humanity itself. Many (perhaps too many) SF stories are driven by human/alien conflict, with authors such as Lem seeing this as a paranoid playing out of "fears and self-generated delusions on the universe".[21] Nonetheless, malevolent aliens committed to the annihilation of the human race and its allies continue to be a popular subject for fiction as in John Scalzi's *Old Man's War* (2005). A further mass-media subsection includes replacement narratives: aliens either duplicate a human identity or co-opt/corrupt our biological forms. In the mid-twentieth century, these were often political allegories (Robert A. Heinlein's *The Puppet Masters*, 1951) but nowadays are more associated with **Body Horror** tropes (*The Thing*, dir. John Carpenter, 1982; the television series *Peacemaker*, 2021).
- **Post-organic intelligences:** Sharing some narrative material with **Robot** stories, post-organic intelligences are aliens who have transcended their biological forms for something technological in nature (space is, after all, famously hostile to squishy organic lifeforms). They have transferred their mind-states to silicon or quantum substrates and, often, something has gone astray in the process. Sometimes they are robots or androids that continue to operate after their creators' extinction. Sometimes they are inexplicable. Consider the Autobots and Decepticons of the *Transformers* franchise (1984–present), energised living metal beings descended from—in a series of mutually irreconcilable origin stories—either consumer goods, a creator-god, or a semi-sentient alien artifact (the latter a narrative convenience that might help novice writers evade extraneous backstory).

---

20. Westfahl, 2005, pp. 14–16.
21. Lem, 1984, p. 247.

Things That are Cool About Aliens

Aliens are one of SF's most versatile tools, allowing writers to deliver serious social commentaries about our world or to craft comedies about the genre's absurdities. Aliens offer the writer a means of looking at humanity through a funhouse mirror (literally in the case of some prevalent representations such as the short or tall Greys with exaggerated heads and eyes) or imagining "something outside of ourselves",[22] which "breaks down reality, often fatally, for us".[23] Stories about extraterrestrials are often tales of extrapolation and speculation but, more than that, they trace "the progress of modern SF from its Romantic origins into popular and finally mass culture".[24] Wouldn't you like to be part of that discourse?

Close Encounters

- **Look inside:** Because we're human, we're limited by our human imagination, which finds it difficult to imagine anything outside of our own experiences and knowledge. This insularity can be a limiting factor. Writers have nonetheless "variously attempted to depict truly alien beings, the products of environments and histories unlike Earth's, sometimes even based on physical substrates other than familiar matter (e.g., radio waves or stellar plasma)".[25] As such, consider the extent to which your alien "adheres to or departs from anthropocentric norms", for this "is a function of the mental operation used to generate the alien".[26] Which is to say it's the writer's job....
- **Worldbuild using our world:** One method to adopt is to base your aliens on something unusual from Earth (extremophiles, for instance, or the spiders of Adrian Tchaikovsky's 2015 novel *Children of Time*). Spend some time thinking about what kind of planet your alien is from and how that might have influenced their biology and society, and how that has shaped your character. The implications of this are manifold! As novelist Becky Chambers asks, if your aliens lay eggs "how does that affect your architecture, or your concept of parenthood, or family, or the typical composition of a household?".[27]
- **Reach beyond our borders:** On the continuum of "like us" to "really *really* weird/alien/not like us", how "alien" do you want your alien to be? The answer is related to what kind of story you wish to tell. For

---

22. Spiers, 2021, p. xiv.
23. Benford, 1986/87, p. 23.
24. Rieder, 1982, p. 27.
25. Killheffer, Stableford, and Langford, 2022, n.p
26. Malmgren, 1993, p. 17.
27. Chambers, 2021, n.p.

instances of human-adjacent beings, writers can handwave similarities by way of "convergent evolution"; but for aliens who "think as well as you do, or better, but differently," we may need to accept that not every aspect of their motivation can or should be explained to the reader.[28] The aesthetic aim of fictional encounters with the genuinely alien is often to explore a transformative sensation, not simply in terms of biological contamination but in how they open the characters' minds. In many ways, alien stories like these are the most difficult and most rewarding to write, fulfilling author and critic Gregory Benford's powerful assertion that the alien in SF is "an experience, not a statement or an answer to a question".[29]

- **Variety is the spice of alien life (no *Dune* pun intended!):** Try to avoid the single-type-of-alien-in-a-species. Your warrior species can, and indeed, should also have farmers and doctors (even Klingons have lawyers!). In fact, non-dominant members of an alien species—say, a decadent artist in a race known mostly as religious hermits—can offer valuable perspective to the writer. Equally, pay attention to issues of diversity within your species. Human beings have representatives of many skin colours, genders, and sexualities; consider including similar diversity in your alien populations.
- **Early humans weren't idiots:** Finally, steer clear of the "Ancient Astronauts" trope whereby human monuments—the Egyptian pyramids or the Nazca Lines—are depicted as the products of alien visitors rather than indigenous ingenuity. It goes without saying that just because White people didn't do it doesn't mean it was aliens.

---

28. Niven, 1987, p. 16.
29. Benford, 2019, p. xiv.

ACTIVITIES

Extraterrestrial art exhibition: Any alien will surely have radically different sensory apparatus than human beings and so will perceive the universe in a genuinely different fashion to us (in the same way that philosopher Thomas Nagel once asked, "What Is It Like to Be a Bat?"[30], his thesis being that it's impossible for us to truly understand how that creature perceives the world). This is obviously a challenge for us as writers so, to practice, imagine you've been invited to an Extraterrestrial Art Exhibition. Describe the art of beings who hear X-rays or carve representations of gravity waves out of dark matter. What kind of art is created by aliens who perceive the world through smell alone? What kind of creative expression is practiced by post-organic intelligences? How do the alien artists explain their own art in an effort to bridge the aesthetic gap with humanity?

Aliens anonymous: Imagine you're an alien who lives on Earth. Every month you meet in a local restaurant with a small group of other aliens from across the galaxy to discuss your experiences of interacting with humans. Draw your participants from the "Who's Who" list above but try to create specific and distinctive aliens underneath those broad categories. This exercise should emphasise your characters' "alienness" (James Tiptree, Jr., for example, often depicted her aliens in various forms: "as bright lights, animals, plants, and sea creatures"[31]). Crucially, you should explore the qualities that make your characters different from humans. You can use them for social critique (what do they think of humanity?) or for comedy (what human behaviour baffles or disgusts them?).

---

30. Nagel, 1974, pp. 435–450.
31. Strother, 2019, p. 273.

BIG DUMB OBJECTS

Writers, like any force of nature, abhor a vacuum, and so it's no surprise that the history of SF is littered with attempts to fill the vast expanses of the universe with objects of immense size. For fictional characters, they are mysteries that hold the potential for transcendence. For the receptive reader, they evoke a sense of awe, wonder, and even terror. For the writer, they set a challenge: go big or go home!

A Short History of Big Dumb Objects

The term "Big Dumb Objects" (or BDOs) was coined by critic Roz Kaveney as a tongue-in-cheek description of Larry Niven's 1970 novel *Ringworld*.[1] Though the heyday of the BDO was the 1970s, use of the term continues for any number of preposterous things that so wow the reader with mystery and radical scale that one is willing to suspend not just their disbelief but their critical faculties more generally. Critics have engaged with them in various ways. For Gary K. Wolfe they're a subset of "manufactured" artifacts "embedding evidence of some specific (usually remote) time and place";[2] for Andrew M. Butler, they're a "colossal novum" or "new thing" to use Darko Suvin's term;[3] while for Raino Isto, their sheer size helps us "see beyond the phenomenological horizon of 'the world'".[4]

While some might prefer that we call these huge objects in space "megastructures", there's a distinction to be drawn here for the SF writer. Humans can build megastructures whereas the size and complexity of BDOs remain speculative in the material, economic, and purposeful senses. So, for instance, ancient Egyptians built the pyramids, which were megastructures to them at the time, while modern humans built the Burj Khalifa, which stands almost a kilometre high, as mega as structures currently get. Such constructions inspire wonder and in many cases admiration, but they're still "architecturally scaled".[5] They don't engender the same sense of the sublime that one associates with SF's essentially godlike BDOs, a trope for which *The Encyclopedia of Science Fiction* has settled on the term "macrostructures" to indicate a further step up from mere *mega*structures.[6] Typically, BDOs are artificial and technological in nature. They seem to present themselves

---

1. Kaveney, 1981, pp. 25, 26, 31.
2. Wolfe, 2012, p. 83.
3. Butler, 2012, p. 53.
4. Isto, 2019, p. 554.
5. Scharmen, 2015, p. 182.
6. Langford and Nicholls, 2021, n.p.

for our characters' investigation, but often our protagonists can barely begin to understand the object's purpose. BDOs thus make our protagonists feel small not just because of their size but because their origin and purpose defy understanding. As readers, we want to know who built them and why. What technological secrets do they contain? What, if any, transcendence do they portend? From such questions are intriguing stories made.

A Spotter's Guide: Spheres and Rings and Disks, Oh My!

Writing about BDOs involves a strong emphasis on literal worldbuilding. Sometimes it can be easier to grab one of the off-the-shelf varieties (especially if you're working to a word limit) and customise it for your story's needs. While these aren't the *only* kind of BDOs, they're among the most common that novice writers can benefit from experimenting with:

- **Dyson sphere:** For many people, this is the ultimate BDO. Dyson spheres are frequently depicted in SF as a solid sphere around a star (often with numerous gigantic entrances for spacecraft) with a radius of approximately one astronomical unit (that being the distance from the Earth to the Sun). The interior of such a sphere would provide a habitable surface vastly in excess of a terrestrial planet. For example, the interior surface area of the Dyson sphere in Bob Shaw's *Orbitsville* (1975) equates to five billion Earths, something that has profound economic and psychological impacts on a humanity previously constrained by planetary limits. The Dyson sphere is usually attributed to Freeman Dyson, who in fact proposed a spherical swarm of solar collectors or habitats encircling a star to collect solar energy. In a classic case of fiction preceding science, Olaf Stapledon had already proposed such a concept in *Star Maker* (1937) with whole solar systems "surrounded by a gauze of light traps, which focused the escaping solar energy for intelligent use".[7] Dyson spheres are a challenge to depict in fiction because it's difficult to relate their immense size to the perspective of humanoid characters. As such, they're often used as signifiers of a civilisation's technical and material prowess (as in the Dyson sphere mentioned as the heart of the empire in Ann Leckie's Imperial Radch trilogy, 2013–'15).
- **Ringworld:** Alongside the Dyson sphere, ringworlds are a quintessential Science Fiction BDO. First described by Niven, a ringworld is a rotating circumstellar macrostructure: essentially an enormous hoop that completely encloses a star at an Earth-to-Sun distance. Again, the vast interior is habitable—in the case of *Ringworld* itself something

---

7. Stapledon, 1999 edition, p. 179.

like three million times the surface area of Earth—with a breathable atmosphere retained by walls thousands of kilometres high along its outer edges. In Niven's *Ringworld,* an inner hoop of occultation panels or sunshades provide a regular day/night cycle. A functioning ringworld could accommodate trillions of lifeforms on a sculpted landscape of mountains, rivers, farmland, cities, and even shallow oceans, all in a thousand-kilometre band arching up and away from your characters in spinward and anti-spinward directions. A beautiful but inherently unstable setting for your stories!

- **Orbital:** Associated primarily with Iain M. Banks's Culture novels, and with the *Halo* videogames, orbitals are essentially miniature ringworlds. Rather than a hoop encircling a star, they're smaller ("smaller"!) rings that orbit a star in the same way a planet does. The diameter of Culture orbitals is generally in the range of three million kilometres, while those of the Halo universe are smaller again at only 100,000km. An orbital-style macrostructure offers a writer many of the benefits of a ringworld with far fewer of the technical problems to explain away for the reader.
- **Alderson disk:** Consider this the SF version of Terry Pratchett's Discworld, only vastly bigger and with a star in its centre (preferable a bobbing star to provide a day/night cycle). An Alderson disk (named for Jet Propulsion Laboratory scientist Dan Alderson) is like a vinyl record several thousand kilometres in thickness and extending, in width, from near its host star to a distance equivalent to the orbit of Mars or further. A thousand-kilometre-high wall would again prevent loss of atmosphere, and both the upper and lower surfaces of the disk would be habitable, at least in the so-called Goldilocks zone where the temperature would be neither too hot nor too cold. Even with this restriction, the human-habitable area of a BDO like this would be on the order of hundreds of millions of Earth-sized planets, with story and conflict potential presented by the possibility of different alien species inhabiting the warmer and colder regions.
- **Shellworld:** A shellworld is a spherical macrostructure resembling a series of nested Russian dolls, often with massive pillars running from the core to the upper surface. Individual levels can be tens of kilometres in height, and the variations between them present a writer with opportunities to bring radically different civilisations and cultures into contact within a single artificial planetary body. Often shellworlds are artifacts of long-lost civilisations subsequently settled by less-advanced species unaware of the dangerous technological secrets hidden in the object's heart. Other variations include the Matrioshka Brain, generally attributed to SETI scientist Robert Bradbury, an immense solar-powered structure comprising concentric spheres of computational substrates

and capable of hosting billions of simulated or uploaded sentient minds (perhaps even "resurrecting" the dead as digital constructs in transhumanist fashion). Charles Stross, in *Accelerando* (2005), presents Matrioshka Brains as a natural stage of the evolution for advanced civilisations and, who knows, we may even be simulated in one right now…

Things That are Cool About Big Dumb Objects

Containing multitudes (some enclose whole planets!), BDOs are an incredibly versatile trope for writers. Characters (and species and civilisations) are drawn to BDOs, which generate stories and conflicts by their very nature. Perhaps your protagonists have intentionally set out to explore the BDO. Perhaps they've crashed there unprepared. BDOs offer a ready stage for adventure stories, generational sagas, quest narratives, war stories, and epic romance. In some respects, they're also haunted house stories in space, their settings scaled up far beyond the decrepit mansions of **Gothic Horror** but equally troubled by secrets and lost souls. BDOs further offer an opportunity to blur genres together, there being no reason why a Dyson sphere or a shellworld can't bring spacefaring and **Swords-and-Sorcery** style civilisations into contact or confrontation. Moreover, BDOs are a wonderful way to generate one of SF's defining characteristics: a sense of wonder. They're an opportunity to write about scales beyond the human, about true structures of the imagination that confound contemporary science and technology, but, lest we succumb to hubris, BDOs can also be used to satirise elements of SF if we're so disposed. Consider J.G. Ballard's short story 'Report on an Unidentified Space Station' (1982) in which a team of astronauts seek refuge on a space station only to discover that it's far larger than they initially believe, eventually realising that it's the universe (and here a sense of awe becomes the kind of "bemused wonder" that Isto sees as central to the trope's effect on us).[8]

Big Things Can Make for Big Problems

- **Scale:** We need to think about how best to communicate the scale of our BDO to the reader. Many writers do this by contriving a reason for their explorers to travel on foot, which emphasises how long it takes to travel within the BDO. Others use careful description of what it's like to experience a BDO on a visual level. Because BDOs are simply too big for our human perspective to accept, they're disorienting. They should be of a scale beyond that which we consider possible to construct and,

---

8. Isto, 2019, p. 554.

thus, their existence (and that of their creators) should frighten us and our characters even if we don't want to admit it.
- **Mystery:** BDOs aren't just dumb because of their preposterousness but also because of their inability to speak to human characters. Silence rather than silliness is part of their narrative operation. Arthur C. Clarke's protagonists, when faced with the inscrutable interior of Rama (*Rendezvous with Rama*, 1973), can only speculate about its purpose. As architect Fred Scharmen explains, BDOs "present an array of incomplete, overlapping, and contradictory associations that cloud their precise meaning, even while they still seem to mean something".[9] Sometimes it's worth having characters champion radically differing origin stories for the objects. Other times we might actively deny our readers the explanations they so crave, which encourages them to explore the object in their own imaginations long after they've read the story.
- **Balancing description and character:** BDO stories tend to be hugely descriptive because of their subject matter and, while it's fun to develop an object, we run the risk of losing ourselves in worldbuilding at the expense of character development (indeed, this is a recognisable shortcoming of some of the classic examples). We need to be conscious of sharing the cool *gee-whizz* descriptions with drama and character, lest the cavernous spaces inside BDOs become, well, empty. It's often useful to begin with our characters engaged in some kind of small task or conversation, ensuring that we start to become invested in them as people before zooming out to or discovering the BDO. Other shortcuts to narrative action that can be moulded into story include the exploration of the artifact, as in *Rama* (the journey through BDOs is often a reflection of a character's "interior journey of self-discovery"[10]) or being trapped inside/aboard the object and seeking to escape, as in the *Star Trek: The Next Generation* episode 'Relics' (dir. Alexander Singer, 1992).
- **Who created the object and when?** If they were aliens or super-advanced AIs, how differently do they think from contemporary readers? How does their technological prowess call human superiority into question or cause us to reconsider our assumptions? On the one hand this could relate to the sheer mechanical stresses upon a BDO that likely exceed what any known materials or engineering could withstand. On the other hand, this might relate to the idea of technology itself. Because while BDOs are very often meta-metallic in nature, it's a big universe and so there's no reason why they couldn't be the product of advanced *biological* science (for example, *The Rise of Endymion*, 1997, by Dan Simmons features an organic Dyson sphere).

---

9. Scharmen, 2015, p. 180.
10. Butler, 2012, p. 56.

- **Innerspace:** How will we address the sense of enclosure associated with BDOs that are so often defined by their interiority? Do such vast but still contained spaces have a psychological impact on our characters? What's it like to wake up every day and see your world curve up above your head on a ringworld or orbital? What's it like to be claustrophobic in a shellworld? Are there Science Fictional ways to compensate for the paradoxical feelings of constraint BDOs can provoke? Greg Bear's *Eon* (1985), for example, sidesteps the huge-but-still-finite aspect of many BDOs by extending the interior of its asteroid ship through billions of kilometres of manipulated spacetime. Maybe you have similar tricks up your interdimensional sleeve?

ACTIVITIES

Inside the soccer ball: Go find a football or a tennis ball or a ping-pong ball. Imagine what it might be like to live on the inside of it. How might the curvature of such a world distort how you think of and describe things such as distance? Perhaps you don't see the gables of nearby buildings but, instead, their roofs as the surface curves away in all directions? What would it be like to be able to point to a river or a city or a desert thousands of kilometres away, and how would that affect your feelings about distinct places? This kind of thinking is important for developing the experiential aspect of a BDO for your characters. How does it make them (and by extension, the reader) *feel*? Spend some time imagining this scenario and write some descriptions of life inside the soccer ball.

Write the history of your Big Dumb Object: In this activity, try to answer some of the questions above regarding who created the BDO, when they did so, and why. Was it designed as a home or a weapon or a scientific experiment? What happened to the creators? Did they become extinct, or did they perhaps abandon it when they ascended to a higher level of existence? What has happened to it in the intervening billion years that it's drifted through space? Has it attracted the interest of other civilisations, or has it begun to malfunction and become dangerous? You don't have to fill in a complete history, and much of this material likely won't end up in your story, but it will *inform* your thinking about what happens and how you describe it to the reader.

ROBOTS, ANDROIDS, AND ARTIFICIAL INTELLIGENCE

Artificial life is a recurring trope in SF and, increasingly, is part and parcel of our everyday experiences ("Alexa, tell me about Asimov's Laws of Robotics."). Yet, in many ways, fiction about artificial beings are stories about *our relationships* with them and thus with each other. The kind of dynamics typically explored include master/enslaved, dominance/marginality, creator/creation, human-machine teams and, on occasion, even romance.

A Short History of Robots

We can trace the distant ancestor of the robot, what we might call Mechanical Eve, to the biblical Eve via "myths of origin of the female human"[1]; Eve was a being made for a man by a male-identifying deity, something that echoes throughout thousands of years of stories. Pre-technological versions of physically embodied artificial life, usually with some degree of autonomy, appear in many mythologies, such as the Jewish Golem, a creature formed of clay and animated by incantation and a series of Hebrew letters carved on its forehead. The eleventh-century Indian story cycle *Lokapannatti* tells of an army of mechanical soldiers ("spirit movement machines") guarding the relics of Buddha.[2] Later, primitive automata appear in Leonardo da Vinci's fifteenth-century notebooks and in the form of the fraudulent chess-playing "mechanical Turk" of the eighteenth century (spoiler alert: there was a person inside it!). Mary Shelley's *Frankenstein* (1818), while arguably not quite depicting the first robot or android (meaning "man like") being in fiction, nonetheless presents a form of artificial life. A better origin, however, is the play *R.U.R.* (1920) by Czech writer Karel Čapek. The title stands for Rossum's Universal Robots, a company that manufactures synthetic workers. Čapek chose the word "robota" to describe the artificial workforce, something meaning "unpaid labourer" in Czech and that, crucial to understanding any number of subsequent robot stories, is usually translated as "slave".[3] Moreover, Čapek's workers eventually revolt and wipe out humanity, an anxiety that recurs throughout stories of artificial life and intelligence to this day.

Just as significant in the robot revolution is the expressionist film *Metropolis* (dir. Fritz Lang, 1927), around whose android–or, technically

---

1. Stableford, Langford, and Clute, 'Robots', 2022, n.p.
2. Mayor, 2019, n.p.
3. Jordan, 2019, n.p.

gynoid, seeing as it presents as female–orbits a whole history of machines modelled after women who are alternatively demonised (Eve), dominated (Ira Levin's *The Stepford Wives*, 1972), sexualised (*Battlestar Galactica*'s Cylons) or liberated (Janelle "I only date androids" Monáe's cyborg alter ego Cindi Mayweather, 2003–'10). The following pulp era offered many robot stories, but the twentieth century's most enduring narrative developments in this subgenre come from Isaac Asimov's mid-century robot stories, collected in *I, Robot* (1950). Asimov's version of artificial life, more positive than others, sought to portray robots as machines rather than in metaphorical fashion, and can be read as a commentary on human morality. Hot on his heels, in 1954, George C. Devol created the first real programmable robot and called it the "Unimate", which, honestly, sounds like someone you spend all of the second semester trying to get rid of.

A succession of famous fictional robots followed. Stanisław Lem adopted a humorous approach in *The Cyberiad* (1965). Meanwhile, Philip K. Dick considered serious ethical and philosophical questions about android empathy and what it means to be human in *Do Androids Dream of Electric Sheep?* (1968), later the basis for the better-known *Blade Runner* (dir. Ridley Scott, 1982), a work that again foregrounds the fear of human centrality being lost in the face of robotic replacement. PKD's androids are fully organic and genetically engineered, so much like humans that they require psychological tests to tell them apart. Also in need of psychiatric care is the artificial intelligence HAL from *2001: A Space Odyssey* (dir. Stanley Kubrick, 1968; based on Arthur C. Clarke's 'The Sentinel of Eternity', 1951), one of the most famous computers—arguably one of the most famous *characters*—in pop culture: a completely logical being driven to murder by contradictory instructions.

In the later twentieth century, cyborgs—or cybernetic organisms, combinations of flesh and technology—further destabilised gender, sex, race, and class, as well as associated social conventions regarding binaries and the body (see Donna J. Haraway's influential 1985 essay *A Cyborg Manifesto*). Cyborgs, after all, are hybrids, and hybridity is a rich vein for SF authors to mine. Martin Caidin's *Cyborg* (1972) solidified the trope, but the ease by which cyborgs can be played by human actors has made them particularly popular on television and film screens. Classic examples include *The Six Million Dollar Man* (1973–'78), loosely adapted from Caidin's novel; *Terminator* (dir. James Cameron, 1984), and *RoboCop* (dir. Paul Verhoeven, 1987). Meanwhile, the African-American DC Comics character Victor Stone, known as Cyborg (created by Marv Wolfman and George Pérez), offers writers a case study in how the Black body in particular is too often portrayed in SF as a "person transformed from a metaphorical machine to an actual one".[4] It's impossible to disentangle Stone's character from the African-American experience of enslavement and, moreover, from larger representational issues stemming from a white supremacist culture. This character's cybernetisation is frequently portrayed as a joyless one that reduces him to a "liminal status between human and tool" (and here we will recall "robota" means "slave").[5] Stone's transformation from dynamic young Black man into "resident chauffeur" and "digitized administrative assistant" has the racist effect of rendering him neither threat nor competition for White characters (indeed, in some iterations, Stone is even sexually defanged by the cybernetic castration that accompanies the loss of his human lower body).[6] He's a cautionary example of how even stories about robots, cyborgs, and AIs are not immune to the malware of unspoken racial prejudice. A more nuanced instance of Black characters interacting with the robotic can be found in Dilman Dila's moving 'Red_Bati' (2020), in which a former robot pet faces an existential crisis when it's consigned to asteroid mining.

Of all the SF subgenres or tropes, robotic characters are the closest to reality in our technology-saturated present in which philosophers seriously debate moral machines and robot rights. We're surrounded by driverless cars, recommendation algorithms (if you like this book then why not buy our others?!), assembly lines of industrial welding arms, and endless social-media bots (only something like 38% of online traffic is generated by humans![7]). Always remember, we're now writing stories about robots in an age when robots can write stories about us.

A Spotter's Guide: Domo Arigato, Misuta Robotto

Robots come in all shapes and sizes, so it's easier to organise them via their function and their relationship to us. As ever, these broad categories can always be mixed and matched:

- **Killer robots:** The fear of a robot uprising waging war on humanity has been a theme of SF narratives from *R.U.R.* onwards. Often overlapping with **Military SF**, killer robots can be mindless automata, self-aware individual units, or even the metal muscle of evil or misguided AI such as Skynet in the *Terminator* franchise (1984–2019) or the Marvel Comics antagonist Ultron. Depending on their programming, they're entirely focused on their mission and often can't be reasoned with (such as the "toaster" Cylons from *Battlestar Galactica*, 2004–'09).

---

4. Sonofbaldwin, 2015, n.p.
5. Hampton, 2015, p. xi.
6. Sonofbaldwin, 2015, n.p.
7. Newmann, 2014, n.p.

This requires our squishy organic protagonists to muster significant force or innovative (often deliberately illogical) tactics against them. The most interesting characters, however, are those that can surmount their programming—even learn to feel—and become something more than lethal machines. Good examples are the character of Paladin in Annalee Newitz's *Autonomous* (2018), or the protagonist of Martha Wells's Murderbot Diaries series (2017–'21).

- **Pinocchios:** Carlo Collodi's 1883 novel following the adventures of a wooden marionette that wishes to be a real boy has proven the model for many SF stories about artificial beings that wish to become human. Pinocchios, such as Data from *Star Trek: The Next Generation* (1987–'94), intrigue us because they want the flawed, messy, human existences that we take for granted. We wonder why they would *ever* want to give up physical or intellectual perfection for eating Pringles in a snuggie after a horrible day at work. As such they offer a vehicle to question our preconceptions about ourselves and our societies (as well as existential conundrums such as "Would we sacrifice super strength to laugh at a joke?"). Asimov's novelette 'The Bicentennial Man' (1976) offers another good example, as does the android child David in *A.I.: Artificial Intelligence* (dir. Steven Spielberg, 2001).

- **Cyborgs:** Do you wear glasses? Have you ever had a metal pin implanted to help a broken bone heal? Well congratulations, you're a cyborg! Cyborgs are in some ways the most realistic intersection of the human and the robotic (and also play into the aesthetic of **Cyberpunk**). Their presence in fiction waxes and wanes but was particularly prominent after both the Vietnam War and the Middle Eastern military misadventurism of the early twenty-first century as maimed soldiers increased the visibility of prosthetics (and led to advances in medical science). Cyborg stories often begin with an injury or mutilation (see the underrated television show *Almost Human*, 2013–'14) after which characters run the risk of alienation from society. Meanwhile, some cyborgs are networked together, such as The Conjoiners in Alastair Reynolds's Revelation Space series (1990–2021), and consequently have difficulty existing in isolation. Cyborgs, like real people with disabilities, are often discriminated against in both overt and careless ways. Marissa Meyer's *Cinder* (2012), a futuristic cyborg fairy tale, follows a protagonist who keeps her prosthetic a secret for exactly this reason.

- **BioBots:** Advanced "robots" made from flesh and blood can be so indistinguishable from human beings that we question what it is to *be* human. Čapek's original robota are synthetic lifeforms grown in vats of chemical batter, but modern examples include the Replicants of *Blade Runner* and the humanoid Cylons of *Battlestar Galactica*, which look and feel human. Science Fiction has always been concerned with the blurring of the natural and the artificial, and biobots allow a writer's artificial characters to "manifest all the vagaries, emotions and individuality" of human protagonists.[8] The collapse of any robot/human division can translate into a breakdown of the enemy/friend distinction, and the best biobot stories raise compelling issues of personal and political responsibility towards the "other", as well as problematising issues of gender and race in fascinating ways.

- **Friendly robots:** Even in a story filled with dangerous mechanical beings, some robots can and will be friends with your characters and, in the process, allow us to examine humanity's relationship with technology. The classic examples are R2D2 and C3PO in the *Star Wars* franchise, but we can also find them in the **Solarpunk** Robot and Monk duology (2021–'22) from Becky Chambers. Another approach is to portray "Centaurs", or human-machine teams in which the AI assesses a situation, and the human character makes the final decision. We might also consider Chaos Robots, the likes of WALL-E or Johnny 5, who mean no harm but get into various calamities along the way. Finally, we have the "professionally friendly" type, the "sexbots", and companion programs (see everything from the male robot TN-3 ["Tony"] in Asimov's 1951 story 'Satisfaction Guaranteed' to the female AI Samantha in 2013's *Her*, dir. Spike Jonze). Your—and your reader's—mileage will vary with regard to the related moral and ethical implications.

Things That are Cool About Robots

As with **Aliens**, stories about robots and AIs are a chance for us to interrogate different aspects of human nature in allegorical fashion. They ask readers to consider how they treat others by telling stories about beings created in our own image. More than that, however, they are stories about how we interact with the technology already all around us, be that prosthetics or smart speakers or robot vacuum cleaners. Robot stories posit a world where the enslaved past is repackaged for the capitalist present; cyborg stories ask us to reconsider how we see and depict the body; while AI stories are often about the level of control we're happy to give up in the name of convenience.

Beware Malfunctions

- **Robot rules:** Some of the most famous "rules" (and we always use that term loosely!) about robot stories are Asimov's Three Laws of Robotics introduced in his 1940s stories[9]:

---
8. Tranter, 2007, p. 53.
9. Asimov, 1950.

1. A robot may not injure a human being or, through inaction, allow a human being to come to harm.
2. A robot must obey orders given to it by human beings except where such orders would conflict with the First Law.
3. A robot must protect its own existence as long as such protection does not conflict with the First or Second Law.

Asimov's intention was to write robot stories different from the *Frankenstein* model of scientist creates monster and monster destroys scientist. In the process he demonstrated how useful it is for a writer to set limits or constraints on their fictional world, with his laws generating much in the way of story material and unexpected—though somehow always logical!— consequences.

- **The uncanny valley:** You know how a robot arm welding a car is clearly just a device, but a robot such as WALL-E is cute and has personality, almost like a pet? This is because robots have aesthetic values, which is something that you as a writer have control over. The closer they come to something recognisable, the more we find them appealing. What you need to keep in mind is that as your robots approach appearing fully human, they can fall into what's called "the uncanny valley" (see **Body Horror** and **Gothic** for more). This is an aesthetic-emotional response to a robot or android that's designed to look like a person but that, let's just say, falls short of convincing on account of dead eyes, plastic skin, stilted movements, and so on. Worse, the effect can create anxiety or even *revulsion* on the part of a human! The uncanny valley is the gulf between human and "Oh, that's super creepy". It's useful to consider this when describing your human protagonists' reactions to your robotic beings.

- **Self-replication:** This is any autonomous machine capable of reproducing itself using raw materials found in its surroundings. Self-replicating (or indeed, self-*repairing*) robots are in many ways analogous to living beings in that they seek to propagate their form, often serving as a metaphor for consumption and environmental destruction. The well-named Replicators in *Stargate SG-1* (1997–2007) are a classic television example. The SF writer can always rely on the risk of malfunction for story material (see Reynolds's 'Galactic North', 1999). Some theorists have also proposed self-replicators whose complexity could grow in the same way biological organisms evolve.

- **The singularity:** In discussions of AI the technological singularity is the hypothetical future point (or perhaps past point in your story) at which technological growth becomes uncontrollable and irreversible, often taking the form of an intelligence explosion when AI becomes sentient and self-aware. Many stories investigate the unforeseeable changes to human civilisation when computerised superintelligence passes just such a threshold and begins to improve itself in runaway fashion. These stories typically play up technological paranoia to depict AI rebellion and the potential extermination of humanity (see: *Powers of X* by Jonathan Hickman and R.B. Silva, 2019) but, conversely, can occasionally show **Utopian** and post-scarcity outcomes (see The Culture series by Iain M. Banks, 1987–2012).

- **Who programs the programmers:** Can a robot be racist? Unfortunately, yes. Robots and AI are only as good as they have been programmed to be, and human programmers are prone to any number of malignant prejudices. Studies have shown that real-world algorithms regularly give preference to men over women and White people over People of Colour, and make biased assumptions about peoples' employment after a mere scan of their faces.[10] The data we feed into our real-world machine-learning algorithms can render them toxic; famously, a Microsoft chatbot "spent a day learning from Twitter and began spouting antisemitic messages".[11] Maybe your AIs have been radicalised by religious extremists (television's *Caprica*, 2010) or, perhaps, your protagonist is a software engineer designing anti-racist modules for robots? As ever, once you've acknowledged the problem, you can write about it.

---

10. Hunt, et al., 2022, pp. 743–756.
11. Buranyi. 2017, n.p.

ACTIVITIES

"What *I* did on *your* summer holiday": Write a short piece from the perspective of a self-aware household robot that is left alone while the family it's assigned to is away for a week. The story can be set in the near-future Earth or perhaps on a **Spaceship** or **Alien** planet. It should attempt to capture the experience of the robot in its own words: How did it spend the time by itself? Did it conduct self-improvement? Did it dress itself in human clothes and attempt to interact with others outside the house for the first time? Did it Netflix-and-chill with a cyber buddy? There's scope here for both pathos and comedy.

CAPTCHA: Did you know CAPTCHA is an acronym? It stands for "Completely Automated Public Turing test to tell Computers and Humans Apart" and was developed as a way to differentiate AI from human. In this exercise, your protagonist is accused of being a very advanced biological robot. They must prove to an investigator that they're human. To do so, they might attempt to describe their childhood or a particularly intense emotional experience. They might engage in philosophical discussion (what even *is* a human being?). They might detail their likes and dislikes. They might even begin to doubt themselves....

MILITARY SF

War stories are as old as narrative itself. As long as people have been fighting, they've been telling stories about heroic deeds or spectacular routs. Military SF, ranging from near-future narratives here on Earth to galaxy-spanning space opera, is merely the latest iteration of that. The subgenre differentiates itself from civvy stories through an emphasis on martial lifestyles, hierarchies, and procedures. Though, at its armoured heart, it's as much about characters choosing honour and sacrifice as it is about big honkin' space lasers.

A Short History of Military SF

Relevant precursors to military SF are to be found in late-nineteenth-century work such as George Tomkyns Chesney's novella *The Battle of Dorking: Reminiscences of a Volunteer* (1871), which describes the destruction of the Royal Navy by the "fatal engines" of an early doomsday weapon. Chesney in turn inspired *The War of the Worlds* (1898) by H.G. Wells, the originator of the **Alien** invasion subgenre that sought to bring then-contemporary military technologies to bear on an extraterrestrial menace (though imperial Britain's maxim guns, artillery, ironclads, and strategies prove largely inferior to the three-legged Martian "fighting machines").

In the pulp era that followed, much military SF was, essentially, naval fiction cosplaying as space opera, often inspired by both real and literary naval heroes such as the two Horatios (Nelson and Hornblower respectively) though, in a curious looping, work such as E.E. "Doc" Smith's Lensman novels from the 1940s would go on to inspire real Combat Information Centres aboard modern naval vessels.[1] In the post-World War II decades, a distinct "militaristic" strand began to develop in American SF, in particular via the juvenile books of former Navy lieutenant Robert A. Heinlein (see *Space Cadet*, 1948) and work by Andre Norton (Alice Mary Norton; see *Star Guard*, 1955).[2] Later again, SF writers began to interrogate various facets of warfare, producing stories weightier than their prior unexamined zap-gun escapism, often in dialogue with one another and with contemporary events. Among the most influential of these was again Heinlein with *Starship Troopers* (1959), essentially a Korean War novel in which "the ideas and the lethal weapons [... ,] sentiments and the battle equipment" of that conflict were "enlarged to the cosmic dimensions of fantastic planetary worlds".[3]

---
1. Peck, 2012, n.p.
2. Stableford and Langford, 'Military SF', 2022, n.p.
3. Clarke, 1979, p. 297.

Starship Troopers has been deemed both fascist agitprop (it glorifies military service as a prerequisite to citizenship) and a soul-searching account of how war is a form of endurance rather than entertainment, albeit one dressed up in a powered armour exoskeleton.

A nuanced rejoinder to Heinlein's militantism is found in Joe Haldeman's *The Forever War* (1976), inspired by that author's first-hand experience during the Vietnam conflict. The novel portrays war as a dehumanising and senseless undertaking that enriches vested interests while leaving the actual combatants alienated from society. It follows a student drafted into duty against an alien force thousands of light-years away from home. Relativistic time dilation during travel means that, eventually, centuries elapse on Earth during his absences, rendering life at home unrecognisable: in "an interesting reply to the 1970s military's ban on homosexuality",[4] gay sex becomes officially encouraged to curb overpopulation; language changes; ethnicity becomes uniform; and, eventually, humanity becomes a new cloned collective. The significance of Haldeman's novel lies in its matter-of-factual dismissal of war-story clichés.

A proliferation of popular and successful work followed. C.J. Cherryh's expansive Alliance-Union series (1976–present) is in some ways the benchmark for space combat, marrying imaginative tactics and technology—such as her predictive "longscan" targeting—to realistic depictions of people making decisions under pressure. Heinlein-style powered exoskeletons appear again in John Steakley's *The Armor* (1984) as they will again in *Aliens* (dir. James Cameron, 1986) and in countless other films and video games. Many books in Lois McMaster Bujold's long-running Vorkosigan Saga (1986–2018) offer a lively feminist take on typical military space-opera plotlines, featuring many martial protagonists, as well as both ship-to-ship and personal combat, a vast range of sinister weaponry, and serial personal and political intrigue.

In the twenty-first century, military SF has thus far largely focused on reimagining themes and tropes from the previous half-century. On television screens, the preeminent example of the era is probably the modern *Battlestar Galactica* (2004–'09), which adapts the campy 1978 original into a bleak, post-9/11 exploration of military and political themes ranging from urban combat to Guantanamo Bay-style due-process violations to ingenious spacecraft tactics (we will never stop being blown away by the Adama Manoeuvre!). The show's interrogation of the so-called War on Terror peaks—in a startling act of cognitive estrangement—during the third season's New Caprica arc in which White protagonists with catalogue-model good looks find themselves cast in the role of refugee-camp suicide bombers. Back on the page, John Scalzi's Old Man's War series (2005–'15) combines successful riffs on the

---

4. Jordison, 2011, n.p.

genre's foundational texts of *Starship Troopers* and *The Forever War* with an inventive perspective on US militantism. Kameron Hurley's *The Light Brigade* (2019) also reenlists themes from Heinlein and Haldeman but adds **Body Horror** and temporal turmoil courtesy of the teleportation technology used to wage intercorporate, inter*planetary* feudalistic warfare. Changes wrought by the protagonist's repeated de- and re-materialisation serve as a metaphor for how war transforms a person, while a **Time Travel** element adds a twistiness reminiscent of Hiroshi Sakurazaka's *All You Need Is Kill* (2014).

Closer to the here and now, techy, jargon-rich military writing is found in Cixin Liu's story 'Full Spectrum Barrage Jamming' (2014), while more substantial examples of near-future high-tech SF war include P.W. Singer and August Cole's techno thriller *Ghost Fleet* (2015) and the novel *New Model Army* (2010) by Adam Roberts. The latter sees the traditional British Army portrayed as a lumbering and ineffective dinosaur when compared to the nimble, networked, democratic decision-making of a rank-less New Model Army fighting for Scottish independence in a story in which the most potent weapon (apart from an occasional nuke) is a wiki.

A Spotter's Guide: Ready for Deployment

Military SF has obvious connections with **Starship** stories, but for the most part it owes its imagery to the real-world history of war and warriors (think about how, as Neil Jordan put it, *Star Wars* [dir. George Lucas, 1977] is "a Second World War aeroplane movie in space"[5]). To that end, we can find several useful analogies:

- **Aircraft carriers in space:** In many ways, visiting a real-world aircraft carrier (there are lots of museum ships!) is the closest many of us will get to going on board a starship. Yet many people will tell you that carriers don't make any sense in space; you'll hear a lot about the lack of need for them (given that the sea/air environmental division—and hence the ship/plane division—of real-world carriers is not reflected in the, eh, space/space division of SF). But you know what? You're writing a story, not personally invading Proxima Centauri, and aircraft carriers in space are *cool*! Speaking of, a carrier inevitably comes with…
- **Space fighters, bombers, reconnaissance drones, or search-and-rescue craft:** A typical sci-fighter looks a lot like a real-life fighter jet. They're small one- or two-person spacecraft that are often aerodynamically inclined (though shout out to *Babylon 5*'s "starfuries" for making the effort to look genuinely designed for their environment).

---

5. Jenkins and Taylor, 1984; reprinted in Zucker, 2013, p. 49.

By convention, protagonist pilots are probably hot-headed mavericks or ice-cold by-the-book professionals. Occasionally they may be cybernetically linked to their craft. Space fighters and dogfights were a huge part of television shows such as *Space: Above and Beyond* (1994–'95) and the reimagined *Battlestar Galactica*. Key considerations for the writer include how to credibly portray the impact of g-forces on pilots and how to address acceleration and deceleration or, if you prefer, the change in velocity known as delta-v.

- **Submarines in space:** Two vessels, often personified by two *captains*, go head-to-head in a tense, claustrophobic game of cat-and-mouse. Undetectability is key, with ships hiding inside nebulas or behind moons or invisibility cloaks (and, for a more realistic approach, consider how your hidden craft might expel very visible waste heat!). Various incarnations of *Star Trek* have done a good trade in these stories, from the original series episode 'Balance of Terror' (dir. Vincent McEveety, 1966) to the *Strange New Worlds* episode 'Memento Mori' (dir. Dan Liu, 2022), which comes complete with jury-rigged sonar and a hull creaking under exterior pressure.

- **Groundpounders:** Infantry stories in SF often find characters invading a planet (sometimes dropped there from orbit), holding territory captured by naval elements, or conducting counteroffensives against a resurgent enemy. This is gritty, messy, in-the-trenches stuff that writers need to sell the reality of via sensory detail: the smell of ordnance or burning flesh, the sounds of weapons fire or screaming causalities, etc. Varied settings offer different challenges: desert worlds lacking cover or water (think Frank Herbert's *Dune*, 1956); jungles filled with alien illnesses and that hamper manoeuvrability; ice planets where exposure is another adversary; or urban warfare where the enemy hides all around. Consider your army's composition, too: standard infantry is good for broad, novel-length perspectives following a character through their career from raw recruit to seasoned soldier (see Marko Kloos's Frontlines series, 2013–'22); but specific missions, good for short stories, often call for black-ops units, shady private contractors, or even genetically engineered super soldiers. A good example of the latter is *Rogue Trooper*, the *2000AD* series created by Gerry Finley-Day and Dave Gibbons following a "Genetic Infantryman" and the three bio-chip-mounted minds on his equipment.

- **Advanced weaponry:** It's probably obvious, but a good military SF story will deploy sophisticated—sometimes egregiously so—weapons systems far in advance of what's available today. These could be anything from satellite beam platforms to killer **Robots** of various types (Terminators, anybody?) to stealth craft, electromagnetic rail guns firing shape-shifting liquid metal slugs, kamikaze cybernetic insects, or conscious fire-and-forget missiles that always remember their mission. The weapons of your war are your best chance to play with the bombastic and imaginative elements of your story or, indeed, to show off your research chops by investigating and extrapolating armaments from the cutting edge of contemporary military science (googling the outlandish projects run by DARPA, the US Defence Advanced Research Projects Agency, is a good place to start!).

Things That are Cool About Military SF

Military SF has always had a strong readership. There are a lot of people out there hungry for action-packed stories of battles beyond the stars (that's a Jimmy T. Murakami reference for anyone keeping track). But, more than that, this subgenre is a chance for us to ask *why* we fight and to consider what war does to individuals and societies. Some people might have first-hand knowledge of military service and writing about it in this fashion presents a chance to process such intensely personal experiences. For others, the allegorical aspect of SF allows us to comment on, critique and, should we wish, protest contemporary or near-contemporary conflicts by asking, *war, huh yeah, what is it good for?*

Battle Lines

To further grant realism to your military SF stories, consider the various components of current and historical militaries and their actions:

- **Diversity:** There's no reason why your fighting force should be homogenous, meaning no reason why it should be all male, all White, or even all human. Navies, armies, and air forces recruit from all strata of their societies; consequently failing to do so in fiction betrays a lack of imagination. Even alien armies composed of insects (the fictional descendants of *Starship Troopers*) or clones (*Star Wars: The Bad Batch*, 2021) differentiate between biological castes or recognisable characters. In the real world, Black sailors were commonplace aboard Royal Navy vessels during the Napoleonic Wars, while women have long fought as deadly warriors all the way back to the Vikings and beyond. A crucial text regarding this is Hurley's Hugo Award-winning essay '"We Have Always Fought": Challenging the "Women, Cattle, and Slaves" Narrative' (2013).[6]

---

6. Hurley, 2013, n.p.

- **Combined arms:** At its most basic, this means that different elements of your fictional military forces support each other. The aim of combined arms is to assault an enemy in multiple ways simultaneously and in a fashion whereby their defence against one attack leaves them vulnerable to another. One of the principle's most realistic depictions (to the point of essentially being a military recruitment video) comes in one of the genre's most outlandish films: *Transformers* (dir. Michael Bay, 2007).
- **Not everyone is in the trenches:** It's sometimes easy to imagine that the military comprises only soldiers, sailors, and pilots, but there are a multitude of roles integral to success in war: engineers, cooks, I.T. support, nurses, lawyers, and even financial administrators (termed in the Royal Navy, rather pleasingly, "Writers"). Telling a story from the perspective of a character with an atypical military role can offer your fiction distinctiveness. Think about the kinds of conflicts that varied aspects of military service allow you to consider. You can also ask difficult questions about the moral and/or ethical implications of rules of engagement, war crimes, military scandals, and so on, such as Jack Campbell (John G. Hemry, USN ret.) does in his JAG in Space series (2012).
- **Logistics:** A space army marches on its ... space stomach? Logistics isn't the sexiest topic, but it's arguably the most important in any military campaign. Consider how your space fleet is supplied. Is there a network of starbases à la the *Star Trek* franchise, or do your vessels manufacture their own supplies from raw material they acquire along the way as in *Battlestar Galactica*? What happens to your characters when a supply line is interrupted by the enemy?
- **Permission to speak freely:** Consider the degree to which you want your fictional military to reflect the hierarchical norms and discipline of a real-world fighting force, because, in many cases, a bit of authorial leniency is beneficial to both your story and characterisation. Television and film offer particularly good examples of this, with many very enjoyable characters—for instance *Stargate: SG-1*'s wisecracking Jack O'Neill or *Battlestar Galactica*'s rebellious Kara Thrace—being unlikely to survive long in a real military unit. Presenting a fictional fighting force that's a little less rigid than reality can give you as a writer the best of both worlds: the trappings of a war story along with the freedom to create engaging and memorable protagonists who don't spend the whole narrative locked up in the brig!

ACTIVITIES

Restage an Earth battle: A time-honoured approach to military SF is to take an engagement from history and re-enact it in space or on another planet. For example, both the television shows *Space: Above and Beyond* (1995–'96) and *Star Trek: Deep Space Nine* (1993–'99) had episodes based on the Battle of Guadalcanal in World War II. For this activity, research a historical conflict (and do go beyond the usual suspects of the World Wars or the American Revolution), considering how the battle's belligerents, objectives, and tactics might be portrayed in Science Fictional fashion (islands become planets, battleships become spacecraft, etc). For extra credit, think about how you might use this as an opportunity to comment on some aspect of the inspiration conflict.

Arm yourself: Develop an advanced weapon and write a story about your military protagonist being briefed on its use (this can be either a portable weapon or something larger installed on a fighter or cruiser). Maybe they have a personal connection to its development via a family member or lover? Perhaps your character has qualms about the weapon's destructive nature? Worth looking at here is Kim Stanley Robinson's alternate history of the Hiroshima bomb 'The Lucky Strike' (1984).

UTOPIA

Utopia is the most political of subgenres. It's about making a point. It's about telling the reader that there is another way, a better way. People dismiss it as boring, but they probably just want you to be satisfied with chlorinated chicken and wage slavery. Don't let them. Join a union; imagine a functional public transport system; show readers that another world is possible....

A Short History of Utopia

Utopia as both a word and a concept in the West originates in a book called *Utopia* by Thomas More (1516). The name literally means "Nowhere", emphasising its fictionality. Though one of the fun things about the word "utopia" is that, depending on how you pronounce it, it can mean either "No Place" ("ou-topia) or "Good Place" ("eu-topia). As a term, it's been used to describe both intentional communities like the one your cousin's hippie friend ran off to, as well as imagined societies portrayed in fiction. More's intent was to have the nations of Europe—England in particular—think about how Utopia's "decrees and ordinaunces" fostered a well-ordered community.[1] As such, the original *Utopia* is a political text written by a politician proposing alternatives to how society around him was organised. In *Utopia*, people work only six hours a day and spend their free time studying literature, science, and philosophy. There is zero unemployment, no money (hello, *Star Trek*), and property is owned collectively.

Any literary utopia, says critic Darko Suvin, is an "historically alternative wishful construct".[2] Which is to say that the best utopia is credibly thought through. Hence to SF, where utopias and **Dystopias** are very important; indeed, there are significant "degrees of kinship" between utopia and SF.[3] In the early history of the subgenre, many works, such as Francis Bacon's *New Atlantis* (1626), Margaret Cavendish's *The Blazing World* (1668), and Jonathan Swift's *Gulliver's Travels* (1726) followed More's model in presenting a utopia as another place. Yet the pivotal shift in utopian writing occurred when authors moved from depicting better places to better times, usually under what *The Encyclopedia of Science Fiction* calls "the influence of notions of historical and social progress".[4]

Indeed, there was quite a lot of such utopian fiction between More and, say, World War I. Hundreds of examples, in fact, though getting hold of them

---

1. Lupton, 1895, p. 33.
2. Suvin, 1992, p. 34.
3. Suvin, 1992, p. 33.
4. Stableford and Langford, 'Utopias', 2022. n.p.

these days is a utopian dream in and of itself! These works often interrogated ideas of technological progress, gender, concentration of capital, etc., with diversions into romantic pastoralism (held back by dreadful it-was-all-a-dream style endings). Among the most notable are Mary Griffith's 1836 novella *Three Hundred Years Hence*; famed artist, designer, and Socialist campaigner William Morris's *News from Nowhere* (1890); Florence Dixie's *Gloriana, or the Revolution of 1900* (1890), which concludes a century in the future with a prosperous and Federalised Britain governed by women; and Chinese intellectual Cai Yuanpei's story 'New Year's Dream' (1904), which depicts a future of "universal human freedom and affluence"[5]. Among the most influential literary utopias written in the United States (itself either a utopian or dystopian project depending on your racial, economic, sexual, or religious position) are Edward Bellamy's socialist inflected *Looking Backward: 2000–1887* (1888) and, moving into a twentieth century marked by diminishing faith in technological utopianism in particular, *Walden Two* (1948) by behavioural psychologist B.F. Skinner.

In more recent times, utopian fiction has been more ambiguous (as in the subtitle of Ursula K. Le Guin's *The Dispossessed: An Ambiguous Utopia*, 1974), presenting "unaccomplished" visions that often fell "short of complete success".[6] Is this, novelist Geoff Ryman asked on a panel at a SFF convention in 2015, "because it so often leads to Stalin or ISIS?"[7] Such an observation puts one in mind of Le Guin's classic 1973 story 'The Ones Who Walk Away from Omelas'. In utopian Omelas, everything is perfect and wonderful ... except for the one child suffering in darkness upon whose wretchedness the city's prosperity depends. And everyone knows it and carries on, being complicit in the child's distress. In many ways, this sounds like the Global North today: yes, we have smartphones and cat memes, but only because a seven-year-old child dug the necessary rare earth minerals out of the ground with their bare hands. We all know it, we're all complicit in it, we all like and subscribe. Le Guin, as ever, was ahead of the curve in realising that both utopia and dystopia contain versions of each other.[8] Many modern utopias follow her lead by drawing drama from the risk of falling short of their own ideals.

One writer who does exactly that is California's Kim Stanley Robinson. Of particular interest is Robinson's Three Californias trilogy (*The Wild Shore*, 1984; *The Gold Coast*, 1988; and *Pacific Edge*, 1990), which depicts three different possible futures for Orange County. They illustrate how the line between utopia and dystopia is surprisingly thin. Subsequent Robinson

---

5. Li, 2013, p. 90.
6. Lauri, 2013, p. 24.
7. Ryman, 2015, n.p.
8. Atwood, 2011, n.p.

work such as *The Ministry for the Future* (2020) engages with utopia as a process rather than an end point. Novice writers should take note that this process is not a straight line; it's often a "struggle" in which characters face "repeated defeats, detours, and backslidings".[9] Speaking in 2012, Robinson distilled this point by saying that we need to "take away a definition of it as a static end state, that sense of 'We're never going to get to that' and 'It might be boring or it might not be but in any case it's not going to happen'".[10] If, he says, utopia is instead defined as "a positive *course* in history then you can shift it over to something like what Joanna Russ called the 'optopia', which is the best possible, given where we are, given our technological base".[11]

As the twenty-first century rolls on it continues to bring a more expansive vision of utopia to readers and audiences. Novels such as *In the United States of Africa* (2006) by Djiboutian author Abdourahman A. Waberi offer a brilliantly satirical reversal of the global North/South divide wherein refugees flee the barbaric slums of war-torn "Euramerica" for the prosperous US of A(frica). That book's utopian message lies not in any easy denunciation of colonialism or commercialism (its world is, if anything, just as impoverished and immiserated as the real one) but instead on acknowledging common humanity and the power of art to bridge cultural and racial divisions. *Everfair* (2016) by African-American author and editor Nisi Shawl offers an equally inclusive utopian vision, a neo-Victorian steampunk world of British socialists and African-American missionaries purchasing the Belgian Congo from its colonial occupier and founding a haven for indigenous populations and formerly enslaved peoples. Meanwhile, on the silver screen, the Wakanda of *Black Panther* (dir. Ryan Coogler, 2018) is a powerful and joyful (that's important) Afrofuturist re-centring of Black experiences as part of the hugely popular Marvel Cinematic Universe. In a depiction that ignited the imaginations of audiences, Wakanda draws its utopian energies from both the future—the advanced technology engendered by the metal Vibranium—and crucially, as the only African country unravaged by European colonialism, from unbroken links to its rich cultural, social, and familial past.

A Spotter's Guide: A Guidebook to the Territory

- **Some broad categories:** The scholar Raymond Williams grouped utopian stories into four overlapping fields: the paradise, in which a happier life is described as existing elsewhere; the externally altered

---

9. Markley, 2019, p. 6.
10. Nolan, 2015, p. 65.
11. Nolan, 2015, p. 65.

world, in which utopia has been made possible by an unlooked-for natural event; willed transformations, in which a new kind of life has been achieved by human effort; and technological transformations, in which utopia has been made possible by a technical discovery.[12] While these are useful for determining backstory, fiction writers should attempt more specificity by narrowing their focus.

- **Post-scarcity societies:** Perhaps the best-known understanding of utopia is the society that exists without economic want or need, what Aaron Bastani called *Fully Automated Luxury Communism* (2019). Such utopias present visions of hope, positivity, and meaningful freedom for everyone (the future that liberals want, etc.). Humanity, in post-scarcity societies, has overcome famine, greed, war, and prejudice. The Culture books by Iain M. Banks are a particularly good example, being an energy-abundant galactic civilisation administered by godlike machines that enable everyday citizens to indulge in whatever art, hobbies, or lifestyle choices that they desire.
- **The snake in the grass:** Some societies appear idyllic but often hide a dark secret, such as the suffering child of Omelas on which the prosperity of the city depends. This is a surprisingly common aspect of well-known utopias. More's defining utopia, for example, still had enslaved peoples. On the surface, the Federation of the *Star Trek* franchise seems to be a utopia but, as a student once remarked to us, "Picard's Enterprise is a utopia; the rest of the Federation isn't". Stories such as these are sometimes called "Critical Utopias", a term coined by academic Tom Moylan (who cited Le Guin, along with Russ's *The Female Man*, 1975, and Samuel R. Delany's *Triton*, 1976). Critical Utopias tend to "dwell on the conflict between the 'originary world' and the Utopian society opposed to it so that the process of social change is more directly articulated".[13] In some ways they are literal calls for real-world revolution.
- **Themed utopias:** Some utopias are defined by a single trait, typically an exaggerated aspect of some real-world political or social movement: ecotopias (after Ernest Callenbach's 1975 novel), religious utopias, philosophical utopias (such as the work of Ibn Tufail), economic, or scientific utopias. They all offer ready-made backdrops for our stories. For us as writers, it is crucial "that we begin to imagine as many different kinds of utopias as possible. A patchwork of different types of utopias for different types of people".[14] Attempting a variety of themed utopias will serve us well.

---

12. Williams, 1978, pp. 203–214.
13. Moylan, 2014, pp. 10–11.
14. Ryman, 2015, n.p.

- **Pocket utopias:** These are specific types of utopian stories in which the utopia is socially, geographically, or even militarily isolated from the surrounding population. Consider, for instance, campus novels, which used to be a subgenre of utopian writing (though the neoliberal corporatisation of universities these days, especially in the UK, potentially pushes contemporary examples into dystopian territory). Once we realise these are an artifact of the distribution of wealth, any very prosperous part of today's world can be considered a pocket utopia, with the palatial abodes in any well-off suburb or gated community as good examples. The Capital from The Hunger Games series (Suzanne Collins, 2008–'10) or the titular space station from *Elysium* (dir. Neill Blomkamp, 2013) are pocket utopias in that only the mega wealthy live there and can enjoy their freedoms. *Black Panther*'s Wakanda is in some respects a pocket utopia, especially when the film counterpoints life in the hidden kingdom with everyday Black experiences in the United States.

Things That are Cool About Utopias

Utopian fiction is a means of expressing personal and political discontent that exists alongside, and is often as effective as, the more obvious practices of activism and protest. It is your opportunity to take a stand against dominant narratives or ideologies. Remember, too, that utopian writing has long had a satirical strain, one punching upwards at problematic and/or prevailing socioeconomic conditions (often shown to be wanting in comparison to the writer's fictional community). Moreover, the genre offers an exciting creative challenge to any writer, because utopia asks writers to critique not just our present moment but our cultural and fictional *imagining* of potential alternatives: what kind of world do *you* want to live in? What kind of future do *you* want to see?

Creating "Perfection" Can be Difficult

- **Common elements:** There is a considerable body of scholarship about utopias but, for our purposes, More sets four general characteristics for the shape of any utopian narrative:
    - They normally describe a journey to an unknown place or time.
    - Their protagonist often, but not always, arrives by way of a shipwreck or a crash.
    - The utopian traveller is usually offered a guided tour of the society and given an explanation of its social, political, economic, and religious organisation.
    - Eventually the protagonist returns home.

A good example is Robinson's novel *2312* (2012). Characters leave their homes and travel through the Solar System. They experience a shipwreck of sorts when their spacecraft depressurises, and they're left drifting in spacesuits. They're given tours of different political and economic approaches, though in *2312*, Robinson replaces More's emphasis on different kinds of religion with technological developments. Structurally so, *2312* checks all the boxes as a utopian novel. Additionally, the novel repeatedly stresses and demonstrates alternate ways of structuring society. In that way, a book like *2312* also shows how utopian novels are political novels.

- **It's not always easy:** Nonetheless, the writer must keep in mind that any good utopian fiction presents the reader with "not the structure of a blueprint" but rather an ongoing "self-reflexive and self-critical process" on the part of the character.[15] The constant construction metaphors in the discourse around utopia are fascinating and informative (and not accidental): a utopia is often a city and is almost always something to be "built". Indeed, *The Encyclopedia of Science Fiction* considers it a "future-historical goal, to be achieved by the active efforts of human beings," and this is a good guide for writers in that utopias don't just appear but instead have been created through struggle.[16] Riffing on this for a moment, one is reminded of how Le Guin describes More's utopia as "a blueprint without a building site".[17]

- **Consider the conflicts:** One misconception about utopias that frequently deters novice writers is the perception that they are "boring" and lack dramatic conflict (especially in comparison with dystopian fiction). This, again, is where fiction intersects with politics. Declaring utopia boring, says Robinson, is "usually a political attack from the right. It's also said by people who aren't living in cardboard shacks. The people who do live in those are probably willing to throw the dice on utopia and see if it's boring or not".[18] It's easy to realise that there can indeed be conflict in utopia (or how, for example, different versions or visions of utopia can also be in conflict with each other, such as in Robinson's own Mars Trilogy, 1992–'96). As Banks once said, "You can still have unrequited love; you can still have unfulfilled ambition in utopia".[19] The basic building blocks of human stories—desire, death, and so on—remain even in a spec-fictional setting that offers (and here is where you as the writer come in!) opportunities for imaginative resolution.

---

15. Moylan, 2014, p. xix.
16. Stableford and Langford, 'Utopias', 2022. n.p.
17. Le Guin, 'Utopiyin, Utopiyang', 2017, p. 85.
18. Nolan, 2015, p. 69.
19. Nolan, 2015, p. 68.

- **Character above all else:** Like **Big Dumb Objects** or **High Fantasy**, utopia is a genre in which we can very easily allow worldbuilding to overshadow character. So, when portraying a world that has moved from immiseration to peaceful prosperity, we mustn't forget to give the reader a "personal journey from passivity to agency in one or several protagonists," which is to say characters beyond the merely didactic.[20] Define the scale of your utopian world by placing a three-dimensional character at the heart of your story. For, as Banks put it, the best utopian stories are those about "someone like us who is, shall we say, slightly better behaved than we are".[21]

---

20. Moylan, 2014, p. xv.
21. Nolan, 2015, p. 65.

ACTIVITIES

Relationship drama in utopia: Challenge the perception of utopia as boring by spicing things up with a little messy drama. As Robinson once said, the utopian writer can "still have Character A falling in love with B falling in love with C falling in love with A. That creates an awful lot of misery as many of us know".[22] For added structural satisfaction, overlay relationship conflict onto an effort to preserve or expand some aspect of your utopian society. What's it like to live in a perfect world but discover your partner is having an affair? Or perhaps romantic rivals approach utopia from differing philosophical stances and your protagonist is torn between the different approaches embodied by their different suiters?

Centenary celebration: More so than many other SF subgenres, utopia is less about prescience than it is about commenting on the moment of the story's composition. So, imagine the world a hundred years from now. Consider the changes that must have occurred to transform our present into your utopian future. Remember that utopia is a *journey* and not a destination, so consider specific moments of transformation that you could dramatise: scientific developments, movements towards economic or philosophic enlightenment, social progression regarding race, gender, or sexuality, and even political reform or revolution. Who are the major actors of these transformations and what are they willing to sacrifice to create a fairer and more equitable world for all?

---

22. Nolan, 2015, p. 68.

DYSTOPIA

More than simply the opposite of **Utopia**, dystopias have evolved into a fertile subgenre of their own. They are a worst-case scenario; they are a warning; they are an arena for resistance. They generate a sense of dread by expressing our fears regarding loss of agency and individuality. You want to write about them? Well, you're not allowed! The government, religious authorities, warlords, corporate executives, or algorithms forbid it! And yet....

A Short History of Dystopia

One of the earliest uses of the word dystopia was by political economist John Stuart Mill in 1868 when he lambasted British policy towards Ireland as "Dystopian" and "too bad to be practicable" (these were, after all, the people who had overseen the Irish Famine twenty years earlier).[1] Old-school examples of fictional dystopias include Walter Besant's *The Inner House* (1888) and Jack London's *The Iron Heel* (1907), but for the good bad stuff one needs to wait for the "terrors of the twentieth century", in particular the devastation of World War I, which made it difficult for people to imagine better futures.[2] A typical narrative pattern quickly developed that is still visible today in SF stories about "the oppression of the majority by a ruling elite" and "the regimentation of society as a whole".[3] We see this in a series of typical tropes such as "the lack of freedom, the constant surveillance, the routine, the failed escape attempt [...] and an underground movement".[4] A further important observation is that "unlike the 'tourist' style narration common to utopias, Dystopias tend to be narrated from the perspective of the imagined society's inhabitant; someone whose subjectivity has been shaped by that society's historical conditions, structural arrangements, and forms of life".[5]

Some of the subgenre's most influential and oft-imitated texts emerged in the middle decades of the century. The first of these is Aldous Huxley's *Brave New World* (1932), the flavour of which is discernible in everything from *The Matrix* (dir. the Wachowskis, 1999) to contemporary conservative politics. *Brave New World* is a tapestry of anxieties over mass production and overpopulation, personal and psychological freedom, eugenics, commodification, and technocratic government control. Huxley presents

---

1. Hansard Commons, 12 Mar. 1868, vol. 190.
2. Moylan, 2000, p. xi.
3. Stableford, 'Dystopias', 2021. n.p.
4. Ketterer, 1989, p. 211.
5. Davison-Vecchione, 2021, n.p.

a world state in which people are grown artificially in vast municipal incubators, are sorted based on intelligence and labour requirements, and are addicted to hedonism in a way that anticipates the short cycle dopamine hits of today's social media and our commercial gamification of sexuality via dating apps and television shows such as *Love Island*. Did Huxley predict our present? If he did, he did so just ahead of George Orwell with *Nineteen Eighty-Four* (1949), a novel in which austerity dominates a Britain known as "Airstrip One", a society under mass surveillance where cameras are omnipresent but independent thought and self-expression are crimes. Orwell's totalitarian government warps language in a manner that popularised many key pieces of dystopian imagery and terminology such as "Big Brother" (not the reality show, but that's where the name comes from!), "Thought Police", and "Memory Hole". A third book, the darkly satirical *A Clockwork Orange* (1962) by Anthony Burgess, also plays with language (in this case a mishmash of Slavic words and Cockney rhyming slang) in its construction of an ironic and dystopian Britain stalked by gangs of violent delinquents. The novel interrogates notions of personal and state violence but is best known for its depiction of behaviour modifications that have inspired any number of brainwashing scenes in dystopian literature, television, and cinema.

The latter half of the twentieth century began to see the dominance of women writers in the dystopian mode, something that should not surprise anyone, and that ascendency continues today. James Tiptree, Jr. (Alice Sheldon)'s Hugo Award-winning *The Girl Who Was Plugged In* (1973) explores "the traumatic appropriation of the human body" along with questions about "oppressive consumer culture and corporate technoscience" that still speak to our present moment of influencers and YouTube personalities.[6] Dominating this period of dystopian fiction, however, is Margret Atwood's seminal novel *The Handmaid's Tale* (1985) set in an authoritarian future America governed by a religious hard right that forcibly subjugates women's reproductive autonomy. Atwood's great achievement was tying her dystopia into America's long Puritanical tradition (such as the Salem witch trials) and the political climate at the time during which it was written, thus making her fictional future feel historically persuasive.[7] She's made no secret about the real-world relevance of her novel, stating that her primary inspirations were "what some people said they would do re: women if they had the power (they have it now and they are)".[8] The result is a bleak, uncompromising, and socio-historically resonant fiction that remains the gold standard for literary dystopias.

The work of Tiptree and Atwood continues to cast a long shadow, and any representative sample of contemporary dystopian fiction proudly displays

---

6. San Miguel, 2018, p. 29.
7. Regalado, 2019, n.p.
8. Temple, 2017, n.p.

their influence. Such books include Suzanne Collins's hugely popular Hunger Games trilogy (2008–'10); Hillary Jordan's *When She Woke* (2011), which is a science fictional re-telling of Nathaniel Hawthorne's *The Scarlet Letter* (1850); Louise O'Neill's *Only Ever Yours* (2014) in which women are no longer born but made to order; Meg Elison's *The Book of the Unnamed Midwife* (2014) in which the surviving women of a post-plague world are sexually enslaved by violent men; Claire Vaye Watkins's timely climate dystopia *Gold Fame Citrus* (2015); and so on. Yet while all these fictional dystopias are generally a step or two removed from the real world, they are often only set "ten minutes into the future of technoscientific innovation" and as such offer a negative version of a reality already riddled with inequality and violence.[9] That said, they frequently contain within them the possibility for change, which we as writers might think of as the "story". Even *The Handmaid's Tale* concludes with metafictional "Historical Notes" taking place further in the future again, something that retroactively positions that dystopia as poised between the timeframe of the reader and the possibility— the *hope*—of a better future to come.

A Spotter's Guide: New Maps of Hell

Raymond Williams, who we met in our definitions of utopia, also proposed a mirroring schema for different types of dystopias that include "the hell", in which a more wretched kind of life is described as existing elsewhere; "the externally altered world", in which a new but less happy kind of life has been brought about by an unlooked-for or uncontrollable natural event; "the willed transformation", in which a new but less happy kind of life has been brought about by social degeneration, by the (re)emergence of harmful kinds of social order, or by the unforeseen yet disastrous consequences of an effort at social improvement; and "the technological transformation", in which the conditions of life have been worsened by technical development.[10] As with utopias, these classifications and elements exhibit significant overlap and are best thought of as starting points to which writers can add detail and specificity. Here are some productive avenues towards doing so:

- **The ideological dystopia:** This contains shades of Williams's "willed transformation", such as *The Handmaid's Tale*, for example, though the "will" in that case is reactionary and conservative. These are the dystopias defined by patriarchies, white-supremacist states, theocracies/ fundamentalist regimes, institutionalised racism, neoliberal capitalism, or authoritarian governments. Writers typically use ideological

---

9. San Miguel, 2018, p. 36.
10. Williams, 1978, pp. 203–204.

dystopias as a story's backdrop against which their protagonist struggles. Ideological dystopias are most often presented as future events, but there is some overlap here with alternate histories (such as the Nazi-dominated dystopia of Philip K. Dick's *The Man in the High Castle*, 1962).

- **The industrial and informational dystopia:** These stories draw attention to the dehumanising potential of technological developments with characters stifling under evil technocrats or algorithms that rob them of choice (often under the illusion of providing it). Occasionally used for satirical purposes (see: *The Circle*, Dave Eggers, 2013), such stories gesture towards how "the industrial revolution turned workers into cogs in a machine," or engage directly with how "digitization turned human users into commodified data" (hello, social media companies!).[11] E.M. Forster's "The Machine Stops" (1909) or Huxley's *Brave New World* offer classic examples of the Industrial Dystopia, but elements of Emma Newman's Planetfall series (especially *After Atlas*, 2015) show how the informational dystopia can be integrated into a variety of adjacent narrative modes. There's also some crossover here with **Apocalypses** (consider the *Terminator* franchise, 1984–2019) and, in terms of imagery and use of language, with **Cyberpunk**.

- **The mirror universe:** Grab your goatee for a world just like our own but in which the prevailing moral compass has flipped: good people are evil, symbols of virtue are corrupt, and/or the villains have won. Such dystopias work intellectually as much as emotionally upon the audience by asking their readers or viewers to take seriously the implications of a world turned upside down. Mirror universes can often be the result of external alteration via **Time Travel** changing the past (as in *Back to the Future, Part II*, dir. Robert Zemeckis, 1989) and work quite well in serial narratives such as comic books or television shows where the inverted world can most readily be contrasted with the narrative status quo. One finds such dystopias played with a campy earnestness in *Star Trek*'s Mirror Universe and as real-world commentary in the fascist America of *Agents of SHIELD*'s Framework.

- **The Orwellian dystopia:** Best summed up by the image of "a boot stamping on a human face—forever," these are greyscale stories involving the denial of truth by malevolent actors.[12] Typical elements include manipulation of public opinion by state-sponsored media, cults of personality, forever wars, and the erasure of personal liberties. In many ways, these are the archetypical Western twenty-first-century dystopias of mass surveillance, wannabe strongmen, outrage politics, a

---

11. Jong, 2019, p. 2.
12. Orwell, 1949 (1983 edition), p. 220.

willingness to lie without compunction, and the deliberate maintenance of poverty and ignorance. All of which are far too common in our contemporary political discourse.

- **The anti-utopia:** This form actively critiques aspects of utopian politics under the guise of dystopian imagery and conventions.[13] Anti-utopias have the aim of making the label "Utopian" "take on the meaning of fanciful, unrealistic, [or] impractical".[14] These frequently appear as stories of utopian endeavours gone drastically awry leading to dystopian consequences. Their rejection of utopianism often occurs "from a position allegedly outside it," offering the writer fun opportunities for formal experimentation via the inclusion of metafictional elements such as mock-academic work, imitations of (social) media, and other textual interventions.[15]

Things That are Cool About Dystopias

Dystopias offer the writer a means of warning receptive readers about aspects of life they feel are heading in the worst possible direction. They allow us to critique things such as income inequality, structural racism, neoliberal capitalism, and the messianic nonsense of everyone from cult leaders to the "disruptors" of Silicon Valley. More important, they're a way of looking at ourselves, at our writing, and at how we're imagining (or not) our futures. In that way the speculations of dystopia can be as political and provocative as those of utopia.

Building the Bleak Future

- **Circumscription:** In a useful observation for any writer, Atwood sees both utopia and dystopia as "often an enclave of maximum control surrounded by a wilderness," citing historical examples in Samuel Butler's anti-mechanical *Erewhon* (1872) and Yevgeny Zamyatin's dystopian *We* (1924).[16] We might similarly see chain-link fences or riot police as the boundaries of contemporary enclaves, imagery that SF and Fantasy can portray allegorically in any number of ways (planetary shields, **Big Dumb Objects** such as Dyson Spheres, mazes, moats, or swarths of ecologically devastated land). Consider how this can generate narrative developments and characters, such as how The Capitol and various Districts in *The Hunger Games* (2008) are carefully kept separate by their totalitarian government.

---

13. Jameson, 1991, pp. 331–340.
14. Sargent, 1994, p. 22.
15. Balasopoulos, 2006, n.p.
16. Le Guin, 2017, 'Ursula K. Le Guin Explains …', n.p.

- **Fight for what's right:** Academic C.R. La Bossiere once noted that "Utopias tend to argue discursively; Dystopias, to argue movingly," and this is worth the consideration of any writer in the subgenre.[17] The didactic quality of utopian writing going right back to Thomas More finds its truest counterpart in the emotional heft marshalled by dystopia's warped worlds. Because the desire for freedom—be that political, economic, sexual, or in terms of creative self-expression—provides a ready-made motivation around which a compelling character can be built. This inherent thematic yearning for freedom in the subgenre has found an avid following among YA readerships in particular. Dystopia's popularity among this audience goes beyond fashionable pessimism and speaks to fiction's power as a means for young adults to wrestle with questions of social justice, state violence, and climate collapse.
- **Playing with language:** Language is obviously the currency of any writer, but in dystopia it's often a tool of coercion within the storyworld itself. The language used by totalitarian governments or fascist regimes is drenched with controlling statements, often outright lies, designed to limit people's knowledge or reshape their perception of reality (consider how Russian propaganda portrayed that country's 2022 illegal invasion of Ukraine as a "Denazification"). Slogans posted in the background of your stories can also serve to quickly create an oppressive, controlling atmosphere (and the more meaningless they are, the more dystopian).
- **The Goldilocks zone:** One less frequently discussed aspect of dystopia is its inherent absurdities, something that offers writers a mechanism for valuable but unexpected tonal shading. Consider the Donald Trump presidency, for example, which according to many veered widely from outright dystopian horror (separating migrant children from their parents) to cartoonish supervillainy (platters of Big Macs in the White House). For every recognisable dystopian image generated by the Trump years (insurrectionists storming the US Capitol, say, or reactionary Supreme Court appointees eroding women's rights) there was a counterpointing farcical development (such as trying to buy Greenland, or a conclave of withered old men touching a glowing orb). While there is no "correct" point on the spectrum between despair and absurdity, any writer will do well to consider how—and how often—to undercut their fictional dystopia with something incongruous.
- **Self-reflection:** This is the key to any good writing, and so, given the state of the world, we might fruitfully ask: are dystopias *too easy* for writers? Are they too obvious? Should we be asking ourselves why we write them (and not *utopias*) in this day and age? As author Stephanie Saulter explains, "we've been conditioned to think the visuals of dystopia are cool. But dystopia is a conservative narrative; it reinforces

---

17. La Bossiere, 1974, p. 290.

the consumer's satisfaction with one's own lot. Utopia is progressive: things could be better. Be dissatisfied!"[18] It's perhaps worth noting here, too, that dystopias do exist. They're not like *The Hunger Games*, though; in many ways they're far, far worse: The Syrian Civil War, Mosul under ISIS, shipbreaking in Bangladesh (arguably one of the world's most dangerous jobs), etc. If you notice a divide here between the rich North and the poor South in terms of real utopias and real dystopias, you're not wrong. The real-life division between the two is heavily based on the unequal distribution of wealth throughout the world.

---

18. Saulter, 2015, n.p.

ACTIVITIES

Ripped from the headlines: One of the best ways to create a convincing dystopia is to take something in a news report or interview or even a history book and extrapolate from it to its worst possible extreme. After all, consider how Atwood has said of *The Handmaid's Tale* that there's "nothing in the book that didn't happen, somewhere".[19] Look at the effects of climate change or the prevalence of intersectional inequalities and think about how they might impact the lives of your characters (as ever, remember your characters and try not to lose yourself in worldbuilding!). Though be warned that investigating some of the dystopian things around us (such as the material seen by social-media moderators or the experiences of child soldiers) can be very upsetting. Do look after yourself when conducting research.

Resistance: Imagine you are a character living in one of the dystopias above. How might you plan a rebellion? Consider what your aims might be: political or environmental change? Raising social awareness of an issue? Bringing down a corrupt company or exposing a dangerous technological innovation? Here it may be useful to go to the library and do some reading about real-life political revolutions or social campaigners as inspiration. More interesting/inspiring than the particular tactics are the personalities of revolutionary leaders. How did they come to prominence? How did they motivate others? What did they do when they achieved their aims? Consider how these can add texture and believability to your own writing.

---

19. Temple, 2017, n.p.

APOCALYPTIC FICTION

We're going to come right out and say it: the end of the world is hella fun to write. Sure that might be insensitive in the midst of <gestures at everything>, but writing apocalyptic fiction means breaking the world as is and building something new in its place. This can be disturbing, cathartic, or just plain old wish fulfilment. If the end is nigh, what have you got to lose?

A Short History of Apocalyptic Fiction

The end of the world has been part of mythology, fiction, and even religious texts for thousands of years (Ragnarök, for example). And although these days we depend on weather forecasting and other technology to help us predict the near future, we aren't immune to getting distracted by some of the older ideas of when the end will happen. Remember when the news was full of stories about the Mayan prophecy that "predicted" the end of the world in December 2012? Or when we were staring down the tunnel of the Millennium Bug (aka Y2K) and the panic that all the world's computer systems were in danger of shutting down because so many systems' dates weren't originally set to tick over from 1999 to 2000? These two examples indicate that not all apocalypses involve world-ending explosions! There's even a Wikipedia page with a list of apocalyptic prophecies and their dates (now *that*'s a great resource for story ideas!).

These days we consider one of the first apocalyptic SFF narratives to be Mary Shelley's *The Last Man* (1826), in which a pandemic ravages the globe and storms cause massive flooding (um, sound familiar?). Soon after, Edgar Allen Poe tackled post-apocalyptic fiction in 'The Conversation of Eiros and Charmion' (1839) and was followed some decades later by H.G. Wells's *War of the Worlds* (1898), in which Britain comes up against giant Martian "fighting machines". The scientific and technical progress at the turn of the twentieth century, along with the fallout from the World Wars, resulted in the further growing popularity of apocalyptic and post-apocalyptic fiction. Since then, writers have gleefully destroyed the word in a multitude of ways.

A Spotter's Guide: Destruction a Go-Go

- **Zombies, Vampires, Robots, Alien Invasions:** Each of these leads to apocalypses in various stories and films. Zombies (Duh! We all end up as food); Vampires (Not the best apocalypse scenario if everyone becomes a vampire and there's nobody left to drink from); Robots (We're already unnerved by the idea of sentience, so it's only a matter of time before our Roombas fight back); and Alien Invasion (We've feared "little green men" invading and using us as food, labour, *whatever* for decades, so why stop now?). For more about each of these particular scenarios, check out their dedicated sections in this book.

- **Plague/viruses:** From the Bubonic Plague to the so-called Spanish Flu to Ebola to COVID-19, pandemics can be grotesque apocalyptic scenarios to write about (break out your gooiest descriptive prose!). Aside from the very real fear of disease, these stories are also metaphors for a dread of globalisation because the diseases cross borders too easily and quickly. There's also a hint of paranoia about science, which either created the disease or can't solve it. Some stories focus on world disruption, while others on survivors. Stephen King's *The Stand* (1978) is a classic of the genre with many film and television versions; Connie Willis's 1992 *Doomsday Book* adds in **Time Travel** as does *12 Monkeys* (dir. Terry Gilliam, 1995); director Steven Soderbergh's *Contagion* (2011) taught us about R numbers way before COVID-19; and Emily St. John Mandel's *Station Eleven* (2014) explores what it's like to live through a viral apocalypse.
- **Nuclear apocalypse:** The development of nuclear weapons changed how we think about the end of the world. Suddenly nations such as the United States and the Soviet Union had the power to wipe out all life on Earth. Their doctrine of Mutual Assured Destruction, apart from being literally MAD, cast a tense shadow over generations (ask anyone who lived through the 1980s). Hence a proliferation of nuclear apocalypse stories particularly in the Cold War period. These are often "reset" narratives because it's a kind of war that kills almost everyone (though Weapons of Mass Destruction (WMD) could also be biological, chemical, seismic, or more outlandish). The point these stories make is that our technology has reached an extreme level of self-destruction *and* humans are short-sighted and kind of awful. We can categorise these into three types: leading up to the war (see director Stanley Kubrick's 1964 classic *Dr Strangelove: Or, How I Learned to Stop Worrying and Love the Bomb*); just after the war (Cormac McCarthy's chilling *The Road*, 2006); and long after the fact (the original *Planet of the Apes*, dir. Franklin J. Schaffner 1968). Louise Lawrence's 1985 novel *Children of the Dust* does all three.
- **Environmental catastrophes:** This type of apocalypse comes in many shapes and lends itself well to the visual mediums of film and television, where the creators can show off their fun new special effects. The message: nature is huge and uncontrollable; humans are puny and arrogant. We can be smashed like bugs at any time, and we're fools to think otherwise. There are a few types we most often see:

- **It came from outer space:** comets, rogue planetoids, solar flares, and our recent obsession, meteors (directors Michael Bay's *Armageddon* and Mimi Leder's *Deep Impact*, both from 1998, lead us to question just what was going on that year that these overlapping disaster films were made!).
- **Earth runs amok:** volcanoes (directors Roger Donaldson's *Dante's Peak* and Mick Jackson's *Volcano* were both from 1997; again, what was going on *that* year?), tidal waves (*The Impossible*, dir. J.A. Bayona, 2013), ice ages (*The Day After Tomorrow*, dir. Roland Emmerich, 2004, complete with global flooding and runaway neutrinos; *2012*, also from Emmerich, 2009), etc. These are often the result of climate change, which is a hot news topic that gets eyes on pages and screens. The stories aren't just set during the event, as in the above list, but long after, as in the *Mad Max* franchise (dir. George Miller, 1979–2013); the first film is about a world suffering oil shortages, but the most recent, *Mad Max: Fury Road*, depicts a world with little to no water or plant life, representing some sort of end-stage environmental collapse; it also has some outstanding worldbuilding plus the Doof Warrior, who is completely bonkers and amazing.
- **Oops, my bad:** occasionally we have a "natural disaster" story where it's our fault due to our irresponsible meddling, as in *The Core* (dir. Jon Amiel, 2003).

- **Dragons:** This isn't a popular apocalypse. Maybe it's too silly? Possibly. But such a ridiculous apocalypse can be awesome, particularly if it brings out more outlandish Matthew McConaughey types to battle the giant fire-breathing lizards (see *Reign of Fire*, dir. Rob Bowman, 2002). Also, Sean Grigsby's Smoke Eaters series (2018–'21) brings these fantasy animals to a Midwestern American city and sics firefighters on them!
- **Biblical/religious apocalypse:** This type of apocalypse usually follows two possible scenarios: either a certain percentage of the population vanishes (Tim LaHaye and Jerry B. Jenkins's *Left Behind* series from 1995–2007) or one certain type of person dies, leaving everybody else unscathed, such as in "gendercides" (the 2002–'08 comic book series *Y: The Last Man* by Brian K. Vaughan and Pia Guerra). Sometimes this is a plague apocalypse, but often it's just unexplained or the explanation is murky. Thematically, it's often focused on showing the indispensability of the people who are gone or exploring the dynamics within the group that's still around and discovering what's revealed about them. Other examples include Aliya Whiteley's *The Beauty* (2014).

- **Nanotech/grey goo apocalypse:** A hypothetical end-of-the-world scenario involving molecular technology in which out-of-control self-replicating robots consume all matter on earth while building more of themselves (called "ecophagy", a word which means the consumption or eating of the environment). The original idea assumed machines were designed to have this capability, while popularisations have assumed that machines might somehow gain this capability by accident. The term "grey goo" was coined by nanotechnology pioneer Eric Drexler in his 1986 book *Engines of Creation*. It's easy to see how this is an extreme version of the robot apocalypse, where we're afraid of what we've created.
- **Social collapse/slow apocalypse:** In this scenario, things fall apart: complex economic systems crumble, everything that relied on cheap fossil fuels no longer works (or there's another type of technological disruption), and there might be a plague of some sort, plus environmental decay, because why not? Here we see the modern anxiety that Western post-industrial society will eventually collapse, that we depend too much on our tech, and that we'll quickly revert to patriarchal modes. For some this can be a cosy, nostalgic catastrophe depicting a sense of relief that we're returning to a simpler way of life, or it can go full-on *Mad Max*. We see this kind of apocalypse in E.M. Forster's story 'The Machine Stops' (1909; yes, the guy who wrote *Room with a View* (1908), *Howard's End* (1910), and other literary classics turned into costume porn starring Helena Bonham-Carter), S.M. Stirling's *Dies the Fire* (2004), and William Forstchen's *One Second After* (2009; an EMP takes out all the tech).
- **Reproductive apocalypses:** The world can't keep going if there are no new people, and problems with reproduction lead to an ageing population, a shrinking workforce, and an inevitable end. Sometimes the problem is low sperm counts, sometimes it's a virus or other medical issue that reduces the viability of foetuses, and sometimes it's a mysterious result of another apocalypse (nuclear, environmental, etc.), but it's easy to see how it represents a fear of the collapse of a recognised way of life, of the expectations we have for "how things are supposed to be". See P.D. James's *Children of Men* (1992) and Jane Rogers's *The Testament of Jessie Lamb* (2011).

Things That are Cool About Apocalyptic Fiction

Apocalyptic fiction is a way to safely destroy the world! It allows us to say, "Hey, this is what'll happen if we keep doing X" or "Y could happen and *whoo doggies it's gonna get bad!*" But it's also a way to show that maybe there's a better way moving forward. It's about problem solving, even if the only solution is to try again differently with new ideas from different people. To that end, it's worth noting that apocalyptic and post-apocalyptic SF is no longer just the remit of manly men who'll put the world back to rights, or at least protect the women and children from whatever threatens them. Recent decades have seen women writers catching up and female protagonists front and centre, with Imperator Furiosa leading the charge.

What to Pack in Your Bug-Out Bag

- **What's your apocalyptic catalyst and outcome?** The cause will have repercussions on the whole story. For example, survivors of a nuclear war will have to contend with radiation, which will negatively affect their health, as well as changes to weather, which will affect food supplies, amongst other things. An apocalyptic event is a major change in our world, and it'll have extreme ramifications, *right down the line*. The saying "turtles all the way down" refers to the mythological idea popularised by Terry Pratchett that Earth is sitting on a giant turtle's back, which is on another turtle's back, and on and on down the line. In genre writing, this is a shorthand for explaining that if you change one thing in the world, that will change something else, and that will in turn affect another thing, etc. So, you must consider all your turtles when fictionally destroying the world!
- **Is it an apocalypse of surplus or of scarcity?** This means that if you have, say, a climate catastrophe, the population will be reduced but resources such as water and food will also become scarce. But something like a zombie apocalypse means fewer humans who will have *more* resources (though they'll have to fight zombies to be able to eat in peace). Think about how this impacts the kind of story you can tell.
- **What geographical area will you cover?** Apocalypses are large scale, but you can't cover every city and country, unless you opt for an epistolary narrative such as the series of interviews compiled in Max Brooks's brilliant *World War Z* (2006). A story of a technological breakdown set in one town can be a microcosm, with the actions and consequences standing in for what's happening on a large scale across the world, but with characters that the reader will come to care about (see television's *Jericho*, 2006–'08). Furthermore, we often think of an apocalypse as the destruction of civilisation across the whole Earth, but individual places also suffer apocalypses, such as the Indian Ocean tsunami of 2004 or the 2010 Haiti earthquake, both of which killed hundreds of thousands and destroyed whole communities. So, while these events didn't destroy "the world", they destroyed *their world*. This is something to consider for your fiction; you don't always have to burn it all to the ground to start over.

- **When will you start the story: before, during, or after the apocalypse?** Apocalyptic fiction is set before and during an apocalypse; post-apocalyptic is set afterward and can also be **dystopic** depending on the apocalypse's outcome. Starting before the event means getting to know the characters in their "normal" lives, complete with day-to-day conflicts (that will definitely become more acute once the bombs drop); starting during the apocalyptic event means you're starting pretty much in the middle of the action, so you'll need to establish your characters and situation quickly; starting after the apocalypse means you're going to be dealing with either immediate issues (finding food, water, etc.) or further down-the-line issues (perhaps the after-effects of radiation poisoning or changes to the environment), which will affect how your characters interact and what their immediate concerns are. That being said, one thing to consider while the world is going to hell in a handbasket around our characters is that *they are bodies*, and bodies often need attention. So much early apocalyptic fiction was usually written by male writers and featured hale and healthy male characters, and if there were women, they were just being "protected" with no mention of any medical needs.[1] While this male-centric view of the apocalypse is changing, it still brings up an important consideration about our experiences as bodies: the great majority of us have at least one condition that requires medicines, many of us deal with chronic illnesses and disabilities, and even those of us who are "healthy" (a word like *perfect* that has no useful definition in the real world!) are going to end up dealing with injuries or illnesses as we age, and some of us will experience menstruation, pregnancy, childbirth, and menopause, all of which will only be so much more difficult to deal with in apocalyptic situations. Focusing on your characters' experiences inside their own bodies as they're dealing with the world falling apart is going to make them more realistic and more relatable to readers as well as increase the stakes, which makes for a better story.

---

1. Angus, 2017.

ACTIVITIES

Turtles all the way down: Let's use the example of post-peak oil. The world uses a lot of oil, mainly as petrol for transportation, but it's used to produce other items, too. We're on track to hit peak-oil output and, after that, the oil fields will produce less and less, which will have huge ramifications on our world. Things won't immediately go *Mad Max*, but the changes we'll experience are vital to worldbuilding. Do an internet search for everyday uses for oil and list those things in your immediate vicinity (such as wherever you are sitting) that use oil or its by-products. What will people have to use instead of these materials? Or what will the loss of these items mean for life as you know it now? This is how to turtle!

Rebuilding: Start your story after it's all fallen apart and decide on what should come after. Answer the following questions to start putting a story together. How many people will be in your settlement? 5, 20, 100? Where geographically is it (desert, mountains, seaside, former-urban)? What problems do your group face, such as lack of food/water, or danger from aliens/zombies/marauders? Who's in charge? Who *wants* to be in charge? What mistakes were made that led to the breakdown that you want to resolve? Clarify the threat to your main character and that character's goal: the threats can be nuclear fallout, starvation, catching a disease, being caught in a fast-moving forest fire, etc. The goal could be to find food or other resources such as water or medicines; to find other people or a specific person; or to get to a safe place, wherever that might be.

CYBERPUNK

Break out your sunglasses and your samurai sword and jack into the exhilarating neon-drenched virtual worlds of cyberpunk! Here, computers are king and computer skills are kingmakers. Hackers rub shoulders with cyborgs, drug addicts, and crime lords in dingy clubs beneath the urban sprawl of post-apocalyptic corporate overlords. Sure, society is collapsing, but with one last big score our bodies can be chrome!

A Short History of Cyberpunk

Precursors to cyberpunk include Philip K. Dick's *Do Androids Dream of Electric Sheep* (1968), Alice Sheldon's *The Girl Who Was Plugged In* (1973), the illustrations of French comics anthology *Métal Hurlant* (1974–'87) and the British *2000 AD* character *Judge Dredd* (first published 1977). However, the subgenre's essential origins are impossible to unplug from the increasing capabilities and possibilities of computer technology in the early 1980s. In these, cyberpunk finds "a metaphor for life, and even consciousness itself".[1] The term was first used by Bruce Bethke in his 1983 story 'Cyberpunk'; legendary editor Gardner Dozois then seized on it to describe some of the most exciting writers of the time. Like **Solarpunk**, it's both a subgenre and an aesthetic. It has an edgy non-conformist feel and is frequently populated by tech-literate—often tech-*enhanced*—antiheroes. The "cyber" part obviously refers to technology, to computer-mind interfaces and virtual worlds; the "punk" part refers to an attitude, a cynical and subversive stance taken by the genre's many malcontents and loners. The gritty, complex, arguably *vital* energy of cyberpunk was seen as both an enlivening of and a "materialist critique" of SF at the time, though its imagery has become ubiquitous in the decades since (see *The Matrix*, dir. the Wachowskis, 1999; and the video game *Deus Ex*, 2000).[2]

The work of two authors in particular catapulted cyberpunk into the literary spotlight: William Gibson with his award-winning *Neuromancer* (1984) and Bruce Sterling with his seminal *Mirrorshades: The Cyberpunk Anthology* (1986). Of these, it's Gibson (who coined the term "Cyberspace") who's probably done the most to shape readers' understanding of cyberpunk's themes and tropes. *Neuromancer* follows a has-been hacker whose nervous system has been ravaged by toxins leaving him unable to access the virtual reality of the matrix (no, not that one!). Cured of his condition to carry

---

1. McFarlane, et al., 2020, p. 7.
2. Fisher, 2018, p. 57.

out one last shady job, Gibson's protagonist leads readers through the subgenre's archetypal world of VR environments, mercenaries, shadowy cabals, digital consciousnesses, and invasive body modification. Sterling's anthology, meanwhile, codified many of the themes evident in the initial wave of cyberpunk short fiction. These include "the increasing cyborgization of experience", invasive prosthetics, the mingling of digital and biological data, globalisation, hard-edged cynical depictions of the near-future, and a ready literary identification with postmodernism.[3]

East Asian influences are particularly conspicuous in this subgenre, likely reflecting American anxieties about Japanese economic dominance in the early-to-mid 1980s (with the key text of cyberpunk in Japanese culture itself being probably Katsuhiro Otomo's manga series *Akira*, 1982–'90). Attentive readers will also note a *lot* of overlap between cyberpunk and **Dystopia**, especially in terms of grim, corporate-controlled, and ecologically ravaged worlds. Indeed, this is a pessimistic subgenre overall, with protagonists who are frequently addicts, freelance hackers, or small-time hustlers in larger criminal enterprises. They often carry crucial data in their cybernetically augmented brains and have no idea of how what they're being asked to do fits into the larger conspiracy. In a sea of information, cyberpunk protagonists are usually the last to know what's going on.

As the subgenre developed, the heteronormativity—indeed, the overt masculinist focus—of its early years began to dissolve in cyberpunk's greater thematic curiosity about countercultures and hybridity (mind/data, human/computer, male/female). As probably the woman writer most associated with the subgenre, Pat Cadigan's contribution deserves recognition alongside that of Gibson and Sterling. After a series of intense short stories including 'Rock On' (1984), her novels *Mindplayers* (1987) and, especially, *Synners* (1991) expanded cyberpunk's boundaries into feminist domains by portraying the subgenre's women as essential figures rather than mere sexualised cyphers. Other good examples interrogating gender, human identity, social hierarchies, and cybernetic relations in this era include Candas Jane Dorsey's '(Learning About) Machine Sex' (1988), Elizabeth Hand's nuanced *Winterlong* (1990), and Marge Piercy's *He, She and It* (1991). Later again, queer characters and spaces began to gain more prominence (see Syne Mitchell's *Technogenesis*, 2002, and Marianne de Pierres's *Nylon Angel*, 2004). Trans identities, too, have a natural home in this subgenre, concerned as it is with collapsing binaries in easily reconfigured virtual or cybernetic bodies.

From the outset, cyberpunk has also been a significant presence in film and anime; Ridley Scott's *Blade Runner* (1982) based on PKD's *Do Androids Dream...* along with *Akira* (dir. Katsuhiro Otomo, 1988) are considered foundational works. Then came the mind-bending Keanu Reeves double bill

---

3. Sterling, 1986, p. xiv.

of *Johnny Mnemonic* (dir. Robert Longo, 1995) based on a 1981 story by Gibson, and, of course, *The Matrix*, which made cyberpunk—and the slide-out Nokia 8110 phone—the definition of slickness for a whole generation. That said, many aspects of the era, such as the spinning telephone booths of *Hackers* (dir. Iain Softley, 1995), can seem kitschy to the contemporary eye.

Once the bleeding edge of cool, cyberpunk has settled into a comfortable middle age with an established canon and a critical framework for literary analysis. It has by now evolved into what we can call post-cyberpunk, a more modern variant that preserves the emphasis on overwhelming technological presence and social ills but tones down the dystopic tendencies for more optimistic and sedate—one might almost say respectable!—characters (see Ian McDonald's *Necroville/Terminal Cafe*, 1994, or *The Diamond Age* by Neal Stephenson, 1995). Yet even today this subgenre continues to develop through the likes of Malka Older's 2016 novel *Infomocracy* ("the most relevant cyberpunk thriller of the past few years"[4]) and Marie Lu's *Warcross* (2017). Change as it may, however, certain elements remain core to the feel of cyberpunk.

A Spotter's Guide: Low Life Meets High Tech

- **The city:** Cyberpunk, a subgenre of back alleys, illegal clubs, neon lights, and homebrew narcotics, is an example of hyper-urbanisation (see Judge Dredd's Mega City One). Its cities are simultaneously vast and yet claustrophobic moody puzzles, impossible for our protagonists to ever truly solve. Hong Kong has long been a huge influence (with Scott describing the LA of *Blade Runner* as "Hong Kong on a very bad day"[5]), especially the dense, ungoverned, chaotically built and now demolished enclave of Kowloon Walled City. Striking economic stratification is in evidence in the cyberpunk city, with the immense glass towers of the elite brooding over the polluted streets below. These cultural melting pots haphazardly combine social, linguistic, and culinary influences from all around the world. In terms of atmosphere, it's usually raining and it's usually night (even the primary setting of the 2020 videogame *Cyberpunk 2077* is the rain-drenched, neon-lit Night City). Beyond the urban limits is often a bleak and contaminated wasteland to which mutants and anarchists are consigned.
- **Criminal elements:** Cyberpunk cities are dangerous places, rife with street-level grifters and widespread criminality, as well as hosting more lethal transnational syndicates (often based in part on the Japanese Yakuza). It's here that the noir stylings of crime fiction

---

4. White, 2021, n.p.
5. Wheale, 1995, p. 107.

are most obviously transposed into the subgenre's high-tech world of grizzled private eyes, dodgy jobbers, twitchy drug addicts, and unlicensed doctors. It's not uncommon to encounter a femme fatale or, indeed, a homme fatale. Predictably, cybercrimes such as account hacking and identity theft are rampant; organ theft, supplying a transhumanist demand for body parts, is also not uncommon (shades of **Body Horror** here). Protagonists are usually small-time crooks forced by circumstances into larger criminal machinations and their consequences.

- **Corporate conflict:** The greed-is-good philosophy of the 1980s is a key strand of cyberpunk's DNA. Vast conglomerates own and run everything. Huge companies, seemingly answerable to no one, profit from the "commodification of human sensory and cognitive functions" (arguably anticipating how contemporary social-media platforms turn our photos and observations into dollars).[6] They carry out hostile takeovers—of rivals, nations, and even minds—as well as corporate espionage both directly and via off-the-books anti-hero hackers, fixers, or tricked-out mercenaries. When faced with such widespread corporate malpractice, many protagonists, such as that of television show *Mr. Robot* (2015–'20), turn to acts of resistance against the establishment (this being the "punk" part of cyberpunk).

- **Tech wear:** In worlds based on reputations and shady deals, cyberpunk characters need to look the real deal. But, more than that, they need to look themselves, brazenly combining elements from a global reservoir of jarring styles and traditions. Clothes are tight, often leather or PVC mixed seamlessly with fetish gear, collars, and masks. Variations on classic suits and fedoras will never go out of fashion for those identifying as men (see *Blade Runner* or *Johnny Mnemonic*), yet the look also embraces trashy t-shirts and panelled gilets that somehow cost a month's pay. Meanwhile, those identifying as women can be seen stepping out in everything from flawlessly tailored skirts and blouses in metallic fabrics to post-apocalyptic military surplus. Combat boots, high heels, baroque collars, trench coats, and layers are all common regardless of gender identity (see *The Matrix*), as are clothes with hand-painted anime characters and East Asian logograms. Classic accessories include transparent umbrellas, iridescent visors, katanas, roller skates, and even live animals.

- **Information as currency:** Perhaps the most important element of cyberpunk is that information has value, which has an appreciable impact on society and culture. In that way, the subgenre's earliest practitioners foresaw the information economy we live in today. A

---

6. Latham, 2020, p. 10.

strong belief runs through cyberpunk that "information wants to be free" of corporate and/or governmental control, something that again reflects the provocative and non-conformist "punk" influence. The moral aspect of this position is often traced to 'The Conscience of a Hacker' (usually known as 'The Hacker Manifesto'), a 1986 essay by Loyd Blankenship published in the underground ezine *Phrack*. A foundational document of hacker philosophy, the Manifesto maintains that there is more to hacking than simply showing off or causing chaos. Computer tech and the information contained therein, it says, should be used for the benefit and freedom of all.

Things That are Cool About Cyberpunk

In some ways, cyberpunk is one of the closest subgenres to the here and now of social-media giants swaying democracies, of a gig-economy workforce crushed beneath the heel of vast online platforms, and of empty commercialism numbing the masses. The themes of hopelessness or being trapped in economic systems ruled by distant corporate overlords are unfortunately as relevant today as they were in the 1980s. Cyberpunk's trick is taking the forces warping our world, following them to their worst possible outcomes, and then offering the reader a protagonist who says "No!"

Dialling up the Future

- **Talk the talk:** From Gibson onwards, cyberpunk has developed a distinct slang that is by now characteristic of the subgenre. Console cowboys and wetwired couriers up and down the sprawl jack into the net to steal data from the corps and we, as readers, just need to keep up! Appending "chrome" to words often indicates some aspect of cybernetics (a "chrome hound" is an enhanced investigator); "meatspace" is the physical world in contrast to Cyberspace; meanwhile some terms (such as "deep dive" or "wage slave") have come into real-world usage. Much of the language cynically or sarcastically mixes mythological references (a "ferryman" is an assassin) with terms drawn from medical science (to "flatline" is to die) and military jargon ("silly putty" is plastic explosive). The biggest influence, of course, is terminology from the early days of hacking and personal computers. There are many online gazetteers to draw from, but feel free to go all out making up your own lingo! And the more outlandish the better. Don't overexplain, though. Remember, your characters *know* this jargon. Allow your readers to work out meaning from context; it'll make them feel part of the scene.

- **Virtual Reality:** VR worlds are an essential part of cyberpunk, but because they're SF they go far beyond today's augmented reality and instead offer a truly immersive "proliferation of synthetic realities, to the point that simulated experience has begun to supplant the real thing".[7] Jacking into VR in cyberpunk is a way for characters denied freedom in meatspace to experience the sensory input of more satisfying or more exciting lives in a variety of different worlds even as their physical forms lie prone in a "state of hypermodern catatonia"[8]. Stories feature long stretches inside digital spaces as varied as photorealistic sites of revolution, to highly stylised infinite fluorescent "grids" that stress the environment's artificiality. Characters may become trapped or "lost" in these VR realms, mistaking them for the real world or actively choosing them over their own reality (examples of both are found in *Agents of SHIELD*'s Framework). VR is thus a powerful tool for the writer who wishes to destabilise their storyworld and their characters' certainties within it.
- **Posthumanism:** It's common for human characters in cyberpunk to have a variety of cybernetic enhancements ranging from data ports used to store valuable information in their brains to prosthetics of various kinds (see the discussion of cyborgs in the **Robots** section). These adaptations often have a sublime beauty, being "strangely alluring but equally discordant, even repellent".[9] They have style, though; they're statement pieces as much as practical requirements for technology-saturated lives. Think about how it'll affect your characters and your imagined culture if machines become an extension of the human body and vice versa. Also important is the ability to upload conscious minds onto the web/net/matrix or onto some sort of physical substrate (in *Neuromancer*, data constructs of human personalities are held on CD-ROM!). This, in some respects, is the most cyberpunk thing of all: human consciousness becoming pure data.
- **Global world, local flavours:** Depending on its origin and setting, different strands of cyberpunk have different flavours. Or, as writer Noah Smith once joked on Twitter, "The cool thing about Cyberpunk coming true is that we got *all* the cyberpunk futures. China: universal surveillance and social control. America: cool gadgets and staggering inequality. Russia: shadowy plots, covert ops, and assassins. Japan: Japan".[10] Think about where you want to set your cyberpunk story and how you might use minutia and detail to reflect that. Maybe you want to

---

7. Latham, 2020, p. 8.
8. Fisher, 2018, p. 55.
9. Goicoechea, 2020, p. 25.
10. Smith, Noah, 2018, n.p.

set it in a dense West-African metropolis and incorporate local cultural elements or allusions to history. Or maybe you're thinking about how a cyberpunk story set in a Siberian mining town during the arctic winter would play out. In all cases, of course, it's crucial to do your research.

- **The present through the looking glass:** Gibson has always claimed that his cyberpunk fiction is really just "writing about the present".[11] This is to say that we can still find possibilities in cyberpunk as creators by deploying it to unpack how technology today is used to concentrate capital and subvert power. Consider how, for instance, elements of the subgenre's original inspiration live on in troll-farms and election-swaying fake news, in hacktivist collectives, in surveillance capitalism, in the dark web, and in cryptocurrency (especially the environmental harmfulness of the latter). Any fiction that addresses these has significant value.

---

11. SPIN staff, 2019, n.p.

ACTIVITIES

Nightlife: This activity is about worldbuilding, about capturing the cyberpunk mood and aesthetic. Write a scene in which your protagonist goes to an underground club to deliver stolen data to a contact. Try to capture the sensory experience of this setting: what is the music like? What is the lighting like? How are people dressed and behaving? What kind of cybernetic enhancements are visible or even just suggested? Is there a sense of menace or hedonism or a combination of both? Who here might be a criminal and who might be an undercover cop? Place your reader in the scene and bring it to life via sensory detail as much as possible!

Enter the matrix: Consider how your protagonist might enter a virtual environment and what that cyberspace might look like. Is it a version of our primary world (like in *Free Guy*, dir. Shawn Levy, 2021) or, perhaps, a heightened overtly computerised realm like in *Tron* (dir. Steven Lisberger, 1982). Maybe it's overrun with targeted ads like the internet nowadays. Perhaps it shares the *Sims*-style aesthetic of Facebook's Metaverse or perhaps it's an old-school text-dominated reality where your characters manipulate literal file folders and windows. Write a scene where your character interacts with a competitor inside this space.

SOLARPUNK

Hope is not lost! We can create a better world by working together. By rejecting the preconceptions of late-stage capitalism, it's possible to imagine a life that's kinder to our environment, our societies, and ourselves. Solarpunk gives form to that idea, not by abandoning modern living for clog dancing and tetanus, but by embracing high-tech solutions to our crises of energy, agriculture, and democracy. This future's so bright, we've gotta wear smartshades.

A Short History of Solarpunk

Asking "what does a sustainable civilisation look like, and how can we get there?", solarpunk first emerged in the early 2000s and, like its stylish cousins **Steampunk** and **Cyberpunk**, arose in opposition to capitalism and authoritarianism.[1] However, unlike steampunk, it rejects the reactionary tendency to retreat from our problems into imagined historical techno-dilettantism, and, unlike cyberpunk, it adopts a blatantly optimistic perspective. Indeed, solarpunk shares an interest in community building, activism, and prefigurative politics (meaning actively modelling the world it wants) with the best of **Utopian** writing (and, as with that subgenre, writers here derive drama and narrative tension from beyond the obvious SF antagonists). Yet whereas utopia is in some ways an intellectual puzzle, solarpunk has a crucial element of practicality and lived experience. Its beginnings as a distinct subgenre and aesthetic are closely bound to, on the one hand, early 2010s online culture (specifically people's abilities to collaborate and share art via Tumblr) and, on the other, the horrifying reality of our contemporary climate crisis. It's the genre of the Anthropocene, the present moment in Earth's history during which the impact of humanity is legible on our ecosystem and climate and, as such, intersects with real-life environmental movements like Extinction Rebellion. "We're Solarpunks," says manifesto writer Adam Flynn, "because the only other options are denial or despair".[2] Indeed, a crucial aspect of solarpunk is that it often takes place on the far side of renewable-energy transition in worlds where climate collapse has been arrested or reversed. Yet it isn't a back-to-Earth movement but instead a field of progressive technology. It's a hopeful subgenre of algae-powered wooden **Robots** and invisible solar panels inside every pane of glass. It focuses on ecological, responsible, and self-sustaining communities

---

1. Springett, 2017, n.p.
2. Flynn, 2014, n.p.

(architects, for instance, love solarpunk!). It's an aspiration, it's a dream, it's a meme, it's a *vibe*.

More than that, the subgenre is predicated on a can do—and, in many cases, *must* do—attitude. It recognises that the industrial and agricultural bases of contemporary society are shakier than we'd like to admit (to paraphrase Alfred Henry Lewis, society is only ever nine missed meals away from anarchy[3]) and so it seeks practical solutions. Where other subgenres centre the nerd—the brains or the bookworm—solarpunk's maker-hero is often the geek, the mechanical tinkerer who's good with their hands and can rewire your wind turbine or build an anaerobic digester to power your electric buggy. Self-sufficiency, sustainability, and solidarity are key in terms of both themes and plot material throughout tales where bulletproof-vest fibres are upcycled into sweaters and seagrass is used to sieve plastic particles from the ocean. A typical solarpunk story envisions an Earthbound or near-contemporary future as radically altered as anything in space opera or Fantasy. In place of vast empires or corporations, solarpunk settings situate the universal in the local. They're usually small egalitarian societies defined by communal ownership and regenerated landscapes. Whole villages float on the sea, entire neighbourhoods overflow with verdant rooftop gardens, stratospheric balloons connect the internet to all, and bicycle-riding gene wizards tend to the vertical farms of co-living agri-topias. Seed vaults and homebrew carbon capture ensure the preservation and protection of the natural world while an emphasis on gender and racial equality, along with artistic self-expression, nourish the human imagination. Thus, the genre boldly defies **Dystopia** by daring to imagine a hopeful and pleasant green existence where things move at a slower pace and technology is subsumed into nature for the benefit of all.

The ancestors of the elements that comprise solarpunk arguably include such SF classics as Frank Herbert's *Dune* (1965), Ernest Callenbach *Ecotopia* (1975), and Octavia E. Butler's *The Parable of the Sower* (1993), as well as Ursula K. Le Guin's *Always Coming Home* (1985). Much of Hayao Miyazaki's recognisable Studio Ghibli aesthetic also anticipates the visuals of the solarpunk imagination (think the beautiful plant-draped houses). As it has developed throughout the early twenty-first century, solarpunk has drawn more and more on Afro- and African-futurism, with examples including the plant-based technology of Nnedi Okorafor's 2005 YA debut *Zahrah the Windseeker*, the advanced Wakanda of director Ryan Coogler's *Black Panther* (2018), and the restorative planetary community of N.K. Jemisin's Hugo-winning novelette 'Emergency Skin' (2019). Elsewhere, books such as Alaya Dawn Johnson's 2013 YA novel *The Summer Prince*—set in a nanotech-empowered Brazilian matriarchy—interrogate the artistic aspects of

---

3. Lewis, 1896, p. 2.

solarpunk; Kim Stanley Robinson's *The Ministry for the Future* (2020) does the hard work of reconfiguring economic and political systems for a post-capitalist future; and Becky Chambers's Monk and Robot novellas (2021–'22) foreground the compassionate side of the genre. Many of the first anthologies of solarpunk writing have given pride of place to writers from the Global South, particularly South America. Reflecting the genre's DIY attitude, much solarpunk currently exists as self-published stories online, in fanzines, or volumes from independent presses (with several edited or co-edited by Sarena Ulibarri). Which is, of course, where you as the writer come in.

A Spotter's Guide: Piecing the Future Together

- **The end of capitalism:** Solarpunk stories are cries of resistance against corporations, centrally controlled infrastructure, patent tyranny, and the present moment of late-stage capitalism/neoliberalism/neo-serfdom. They frequently feature worker-owned enterprises and characters banding together to rebuild a world that's been destroyed by the fossil-fuel industries. Work in these stories is portrayed as meaningful and contributory rather than an endless parade of bullshit jobs (yes, that's really the term). Solarpunk offers an alternative to our world of market forces and artificially sustained inequalities, of shortages and econo-political shenanigans. Homelessness is a rarity in solarpunk stories. Digital nomadism is common. There's enough to go around because people don't hoard their wealth or their technical developments. Some might call it socialism, some might call it the Green New Deal, but to solarpunk protagonists it's simply the only way we can all survive.
- **Community-based projects:** Solarpunk stories are about communities coming together to improve themselves in a sustainable fashion. Indeed, Flynn maintains that what lies at the core of solarpunk is "infrastructure as a form of resistance".[4] What this means in a spec-fic context is groups of characters standing in opposition (what Flynn calls "local resistance") to social, economic, and cultural hierarchies, those being governmental, financial, or corporate hegemonies. However, this isn't usually the armed resistance of so many libertarian wet dreams but, instead, one predicated on community support enabled by reappropriated technologies; it's a resistance to energy monopolies (by, say, local photovoltaic farms supplying neighbourhoods or streets), to banks (by forming credit unions or barter networks), or to institutional inequalities (by setting up volunteer coding schools or opening makerspaces). On the crucial creative side of things, solarpunk looks— as the poet Patrick Kavanagh once advised—not to the values of the

---

4. Flynn, 2014, n.p.

shiny and distant metropolis of, say, cyberpunk, but instead to the social and artistic validity of their local, and often intentional, communities.

- **Get the look:** Loose-fitting fashions with a neo-peasant aesthetic dominate in solarpunk. The clothing in the fiction and cosplay is often repurposed or lovingly repaired from garments that would otherwise be thrown out, so it's an ethical stance as much as style. It's a rejection of so-called fast fashion for sustainability and individual flair, and, in that way, there's no single type of solarpunk clothing style. It varies from modernised traditional dress (see *Black Panther*) to new items from independent creators, from primitive futurism to 3D-printed garb, and from earth tones to rich bright colours. The more advanced materials are often self-cleaning or antibacterial. Accentuate with a messenger bag for a homemade computer tablet or a pair of Bluetooth earrings upcycled from junked metals. Love and mend and wear until well worn out.

- **Urban agriculture:** Much real-world farming these days is industrial-scale agribusiness that has a significant impact on our ecosystem and is divorced from the eventual consumer. By contrast, solarpunk stories centre more intimate operations in which people (and robots) can get their hands (and articulated joints!) dirty. These can be rooftop farms growing fruit or berries tended to by drones, off-grid solar-powered vertical farms repurposing any number of discarded "single use" containers, or even free-range chickens (see Gregory Scheckler's story 'Grow, Give, Repeat', 2018) sometimes tracked on the blockchain as they peck their way through futuristic town centres. Often drawing on the principles of permaculture, urban agriculture in solarpunk is a labour of love as much as an environmentally conscious exercise in fulfilling communal needs.

- **Radical imagining/subversion:** To write or be solarpunk, argues academic Jennifer Hamilton "is to mount a resistance to the mainstream present by imagining an alternative future".[5] It is, after all, a *punk* movement. It wants to show us that a better world *is* possible (and that you can have a good time breaking away from the status quo). It's unapologetic about wanting to make space in the world for BIPOC and LGBTQI+ people. Writing solarpunk is thus taking a stand against not just contemporary hierarchies but also against dominant narratives of doom and gloom. It has an activist element and strives to bring about an end to the Industrial Age. Its concern with empathy and compromise are, unfortunately, radical and subversive in our early twenty-first century. Moreover, its themes of environmental responsibility dovetail with a concern for social justice recognisable in things such as the Black Lives Matter and Occupy movements.

---

5. Hamilton, 2017, n.p.

Things That are Cool About Solarpunk

Solarpunk offers a literary and artistic framework for influencing today with imagery of a better tomorrow, not by being idealistic but by attempting to answer real questions about how we can achieve sustainability and respond to the climate crisis (if you want an academic perspective on this, check out what's called the Energy Humanities). Solarpunk is for you if you want to write about our symbolic relationship with nature and wish to foreground stories of individual creativity contributing to community accomplishment. Techno-optimism lies at the core of solarpunk and, in an increasingly dystopian real world already saturated in equally dystopian defeatist narratives (both in fiction and reality), there's a lot to be said for giving readers *hope*.

You'll Have to Get Crafty!

- **Do it yourself:** The DIY impulse is an essential aspect of solarpunk. The subgenre is filled with tinkerers building solar-charged powerwalls from wrecked electric cars that would otherwise be junked and with green philosophers overcoming government inadequacies with practical local action. The key thing is that solarpunk characters are always learning and putting that education into practice, not just by producing punk zines to share ideas for fostering radical communities but also physically building anti-racist urban spaces. These are stories filled with 3D printing, computer-aided design (CAD), and computerised machining that has democratised manufacturing, increased resilience, and enabled self-sufficiency by allowing anyone to be a maker. In general, solarpunk has human protagonists, as stories of alien intervention, while not unheard of (see Cadwell Turnbull's Afrofuturist novel *The Lesson*, 2019), move away from solarpunk's emphasis on humanity sorting out its own shit (or, presumably, recycling it into some kind of feedstock or manure).
- **Renewable energy:** The clue's in the name! Any solarpunk story is underpinned by responsible, renewable power sources (or at least the transition towards them). It's not unusual to write about wind power (either static turbines or floating inflatables tethered to the ground) and wave/tidal power, but the most common source—for it's the most decentralised—is solar power. Perhaps this is transmitted to homes via genetically engineered cybervines that plug directly into home appliances or computers. Perhaps it's generated by individual homes themselves. Solarpunk stories are also filled with ocean-going tankers propelled by computer-trimmed sails, by futuristic airships going

wherever the wind takes them, and by modular, locally produced and maintained electric buggies—or even legged vehicles!—running on batteries, though remember that distance and speed often become limiting factors in these stories (which is partially why there's such a concentration on the local). What goes in the tank will vary from story to story, but the important thing is that it doesn't cost the Earth.

- **Nature and tech in harmony:** Solarpunk is less about a pre-industrial agrarian return to nature than a philosophy of *post*-industrial working *with nature*. These are stories of techno-eco-speculation. They're filled with leafy vistas, even in urban spaces, but subsumed within are technological devices ranging from the upcycled remnants of our own civilisation to newly developed advancements such as nanotech, AI, or biomimic robots. Most solarpunk stories take place in a world where the built environment has been withdrawn, where rewilding is commonplace, and necessary infrastructure—such as manufacturing, recycling, distributed AI, or even high-speed rail—has been moved underground. Buildings are constructed out of carbon-sequestering metamaterials and bedecked with living facades that further clean the air as symbiotic biotech blurs the boundaries between the cityscape and the natural world. Telepresence robots take the place of transcontinental air travel, and, in the most advanced examples, highways have been ripped up and replaced with greenways or animal corridors (though transport options remain for those with disabilities; this is, after all, an inclusive society). People contribute time and scientific expertise to local farms or wildlife conservation projects, seeing nature as a companion and not something to be colonised and commercialised.

- **Art Nouveau influences:** Solarpunk's roots in art run suitably deep. In particular, a significant influence on the subgenre's feel is the Art Nouveau of the late 1800s and early 1900s, a style that stressed a commitment to fine detail and artisanal qualities. Unsurprisingly for solarpunk, leaves and vines and natural tones predominate in a rejection of mass industrialisation. Crucially, Art Nouveau was informed by the German concept of "Gesamtkunstwerk" or "total work of art", the idea being to make everything beautiful for everyone rather than just a few rich sponsors.[6] Solarpunk has absorbed this intention fully with accessible splendour inherent in imaginary worlds of stained-glass solar panels and skyscrapers with sweeping organic lines. Remember, characters in solarpunk don't just make things, they make *beautiful* things.

- **Beware "greenwashing":** Emphasising the "punk" aspect of the subgenre, a solarpunk story generally benefits from standing for something. It's a meaningful artistic movement grounded in a desire

---

6. @InvaderXan, 2018, n.p.

for—even anticipation of—real change, focusing not on what we have to lose but on what we have to gain. It's not enough to simply slap some synthetic ivy on the outside of a building and be done with it. The solarpunk readership appreciates commitment and will delight more than most in your use of convincing detail and technology. Authors in this subgenre will thus gain a lot from immersing themselves in online discussions and innovations in this exciting and still developing field.

ACTIVITIES

Problem-based learning: Write a story where you're apprenticed to an itinerant gene merchant in a solarpunk future. You and your mentor have just arrived (in your mobile wooden lab) to a village where a disease is wiping out the lush local plant life. Your mentor sets you the task of identifying this disease and, if possible, finding a cure. This requires you to interact with a variety of village inhabitants and, in this way, you offer the reader a cross section of this advanced solarpunk community. Who will you meet?

Biography of a piece of tech: Pick a piece of technology in your home today. Maybe it's your computer or your phone, maybe it's your refrigerator or your car. Consider its future. What might happen to it or its components in a solarpunk future that takes the landfill or the scrapheap out of the equation. How might it be upcycled or recycled? How might it be incorporated into a more sustainable life going forward? Be innovative and don't get too hung up on what's possible right now! Think of your tech as a protagonist and try to make its story as compelling as that of any character.

CHAPTER TWO

FANTASY

What is Fantasy?

Fantasy is sometimes misunderstood. Too many people automatically think it's nothing but unicorns, elves, magic, and quests. But Fantasy has a longer history than Science Fiction: basically, many of our earliest stories were Fantasy. Go to any large library and you'll find shelves *full* of books about the genre's evolution and significance (and, if you are into the literary criticism side of things, these are often fascinating texts). Of course, we know that you just want to get to *the fun writing stuff*, the reason why you picked up this book in the first place, but stick with us for a bit longer.

Imagine it's late autumn and you're in a wooded area, clomping or rolling through leaves of various colours, shapes, and sizes on the ground. If you gathered up an armful, how difficult would it be to match each leaf to the tree it came from? And then to the branch it fell from? That's the challenge of describing how Fantasy evolved because its history is closely aligned to various cultures' folktales or fairy tales. In his essay 'On Fairy Stories', J.R.R. Tolkien explains that "It is indeed easier to unravel a single *thread*—an incident, a name, a motive—than to trace the history of any *picture* defined by many threads."[1] What he means is that it's easier to take one element of a story, such as the motif of a magic mirror found in 'Snow White', and attempt to follow that thread back to its source than to find where a whole story came from.

Though if it's so complicated, what's the point of mentioning it here? Well, for one thing, it's because its complexity is opportunity. As writers we get attracted to (okay, obsessed with!) those shiny elements in stories: the dragons, the legendary swords, the names of make-believe places. As writers we know how those elements made us feel as young (or old) readers, a feeling that isn't dependent upon understanding where the thing came from. So, we might not know where this element or story originated, but we know the magic it holds and use it to attain our objective of capturing an audience.

---

1. Tolkien, 1988, p. 21 [in footnote] (his emphasis).

Yet with that complexity—the inability to easily label something or put it in a box that fits it *just right*—comes uninformed ideas. And, as writers, if you haven't come across these myths of what Fantasy is and isn't, you will soon, and our job is to help you navigate those myths. Let's break some down.

Myth 1 - Fantasy is just escapism: Tolkien has been misquoted in his exploration of escapism (his argument was paraphrased in an Ursula K. Le Guin essay as "fantasy is escapist and that is its glory"[2]). However, the gist of what he said on the topic is rather important here: that losing ourselves in another realm via Fantasy might be escaping, for a while, from the noise and machinery of the real world, but it's a way for the reader to reconnect to that which is most important: nature and the natural world around us. Tolkien saw Fantasy as "a natural human activity".[3] He explains that "it certainly does not destroy or even insult Reason; and it does not either blunt the appetite for, nor obscure the perception of, scientific verity" because we use Fantasy to see things: "For creative Fantasy is founded upon the hard recognition that things are so in the world as it appears under the sun; on a recognition of fact, but not a slavery to it."[4] For Tolkien, at least, Fantasy was closely connected to our world.

Myth 2 - Fantasy is just for kids: Since our earliest days as storytellers and story listeners, tales from *The Iliad* and *The Odyssey* to *Beowulf* have been for everyone. The earliest fairy tales, as you'll learn in the **Folktales and Fairy Tales** section, weren't specifically for children (that happened later). Something shifted, though, in our Industrial Age, with production and capital becoming society's narrow focus. Adulthood is now foisted upon us with the command to set aside "childish things" that aren't immediately linked to the commodification of just about everything around us (like how our parents want us to "have real jobs" and make money!). Think of Fantasy as a way for us to reconnect to our ancestors and the myths, legends, and folktales that were important to them. Our love of the Fantasy genre is a continuation of that.

Myth 3 - Fantasy doesn't mean anything: We gotta call shenanigans on this because all writing, all stories, mean something. Fantasy, like Science Fiction and Horror, is a great way to explore our own culture or society; we use these genres to approach things "from the side" instead of head-on, as with mimetic fiction (that which represents our "real world"). In

---
2. Le Guin, 1979, 'Escape Routes', p. 204.
3. Tolkien, 1988, p. 55.
4. Tolkien, 1988, p. 55.

her essay 'The Child and the Shadow', Le Guin explores the function of Fantasy and argues that as we grow and mature, we begin to realise that the darker parts of ourselves—the shadow—exists inside us and that "most of the great works of fantasy are about that journey [of realisation]; and that fantasy is the medium best suited to a description of that journey, its perils and rewards".[5] She claims that "fantasy is the language of the inner self"[6] because "the great fantasies, myths and tales are indeed like dreams: they speak *from* the unconscious *to* the unconscious in the *language* of the unconscious—symbol and archetype".[7] Fantasy, then, allows us to explore the deeper concerns about being a human—relationships, family, pain, grief, etc.—in a way that we often can't in the language of our day-to-day world.

Myth 4 - Fantasy is formulaic: Fantasy might contain various tropes that are repeated from story to story, but, unlike other genres such as Romance or Crime, you don't automatically know how the story will end (with a Happily Ever After or the murderer being caught). Same with Science Fiction and, to a point, with Horror. We've mentioned before, these are really "modes" rather than genres because they don't follow formulas, which make them into "discussions" that you, as a writer, will join.[8] (Note: Despite this theory of "modes", we use the terms "genre" and "subgenre" because they're the relevant marketing categories in the publishing industry.)

So, now that we've explored some misconceptions of one of our favourite genres, let's take a closer look at some popular subgenres of Fantasy and get writing!

---

5. Le Guin, 1979, 'The Child and the Shadow', p. 65.
6. Le Guin, 1979, 'The Child and the Shadow', p. 70.
7. Le Guin, 1979, 'The Child and the Shadow', p. 62 (her emphasis).
8. Mendlesohn, 2003, pp. 1–2.

FOLKTALES AND FAIRY TALES

We're all familiar with the Disney films *Snow White*, *Cinderella*, and *Sleeping Beauty*, and some of us know those stories from books. But there's more going on beneath the surface than you might have first suspected, and their links to the Fantasy genre are very strong: in many cases, older tales—folktales—are "taproot texts". And rewriting fairy tales, or writing stories inspired by folktales, remains very popular in the Fantasy genre! Once upon a time....

A Short History of Folktales and Fairy Tales

Fairy tales seem simple; it makes sense that "stories for kids" should be simple, but the truth, as ever, is much more complicated. There are as many studies and books about the origins and evolution of fairy tales as there are tales themselves, so condensing the history results in a shallow glance at best. Below you'll find some resources to consult if you want to know more.

Folktales were originally oral stories that were handed down from generation to generation as a way of passing along a culture's values, history, etc., and to instruct or warn listeners about various situations or dangers.[1] Within the folktale category are numerous types of materials, from myths and legends to lullabies and limericks, but for our purposes we'll only consider fairy-tale type stories (and yes, that's vague, but this is a big, rambling topic and we only have so much space!). Some researchers claim that the original folktales are thousands of years old, "as far back as the Megalithic period".[2] In many cases they form what's called "taproot texts", those being stories from very long ago that are themselves the "root" of later tales in the Fantasy genre.[3] Because of the close relationship between the very old folktales and the more recent fairy tales, it isn't a stretch to consider folktales as taproot texts for the fairy tale as we know it today, and then to extend this idea to thinking about fairy tales as taproot texts for more contemporary Fantasy stories and novels.

Charles Perrault's 1697 collection of fairy tales, *Contes du temps passé avec des Moralitez* (*Tales of Olden Times*), also more familiarly known as *Mother Goose's Tales*, helps illustrate this point.[4] Published in France, the book contains only a handful of fairy tales, based on the folktales that

---

1. Warner, 2014. p. xvi; Zipes, 1992, p. 5.
2. Zipes, 1992, p. 5.
3. Clute, 1997, 'Taproot Texts', n.p.
4. Ashley, 1997, n.p.

everyone—from peasants to the upper classes—knew at the time.[5] Several are still recognisable to us today, being the primary source of 'Sleeping Beauty', 'Puss in Boots', 'Cinderella', and others. In a nod to the desire that these tales have "social value"[6], Perrault "added moralitiés to make the lessons of his tales clear"[7] so "that the manners and mores of the young would reflect the social power, prestige, and hierarchy of the ruling classes".[8]

These fairy tales, then, were meant to entertain but also to establish—in literature for children and adults—the status quo of society at the time. If you think about the setting of many familiar fairy tales—with their royalty and peasants, castles and kingdoms—you'll recognise how Perrault's time inspired those stories and "essentially reflected late feudal conditions" in Europe.[9] We can see, too, the huge influence that Perrault's tales had on Disney: you can trace "a direct line from the Perrault Fairy Tale of court society to the Walt Disney cinematic Fairy Tale of the culture industry" without any difficulty![10] This is why tales such as 'Cinderella' and 'Beauty and the Beast' share similarities; despite their original folktale's source, when Perrault wrote them down they became linked to a certain place in a certain time, and those elements of setting and character types are now part of how we recognise them as fairy tales.

In the nineteenth century, academics and cultural researchers Jacob and Wilhelm Grimm (the Brothers Grimm) investigated and recorded folktales to find the "pure" original national identity of Germany they believed existed in stories from the past.[11] Like with Perrault, some of their tales came from the lower classes, but many they collected from members of a well-educated middle-class and even aristocrats.[12] The Grimms, however, saw these tale-tellers as "only mediators of the treasures of ancient storytelling of ordinary people".[13] While Perrault's tales perpetuate the status quo of his seventeenth-century French society, the tales in the Grimms' earlier editions often boost what academic Jack Zipes calls an "'underdog' perspective": the "innocent" protagonists "must prove their integrity and demonstrate virtues such as kindness to be worthy of a reward".[14] In later editions, the tales changed "to accord with middle-class notions of taste, decorum, and style". [15]

---

5. Zipes, 1991, p. 8.
6. Zipes, 1991, p. 9.
7. Warner, 2014, p. 114.
8. Zipes, 1991, p. 9.
9. Zipes, 1992, p. 6.
10. Zipes, 1991, p. 17.
11. Zipes, 2014, p. xxv.
12. Zipes, 2014, p. xxxiii.
13. Zipes, 2014, p. xxxii.
14. Zipes 2014, pp. xxxv–xxxvi.
15. Zipes, 2014, p. xxxvii.

It's important to note here the authorial *intention* of figures such as Perrault and the Grimms. In both cases, and with some writers who followed, such as Hans Christian Andersen, literature for children was written not just to entertain but also to teach and socialise young readers. The message isn't always plainly stated, and the supernatural element—often some sort of magic—isn't the focus of the tale, with the characters often taking it for granted. To clear up any confusion, another type of tale—the fable—is similar in some ways to folktales and fairy tales, but different in that the supernatural element is often embodied in a speaking animal, and the tales were usually written with the sole purpose of teaching lessons. Aesop's Fables are the most well-known, with tales such as 'The Ant and the Grasshopper' (lesson: prepare for winter or starve) or 'The Tortoise and the Hare' (lesson: life is a marathon not a sprint) becoming popular enough that most of us came across them as twentieth- and twenty-first-century children.

Beloved Fantasy author J.R.R. Tolkien also mused on the source and function of fairy tales. In his famous 1964 essay 'On Fairy Stories', he attempts to define the fairy story (fairy tale) by first examining the source of the idea of fairies and elves. He concludes that it's more difficult than at first assumed:

> The definition of a fairy story—what it is, or what it should be—does not, then, depend on any definition or historical account of elf or fairy but upon the nature of *Faërie*: the Perilous Realm itself, and the air that blows in that country. I will not attempt to define that, not to describe it directly. It cannot be done. Faërie cannot be caught in a net of words; for it is one of its qualities to be indescribable, though not imperceptible. ... For the moment I will only say this: a 'Fairy-story' is one which touches on or uses Faërie, whatever its own main purpose may be: satire, adventure, morality, fantasy.[16]

Tolkien goes on to argue that many of the tales collected as fairy tales shouldn't be because they don't have anything to do with *Faërie*.[17] You see how this seemingly simple topic is very similar to an onion: the more you peel away at it, the more your eyes sting! So, let's shift away from thinking about their source to considering the stories themselves.

A Spotter's Guide: What Makes a Fairy Tale Feel Like a Fairy Tale?

There's something intriguing about fairy tales in the way we recognise them as such. They have this certain "feel" that's difficult to define or pin down, yet they contain elements we recognise:

---

16. Tolkien, 1988, p. 10.
17. Tolkien, 1988, p. 11.

- **Fairy tales take advantage of motifs:** a motif is a thing—an image, item, idea, character, colour, etc.—used repeatedly in a story to help support or strengthen the theme. We see a lot of motifs repeated across Western fairy tales in particular: the rule of three; colours symbolic of purity (white), death or love (red), evil (black); animals that are actually cursed humans; lost children; wicked witches; etc. Sometimes the motif is a symbol, and it's that symbolism that we remember and that we recognise when an author undertakes rewriting a fairy tale. For example, Angela Carter retells 'Snow White' in her story 'Snow Child' (1979) as Neil Gaiman does in 'Snow, Glass, Apples' (1996), and Cat Hellisen does in *Cast Long Shadows* (2022), and their stories are different from the tale as we know it: the former contains some really dark elements such as necrophilia, and the latter two are told from the point of view of the stepmother. But the motifs of the colours and of the relationship between a girl and her stepmother are there and help us recognise the origin story each author is playing with.
- **Fairy tales speak across generations:** Fairy tales and folktales contain within them themes that we often recognise as basic human experiences, such as jealousy of the young as we age (as seen in 'The Snow Child') or how underestimating others' evil intentions can lead us to make bad decisions (as in 'Snow, Glass, Apples'). These tales have been passed down for millennia because there's something about them that speaks to us in a way that's difficult to vocalise, but that longevity means you're starting with something that readers will have some familiarity with.
- **Fairy tales seem familiar:** Even when we're unfamiliar with a particular fairy tale or folktale, though, there's this certain texture and ambience that a retelling has that somehow hearkens back to a time before, and, as humans descended from uncounted generations before us who told stories around fires, we see something there that's familiar. Tolkien's take on it helps us better understand that being unable to explain something so simple yet mysterious is perhaps why we love them:

> The realm of fairy-story is wide and deep and high and filled with many things: all manner of beasts and birds are found there; shoreless seas and stars uncounted; beauty that is an enchantment, and an ever-present peril; both joy and sorrow as sharp as swords. In that realm a man may, perhaps, count himself fortunate to have wandered, but its very richness and strangeness tie the tongue of a traveller who would report them. And while he is there it is dangerous for him to ask too many questions, lest the gates should be shut and the keys be lost.[18]

---

18. Tolkien, 1988, p. 3.

Recent successful books that use folktales and fairy tales as source material include Catherynne Valente's *Deathless* (2011; the Russian Revolution mixed with a Russian fairy tale); *Children of Blood and Bone* by Tomi Adeyemi (2018; based on West-African folklore and mythology); *Daughter of the Moon Goddess* by Sue Lynn Tan (2022; inspired by the Chinese legend of the Moon Goddess); and *The Hazel Wood* by Melissa Albert (2018; contemporary Fantasy with some creepy fairy-tale elements).

Things That are Cool About Folktales and Fairy Tales

Fairy tales are weird. Think about it: a mermaid gives away her voice to become human? A girl dies of a cursed apple and is entombed in a crystal coffin? A grandmother freed, still alive, from the inside of a wolf? If you're here because you want to try your hand at Fantasy writing, fairy tales and folktales contain some of the most imaginative storylines and motifs you'll ever find! It's fun to take a story that's so familiar and see how you can build a new one using its themes and related motifs in a new way. Changing things up, such as setting the story of Snow White in our own time, gives you the chance to experiment inside a familiar context, which can feel safe when you're just starting out.

Beware the Poisoned Apple

- **Magic systems:** In the **Witches** section, we discuss magic systems in more detail. In fairy tales, though, the magic is often just *there*, as Tolkien explained. It's rarely controlled because it's a wild force, so dabbling in folktales and fairy tales gives you the chance to explore magic as a force that doesn't follow clearly listed rules or restrictions like in some magic systems. However, any magic system should still have some internal logic so that, for example, you don't give a non-magical character sudden magical powers at the end of a story to get them out of trouble (better known as *deus ex machina*, or "ghost in the machine", this is a way of pulling the rug out from under the reader).
- **Folktales and fairy tales from non-western cultures:** If you're reading this book, you're reading it in English and so your experience of these types of tales will mainly be those from Western Europe, but there are so many others out there. It's okay to want to retell an old favourite, especially if you want to approach it in a new way or use it to explore a new theme (like Carter, Gaiman, or Hellisen have done). But do keep in mind that there's a lot of folklore out there to discover and re-introduce to the world.

- **Fairy tales and a "moral message":** Above we explained that early written fairy tales, based on folktales, were often tweaked to include instruction or even just representation (even very subtle) of how people *should* act (to teach bravery or loyalty, for example). Retelling fairy tales for our world now doesn't mean you have to change those basic themes or use the practice to try to teach a new moral lesson; in fact, it's best if you shy away from anything that's didactic as it can turn any story into a lecture. But do consider the theme(s) of the original story and how those can be transferred or tweaked for the new setting.

ACTIVITIES

Retelling an old tale: Choose your favourite fairy tale or folktale. This can be one you read as a child or one that was made into an animated (or live) film. Write down its general structure and list the motifs (the repeated images or ideas) found within. Then, describe the theme(s) it explores. Once you have this information available, change things up. Choose a different time and even place to set your retelling. To make things easy, you can choose your own time and place, even down to the specific neighbourhood. Now it's time to cast your characters. How can you put them in similar conditions to the original story if they're now in a new setting? For example, your new Cinderella isn't likely to be a servant who sleeps in the ashes, so how can you make her familiar enough that readers will recognise her? Is there any way you can genderflip anyone? Who or what is the magical character? And why or how are they magical? Consider how the theme(s) you've listed will work in your new setting; they might fit right in, or you might need to adjust them slightly. What motifs and other elements can you transfer over to the new setting and which ones will you need to change to fit? For example, Cinderella can't go to the ball in a coach and horses, but perhaps her fairy godmother magics up a Rolls Royce with a chauffeur. If you fancy an advanced version of this, consider how you can combine a fairy tale/folktale retelling with a large historical event, such as Valente does in *Deathless*. Is there a particular historical event that you're fascinated by? Write that down, and then consider, for instance, how the general population lived alongside. Telling a regular person's story via the vehicle of a fairy tale or folktale in the same culture would give you a new spin on an old tale and on history.

Finding a new tale: Do a bit of research to explore folktales, myths, and legends from other cultures or places. Social media often has threads on this such as #FairyTaleTuesday, #FolkloreThursday and #FolktaleFriday, great resources that include images from art and books. When you find a tale you like, do the same thinking activities as above: who are the characters, what are the themes and motifs, etc. For this activity, you might want to retell the story in its own setting or shift it to a different place and time. If you stick in the original setting, you'll need to do a bit of research into the place, culture, and time period. The activity in the **Historical Fantasy** section can help with this.

WITCHES

Witches and witchcraft are a huge part of folklore, fairy tales, "true" histories, mainstream literature (Shakespeare, anyone?), and contemporary Fantasy. Not only are there some cultures that still believe in malevolent magic and that attack women (and sometimes men) accused of witchcraft, but wicca/witchcraft is a religion with practitioners around the globe. Witches are thus figures that spill out of fiction and into real life, so grab your broomstick and let's take a ride....

A Short History of Witches

Witches come in all shapes and sizes (and all kinds of hats!). Nonetheless, there are some commonalities that recur again and again because witches are usually women whose femininity, knowledge, and confidence is a provocation to (masculine) society's accepted boundaries. Witches are outliers in patriarchal cultures where women are expected to be chaste and humble, to follow directions, to "be nice", to want nothing more than to be married and be mothers (even if they also must have careers and work; and that dichotomy sets up oh so many problems), or to defer to their male relatives (fathers, older brothers, husbands). Witches are by turns depicted as too ugly (physically and morally), too beautiful and sexually alluring (so presenting a temptation to others), too knowledgeable, or too unwilling to follow (male) instruction. Witchcraft, then, is about power: female power, to be specific. In a patriarchal society in which women have less power than men, or indeed no power at all, harnessing unseen magical forces is one way to acquire some agency over oneself and others. In her book *Fantasy: The Literature of Subversion*, Rosemary Jackson rightly argues that "fantasy characteristically attempts to compensate for a lack resulting from cultural constraints; it is a literature of desire, which seeks that which is experienced as absence and loss".[1] It's easy so to see why stories about witches and witchcraft continue to be popular. Characters—and through them, readers—can find agency in a world or society in which they have little to none.

The word "witch" has its roots in Old English (wicca, wicce)[2], but the concept has a legacy much older than just that. Stories of women who practice magic are found throughout history, with misogyny and ageism constants throughout their depictions in art and literature. The flip side of this is the wizard, who is often portrayed as a kindly, helpful old man. The history of

---

1. Jackson, 1981, pp. 3–4.
2. Online Etymology Dictionary, n.d.

witchcraft (including paganism and wicca) is too long and complex to fully cover here (for an in-depth look at the British practice, see Liz Williams's *Miracles of Our Own Making: A History of Paganism*, 2020), but let's touch on some of the more important points.

The traditional Western/Christian view of a "witch" was a person who made a deal with the Devil for "unnatural" supernatural abilities, often depicted as an exchange with Satan for sexual favours.[3] In the early modern period (which started between 1400–1500, that being the end of the Middle Ages, and continued until around 1800 when the more rational ideas of the Enlightenment and industrialisation took hold) the "handbook" on how to recognise witchcraft and witches was created: the 1486 *Malleus Maleficarum* (*Hammer of Witches*) written by German Catholic clergyman Heinrich Kramer (a co-author, Jacob Sprenger, is also listed on later editions decades after his death, but his contribution has been contested). It was this book that set the scene for the witchcraft trials that sprung up in secular courts throughout Europe, cementing ideas of what a witch was and how to deal with her crimes. The invention of the printing press a few decades earlier contributed to the *Malleus*'s widespread use, while religious volatility between Catholic and Protestant factions in Europe fuelled even more concern about witchcraft as a driving force of evil against the "true" faith (that being whichever one an accuser followed). The fear of witches—alongside the punishment of mainly women for their transgressions against the patriarchal rules of society and the church in Britain and the American colonies—was further strengthened by the belief held by King James I of England (formerly James VI of Scotland) that witches were conspiring against him personally[4], a view expressed in his treatise *Daemonologie* (1597)[5] and enhanced in the King James Bible, first published in 1611. The King James Bible is still used to this day and carries the admonition "do not suffer a witch to live", supposedly translated from the original "poisoner" or "sorceress".[6]

The arrival of the Victorian era, however, brought new perspectives to bear on the figure of the witch as both a person and a cultural construct. In the mid-nineteenth century, during the development of the new sciences of psychology and sociology, Scottish journalist and novelist Charles Mackay published *Extraordinary Popular Delusions and the Madness of Crowds* (1841), a history of mass hysteria that included discussion and analysis of what he called "Witch Mania". Countries all across Europe, he recorded, "ran mad upon this subject, and for a long series of years furnished their tribunals

---

3. Eaton, 2021, n.p.
4. Goodare, 2019, n.p.
5. The British Library, n.d., n.p.
6. Adu-Gyamfi, 2016, n.p.

with so many trials for witchcraft, that other crimes were seldom or never spoken of. Thousand upon thousands of unhappy persons fell victims to this cruel and absurd delusion," with the motivation behind such accusations often less pious religiosity and more petty revenge between squabbling individuals and groups.[7] This relates to an argument made by more recent researchers that midwives and healers were often accused of witchcraft by the Catholic Church, upset that these individuals would help relieve a labouring woman's pain (against the punishment that Eve's original sin supposedly laid on the head of all women), as well as male physicians who were looking to undermine the competition in order to maintain not just the power of the patriarchy in a situation that had been historically for women only, but also build a monopoly in the growing realm of "modern" medicine.[8]

From the late Victorian period until today, the image of the witch—old or young—was adopted by advertising, that industry that underpins social mores to sell products with a touch of magic dust. Artists and writers are often drawn to the idea of the witch because it offers drama; the creators are free to spread their wings and come up with all kinds of bizarre imagery, as we can see in the proliferation of art and photographs of witches in the nineteenth and early twentieth century. The demonisation of women (the "old hags") clashed with the rise of the use of images of the beautiful seductress witch in advertisements for "magical" beauty and cleaning products. And all this coincided with the rise in interest in the occult and spiritualism, as shown by the popularity of mesmerism, mediums, seances, and other attempts to touch the "other side" in the late nineteenth century, which exist today in popular entertainment from ghost hunters to the proliferation of television shows about witches (everything from *Bewitched* to *Charmed* to *The Chilling Adventures of Sabrina*).[9]

A Spotter's Guide: A Coven of Witches

In literature, writers have long experimented with the dichotomies of the witch as young or old and truly demonic or beneficial, or even a caricature:

- *Macbeth:* First performed in or around 1606, William Shakespeare's trio of "weyward sisters" deliver some of the most famous prophecies in all of literature (that Macbeth will become king but that a destructive downfall also awaits him). The Weird Sisters as portrayed by Shakespeare skew to the hag-end of the spectrum, caricatures described as physically disgusting and ugly. They are stirrers of both pots and trouble, seemingly

---

7. Mackay, 2021, n.p.
8. Climo, 2019, n.p.
9. Luckhurst, 2014, n.p.

only interested in mayhem and mischief. Their depiction was, for many centuries, the standard approach in literature.

- ***The Wonderful Wizard of Oz***: L. Frank Baum's modern classic (1900), often published nowadays as just *The Wizard of Oz* and the basis for the beloved 1939 musical film (dir. Victor Fleming). The story follows young Dorothy who's transported to a magical realm where, amongst others, she encounters Glinda, the Good Witch of the South, and the iconic green-skinned antagonist the Wicked Witch of the West. Baum's approach to witchcraft was revolutionary in that he based the moral character of his magical practitioners not on exchanges with demonic entities but, instead, on how they *chose* to utilise their powers. It was one of the first efforts to decouple stories about witches from censorious religious objection.

- ***Discworld***: Terry Pratchett's seminal fantasy series (1983–2000s) features many witches and witchcraft practices. Wise as ever to the folkloric roots of his material (as well as to infamous portrays of witches throughout literature), Pratchett depicts these figures more as medicine women and repositories of community knowledge. Moreover, magic for Pratchett is intertwined with belief itself. The very act of dressing and acting like a witch, what he calls 'crone-credibility' (*Equal Rites*, 1987), makes you a witch in Discworld. And the more warts you have, the more people believe in you!

- ***Hocus Pocus***: A much loved fantasy comedy from 1993, *Hocus Pocus* (dir. Kenny Ortega) is the deeply silly tale of a trio of mischievous witches (shades of *Macbeth* here) famously played by Bette Midler, Sarah Jessica Parker, and Kathy Najimy. They're accidentally resurrected on Halloween in Salem, Massachusetts (yes, that Salem!), and proceed to terrorise a group of children in the modern world. This family-friendly fare is a long way from, for instance, the horrifying imagery of the Middle Ages, and represents a further domestication of the witch imagery, now easily parodied for comedic effect.

- **The Magicians series (2009–'14):** Perhaps best described as *Harry Potter* with sex, drugs, and rock'n'roll, The Magicians series by Lev Grossman updates the Potter notion of an old-world magical boarding school for a new-world magical university. It features many different kinds of magic practitioners, among them "hedge witches": magicians without formal education at a magic school (either those who failed the entrance exams or were simply expelled). "Hedges", as they are known, are an underground magical movement, coveting specialist knowledge and piecing together spells from numerous dubious (and often online) sources. Such homemade magics can often be quite dangerous, and their practitioners are usually derided by the books' classically trained characters, something that introduces potent questions of classism and elitism into magical education.

Things That are Cool About Witches

Witches and witchcraft exist in many historical and cultural contexts outside of Europe and North America. Examples include the witch doctor/healer of South Africa (from the Zulu people); the witch camps of Ghana; the mangkukulam of the Philippines; and Mexico's Santa Muerta, among many others. While some of these cultural practices align in ways with those noted earlier from Western/European culture, in other ways they are very different and open you up to push the envelope a bit on the stereotypical image of the witch that you've likely grown up with. As discussed in more depth in **Supernatural Horror**, do be careful of cultural appropriation, or of using another culture's beliefs in a racist or other offensive way. Like with other character types such as **Zombies** or **Vampires**, witches go through popularity swings, but because of their wide cultural significance and the use of magic in some form or another in the Fantasy genre in general, readers don't tend to get as bored of them as other tropes. We can link this back to how Jackson (earlier in this section) describes Fantasy as about desire, and we all desire power.

Nobody Said Magic Would be Easy

Because witchcraft is about magic, the nuts and bolts of the magic and its consequences—the magic *system*—must be considered. A magic system is a set of rules for spells, incantations, and magic sources, sort of like worldbuilding but for the magical element. The Fantasy genre contains various types of systems, but they tend to fall into two camps:

- **Natural/wild magic:** One example is Williams's Fallow Sisters series (2020–present) in which British folklore and pagan practices are part of everyday life. While pagan practices contain guidelines and rules, and use natural ingredients such as herbs, the wild magic in these books is strongest in the "thin places" where the fey world bleeds through and in the living embodiment of stars that appear in the family's house. This is magic that's uncontrollable and not fully understandable because it isn't human.
- **Skilled/controlled magic:** This type can be found in various books such as the Harry Potter series; consider the consistently Latin-sounding spells and the use of herbal concoctions, magic wands, and rules about who can use magic and when. Another example is Grossman's

The Magicians series (books 2009–'14; television series 2015–'20), in which the magicians have some innate talent but learn the rules of magic in an academic setting as opposed to it being part of a religious or spiritual practice. In this series, the magic comes from gods, but the humans know its rules and consequences, and they have control of it; the main battles are between practitioners and their various levels of power or knowledge.

Of course, a magic system isn't just about its source but also its cultural and historical place in the story's world, as well as the consequences of using it:

- **Rules:** Consider the magic the same way you would any element of "regular" worldbuilding: magic is a part of the world you build and so will have a history as well as an influence on the society. These rules run the gamut from who's allowed to use magic (Is it genetic? Related to social class? Education? Something else?), to how those magic users are identified (Do magic users have to identify themselves as such, or is there something about their physical make-up or clothing that identifies them?), to how it has affected the world (If only some people have magic, are they controlled or do they have control? Is magic used only among people, or is it also used to power engines, for example?).
- **Consequences:** H.G. Wells supposedly said "If everything is possible, then nothing is interesting"; this goes for magic because if a character can do anything, with no consequences, the reader will get very bored very quickly. So, consider what doing magic requires of the witch: does power or energy have to be saved up, or is it lost very significantly after a spell is cast? Is there a rule for the magic similar to that in the physical world that every action has an equal and opposite reaction? Adding in consequences for the magic means the character must consider when and how to use the power, which will make for a more interesting story.

ACTIVITIES

Desire is a double-edged sword: Write about a person who discovers that they're a witch, but instead of being able to use their magic for their own desires they can only use magic to fulfil others' desires—good or bad—with consequences for each. How will the character decide who to help, or who to harm, and where is the line between not doing magic for oneself but fulfilling another's desire that aligns with their own? What consequences will the witch encounter by crossing that line? Is it even worth it?

Build a magic system: One fun way of building a world in which witches exist is to take a specific historical event—the time and place and situation—and add in witchcraft. First, choose one of the following events: the Battle of Little Bighorn (1876); the sinking of the *Titanic* (1912); the assassination of Archduke Franz Ferdinand in 1914 (the catalyst for World War I); the Wall Street crash of 1929; humans landing on the moon (1969); the Chernobyl disaster (1986); the Indian Ocean Tsunami (2004). The location, actors, and specific situations surrounding the event will lead to questions about how the witches will "fit in" to the already familiar world and how their powers might be used to change the outcome of the event. Revisit the questions above where we describe magic systems to help you along in making decisions.

HIGH FANTASY

Brave knights on horseback and kings in exile! Wizards waving staffs around! Badass heroines and goofy bards! Towers, castles, and swords, oh my! High fantasy is what most people think of when they think of Fantasy fiction. It usually takes place against a broad sweep of fictional history and imagined geography. It often features a huge cast of characters—some magical, some fighters, some not—with a common goal. It's about good vs evil, light vs dark. So, assemble your fellowship and let's set out on our own epic adventure!

A Short History of High Fantasy

High fantasy is sometimes known as epic fantasy (though even when palace politics are peeled away from vast quests across continents, the similarities between high and epic are *significant*). The subgenre as we know it today, especially in the West, is heavily influenced by the chivalric romances of Middle English (see the divisive—it's *awesome*—film version of the fourteenth-century *Sir Gawain and the Green Knight*; dir. David Lowery, 2021). These were largely quest narratives with noble heroes, larger-than-life supernatural antagonists, and a touch of pent-up sexual tension. Often, they incorporated and reimagined even earlier legends, characters, and folk motifs into their narratives, such as in Sir Thomas Malory's fifteenth-century *Le Morte d'Arthur*, which wrestled a variety of English and French tales about King Arthur and the Knights of the Round Table into a coherent story. As such, the loose interconnection of chivalric romances, as well as their propensity for reimagining earlier work, makes them in some way analogous to modern-day comic-book universes. A history of these would occupy a whole shelf of books (and in many libraries does), but for the novice writer it's enough to be aware of the modern, subgenre-shaping works and some of the contemporary standouts. Think of them as landmarks on the unfurled parchment map of a vast imagined landscape!

The most influential of these figures is probably professor and linguist J.R.R. Tolkien, who arguably set the stage for the entire Fantasy genre in the latter half of the twentieth century. Tolkien liked to tell his children bedtime stories, one of which became the basis of *The Hobbit* (1937), the classic story of little people making big differences in the world. The popularity of *The Hobbit* led Tolkien's publisher to urge him to write a sequel. Thus, *The Lord of the Rings* (1954–'55) came to be. Composed between 1937 and 1949, this huge project drew on stories and invented mythologies that Tolkien had been writing since around 1917. But Tolkien also studied Old

English, other Germanic languages, and even Finnish, the practice of which introduced him to the mythologies and histories of these cultures, which in turn influenced the development of the realms and histories of his fictional Middle-earth.[1] The result is an epic tale of hobbits, men, elves, dwarves, orcs, wizards, and even sentient trees called ents, uniting to defeat an evil we would nowadays characterise as fascist. It's been read as an allegory for World War I, in which Tolkien fought, and as work intended to reignite society's self-reflection about warfare, honour, and how to "recognise" evil. Rooted in *centuries* of fictional history, the book includes poems and songs, more than one conlang (a constructed language created for fictional worlds), myths, prophesies, battles, romance, and magic. *The Lord of the Rings* achieved cult status (especially in the 1960s and 1970s), and its comprehensive worldbuilding has been a highwater mark for Fantasy ever since, something only bolstered by director Peter Jackson's blockbusting film adaptations (2001–'03). Tolkien's work in fact made such a long-lasting impact that the modern literary genre has had a difficult time evolving beyond his direct influence.[2]

One of the more prominent early attempts to strike a different tone—one based on Christian theology rather than Northern European mythology—came from Tolkien's fellow academic, writing group buddy, and friend, C.S. Lewis, who produced the other great fantasy series of the mid-twentieth century: *The Chronicles of Narnia* (1950–'56). These books tell of a group of siblings who venture through the back of a wardrobe into a magical realm where time runs differently, where animals talk (Aslan the lion represents Jesus, in case Lewis was too subtle about that), and where the children become kings and queens. Like *The Lord of the Rings*, these books found instant popularity—for a time more than that of *The Lord of the Rings*—and have sold millions of copies. Their themes, as well as the non-sequential structure of the series, have inspired writers, academics, artists, and other creatives ever since.

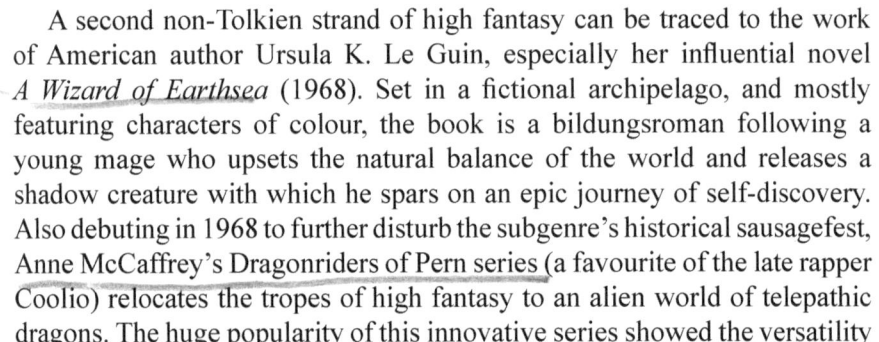

A second non-Tolkien strand of high fantasy can be traced to the work of American author Ursula K. Le Guin, especially her influential novel *A Wizard of Earthsea* (1968). Set in a fictional archipelago, and mostly featuring characters of colour, the book is a bildungsroman following a young mage who upsets the natural balance of the world and releases a shadow creature with which he spars on an epic journey of self-discovery. Also debuting in 1968 to further disturb the subgenre's historical sausagefest, Anne McCaffrey's Dragonriders of Pern series (a favourite of the late rapper Coolio) relocates the tropes of high fantasy to an alien world of telepathic dragons. The huge popularity of this innovative series showed the versatility

---

1. Doughan, 2021, n.p.
2. Doughan, 2021, n.p.

of high fantasy, and the initial novel, *Dragonflight*, saw McCaffrey become the first woman writer to win both a Hugo and a Nebula Award.

Meanwhile, back on Earth, American game designers and Fantasy fiction fans Gary Gygax and Dave Arneson rolled a natural 20 and created *Dungeons & Dragons* in 1974. This tabletop Role Playing Game (RPG) features character types from Tolkien's stories, magical systems and rules borrowed from the Science Fantasy works of Jack Vance, as well later licensed elements and characters from Fritz Leiber's Fafhrd and the Gray Mouser series (1939 onwards; see **Sword and Sorcery** for more). No one should be too cool to admit the crucial importance of *Dungeons & Dragons* to the high fantasy subgenre. Kids who grew up reading the *LotR* and *Narnia* books could suddenly act out similar adventures, playing a specific role with its associated rules and characteristics, allowing fans who had once only imagined being in an epic narrative the opportunity to perform it and even expand it into other stories with connected battles, dangers, and magic spells. As much as the novels of Tolkien and Lewis, *D&D* has proven to be a cultural phenomenon (consider its appearances on television shows such as *Community* and *Stranger Things*).

In the latter half of the twentieth century, high fantasy continued to build on what had come before, often with an emphasis on trilogies and series. Examples include Katherine Kurtz's Welsh-inspired Deryni series (1970–2014); Jack Vance's spectacular Lyonesse Trilogy (1983–'89); Mercedes Lackey's expansive Heralds of Valdemar series (over 30 books, beginning in 1987); Robert Jordan's Wheel of Time series (1990–2013, though finished by Brandon Sanderson); Polish author Andrzej Sapkowski's Witcher saga (1990–2013); and George R.R. Martin's monstrously successful Song of Ice and Fire series (1996–present), which combines high fantasy with a strong emphasis on **Grimdark**. More recently again, the subgenre has finally—*finally*—begun to shed its emphasis on European mediaevalism for more imaginative representations of gods, mortals, and palace intrigue. Among these, the work of N.K. Jemisin, in particular her Inheritance Trilogy (2010–'11), stands out as exemplars of the form. Much twenty-first-century work also draws on a wider pool of cultures and perspectives from across our real world. The rich histories and mythologies from across the African continent, for instance, have been inspiration for much well-received Fantasy fiction. Representative examples include the "not even remotely European" Dark Star books of Marlon James (2019–present),[3] and 2021's *Son of the Storm* by Suyi Davies Okungbowa, a sweeping tale set in a world inspired by the pre-colonial empires of West Africa.

---

3. Eddy, 2019, n.p.

Element Spotlight: Building a Believable World

High fantasy is a worldbuilding smorgasbord: stories in this subgenre are set in secondary worlds (as described in **Historical Fantasy**) that usually require imagining from the ground up. Tolkien called this practice "subcreation", and subsequent scholars have interpreted his thinking on the matter as an almost "theological understanding of literary creation as participation in the divine act of creation".[4] Talk about the author as God of the storyworld! Yet the important thing here for us is that the details usually build upon each other; for example, what someone wears depends on the weather and materials as well as social mores about dress for certain classes in the social hierarchy. As Mark Wolf explains in *Building Imaginary Worlds*, a fantasy setting is one of creative invention, yes, but it still has to follow rules to be fully believable by the reader. He breaks the rules down into three main types:

- **Internal logic:** Changes from our own world to a secondary world (be they naming conventions, changes to the physical geography or culture, or even radical re-imaginings of the laws of physics) must show causality, or internal logic, to work; that is, any action must have consequences[5]. A good example of this is how the irregular weather patterns of the world in Martin's Song of Ice and Fire series has consequences on the level of narrative and even character.
- **Completeness:** The fictional world must give the illusion of completeness, which includes everything from the small-scale inventions (food, clothing, shelter for survival) to those on the larger scale ("Governance, economy, food production, shared form of communication, defense against outsiders").[6] A world that has evidence of a past is also complete. But this doesn't mean that you, as worldbuilder, must imagine *every* little thing, only that audiences find the world to be sufficient for the story.
- **Consistency:** The fictional world must make sense, with "details [that] are plausible, feasible, and without contradiction. This requires a careful integration of details and attention to the way everything is connected together".[7]

So how do you tackle building a new secondary world? It can be daunting, but, like eating a vegan elephant alternative, can be done in small bites. There are several elements to consider:

---

4. Del Rincón Yohn, 2021, p. 18.
5. Wolf, 2012, p. 37.
6. Wolf, 2012, p. 39.
7. Wolf, 2012, p. 43.

- **Naming conventions:** One tradition in Fantasy fiction is to make up complicated names. This is a good substitute for naming someone in a secondary world something like, say, Christian, which would immediately ping a reader's understanding and have them assuming the world contains Christianity (this goes for names from any religion). Likewise, using names for characters from specific places or cultural backgrounds—an Alexander and a Fatima, for example—will lead readers to wonder if this world has a Greece and an Arabia, as well as wonder about the story of their families' migration if, for example, Alexander or Fatima are in a place where there are other characters with names we recognise from Nigeria or Japan or any other Earth locale. So, names of characters and places need to have some internal logic and consistency. One note about languages and conlangs though: Tolkien created languages, but he was a linguist with decades of experience. It isn't necessary to do the same to create a believable world! Just try to be consistent.
- **Physical geography:** The fun that creators have with worldbuilding is why so many Fantasy books contain maps! You can create worlds with deserts or beaches, mountain ranges or prairies, or all types of ecosystems. Even though so many Fantasy books include maps, you don't always have to create new planets with several landmasses; instead, you can worldbuild a single contained environment, such as a spaceship or a rabbit warren (think 1972's *Watership Down* by Richard Adams). Just remember that ecosystems and their weather are going to affect things such as what animals/plants exist there, how people travel, etc. (this is the Turtles All the Way Down rule we discuss in **Apocalyptic Fiction**). Try sketching out your imaginary landscapes to give yourself a sense of what kinds of journey your characters are undertaking. And remember, if you find this difficult, feel free to mix and match real-world examples. Martin's fictional continent of Westeros, for instance, is simply an enlarged and inverted version of Ireland attached underneath a modified version of Great Britain.
- **Plants and animals:** What grows and thrives in a certain ecosystem affects what characters eat, their clothing and housing materials, and even their jobs. Do you have sheep in your world? Then you'll have wool. But if you don't have sheep or certain types of goats, and no imports from another place, then nobody will wear wool, and the existence of knitting might be inconsistent with the world.
- **Character types/various races of people:** Following in the footsteps of Tolkien and *D&D*, it's fun to populate a world with lots of types of characters aside from "plain old humans". Two things to keep in mind though:

- **The character's role in that world:** The world is going to affect the characters and vice versa, and how a character interacts with your new world will depend a lot on whether they are, as Jeff VanderMeer lays out in *Wonderbook*, "a native of the culture", a "tourist or visitor", or a "conqueror or colonizer".[8] Using *LotR* as an example, the Hobbits are natives of an agrarian world; they might take it for granted but they interact with it for their food and shelter and understand it. The Orcs, meanwhile, are conquerors that don't grow crops or raise animals and only see forests as something to destroy and use.
  - **Representations of race or colour:** Be careful of splitting character types along race lines in which any characters with dark skin are evil (it should be noted that Tolkien did run afoul of this). Some authors have tried to subvert this (white=evil and dark=good) but it rarely works out well on the page or off because it is still a binary. To be realistic and compelling, fictional characters should be complicated rather than cardboard cut-outs to stand in for ideas. Equally, it's worth remembering that *of course* elves or hobbits or dwarfs can be People of Colour. Internet trolls—themselves a specific character class—will give you all sorts of nonsense reasons why they can't be, but that's just racism. It's *your* world; if you want a Black elf or an Asian monarch, you get to write that.
- **Systems:** This includes the government, financial systems, education, travel/transport, any type of religion and its internal hierarchies, etc. Systems are how societies function, but not all worlds will have each of these as a fully considered, identified entity; for example, an agrarian world with cart tracks that have developed naturally because of people taking the quickest path through a forest (in contrast to our modern highway systems) might even lack toll roads or any transport rules at all.
- **Culture:** Culture is what characters make and includes not just physical things (everything from eating utensils to buildings), but also those non-tangibles such as myths, legends, social mores, songs, superstitions, religious practices, and so on. Each character type in your world will have their own set of cultural practices and beliefs.
- **Off-screen concerns:** While a lot of worldbuilding ends up on the page, some of it isn't ever explained but is still going to influence the world, which makes it important for you as the creator to know. Ask yourself questions such as how is food moved around and what do characters eat off of or with? Where does garbage go? Who makes clothes, weapons, etc.? What materials or resources are imported? From how far away and to what expense? What "native" materials/resources are exported?

---

8. VanderMeer, 2018, pp. 216–217.

Things That are Cool About High Fantasy

Who are we kidding? *All* of the things about high fantasy are cool! Here you get to stretch your writerly wings and don't have to hold back. Your cast of characters can be huge and your world as full of imagination as possible. Plus, because these books tend to be on the longer side, you don't have to watch the word count as closely as you would with other subgenres and so can create subplots, side quests, and complex histories to your heart's content. What's more, you're part of a tradition. High fantasy is the classic example of what we mentioned earlier about new work always being "in conversation" with existing books and stories. Writing your own high fantasy tale means that you—yes, *you!*—get to add your take to a subgenre developed by Tolkien, Lewis, Le Guin, and McCaffrey, among others.

Sometimes the World is Too Big

- **Falling down the bunny hole:** All of that said, try not to worldbuild to the detriment of the story. Wolf, for instance, argues that you can have a world without a story but not a story without a world.[9] Because sure, worldbuilding is fun, but don't forget that it's just the *setting* for your characters to live in. Spending months or even years creating intricate government systems and shipping conglomerates and detailed explanations for how the sewage system of your fantasy city operates is only setting the scene in which your characters need to act out their lives. Remember, the real worldbuilding is the characters we invent along the way.
- **Tolkien with the serial numbers scratched off:** One real danger of writing high fantasy is just rewriting what's come before. This is a danger not just in the larger "good vs evil" themes but also in smaller ways, especially by populating worlds with stereotypical elements such as the buxom tavern girl, stew for every meal, and bags and bags of gold coins (which, honestly, would be *way* too heavy to be practical!); Diana Wynne Jones created the ultimate collection of these derivative elements in her *Tough Guide to Fantasyland* (1996).
- **Don't "call a rabbit a smeerp"[10] and be careful of "fat writing"[11]:** There's an invaluable source of learned experience for SFF (and other) writers called the *Turkey City Lexicon* available online, and among its guidelines are two that can be applied especially to high fantasy and its related worldbuilding and writing style:

---

9. Wolf, 2012, p. 29.
10. Blish, n.p.
11. Freiheit, n.p.

- **Call it what it is:** If, for example, there are animals in your world that look just like rabbits, just call them rabbits instead of making up a name for them. Making up a silly name is just going to distract a reader who will wonder why you went to all the trouble with a rabbit. Apply this rule widely!
- **Step away from the thesaurus:** There's a lot to be said for interesting word choice and, indeed, for teaching your reader a new (to them) word, but it's often best not to overdo this. Be sparing with fancy language when simpler words might suffice. This is especially important in high fantasy, which can tend toward over-complicated sentence structures when a writer is trying to make the characters sound archaic (thees and thous and so on!), and that can end up on the purple end of the prose spectrum if not kept under some control.

ACTIVITIES

Build a cast of characters: Consider species from Tolkien's Middle-earth. You have Elves, Hobbits, Dwarves, Orcs, Goblins, Dragons, Wizards, and Humans. To these we might add character classes from D&D such as Paladins, Clerics, Bards, and Thieves. Pick four of these character types and describe the history between their races and the D&D classes in your fictional world: How have Dragons historically interacted with, say, Elves? What if a Wizard was a Thief? Can a Human and a Goblin ever be friends (or, who knows, maybe more)? Think about the forces of history, society, and class, and how they might complicate these relationships. Pick the most promising relationship you have devised and write a scene where said characters meet and interact.

D&D after-action report: If you have a writing group, or even just a few friends interested in Fantasy fiction, gather together for a game of *Dungeons and Dragons*. When it's over, each of you should write a first-person account of the campaign from the perspective of your character. The aim here is not for an accurate or objective retelling; each character will likely see themselves as the hero (and may have grievances with other characters!) so the accounts will surely differ! Share, discuss, and even workshop these pieces amongst the group.

SWORD AND SORCERY

It's got swords! It's got sorcery! It's what it says on the tin! Only … there's more to it than that. Sword and Sorcery is a venerable subgenre overlapping and influencing many others. It's a stirring field of bold heroes undertaking dangerous personal quests, finding romance, and defeating supernatural foes. So, grab your blade, summon your trusty sidekick, and let's ride!

A Short History of Sword and Sorcery

Sword and sorcery shares a lot of creative DNA with **High** (or Epic) **Fantasy** but distinguishes itself by a narrow focus on a single hero instead of a group with a common quest or goal. The tales highlight a warrior character fighting supernatural beings in a secondary-world setting, sometimes for monetary gain but sometimes as part of a vendetta or other personal motivation. This contrasts with high fantasy's larger stakes, such as the fate of the world. What this means in a practical sense is that you get to write lots of battles and lots of monsters, sometimes interspersed with wry humour and even a romantic subplot. Because of their nature of focusing on a single character—or occasionally a pair—up against enormous odds, sword-and-sorcery tales tended to be quite episodic and started as short stories or novellas instead of long-form fiction.

    As a recognisable form, this subgenre has old roots, drawing from tales of heroes and monsters in various mythologies (*Beowulf*, and Norse and Greek mythology, etc.), to historical fiction (see **Historical Fantasy** for more), to the swashbuckling rogues of Alexandre Dumas's *The Three Musketeers* (1844). Sword and sorcery as we know it today, however, owes its characteristics to the SFF short-story boom in the early-to-mid twentieth century, fed by the numerous "pulp" publishers and magazines such as *Weird Tales* (1923–present; the magazine has existed on and off, in some form or another, along with title changes, for nearly 100 years) and *The Magazine of Fantasy & Science Fiction* (1949–present; usually shortened to *F&SF*). These were called pulps because the paper used, made of wood pulp, was inexpensive[1]; however, this moniker often led to a belief that the content wasn't worth much more than the paper, an attitude SFF/H sometimes still finds itself fighting against (boooo!).

    The pulps were the realm of singular heroes, from Conan the Barbarian by Robert E. Howard (1930s) to Jirel of Joiry by C.L. Moore (1960s) to the Fafhrd and the Gray Mouser tales by Fritz Leiber (1930s–'80s), the writer

---

1. Britt, 2020, n.p.

who coined the subgenre's name.[2] Howard in particular, whose Conan tales are generally taken as the catalyst of the subgenre, was a prolific writer, toiling during the Great Depression, which meant writing what would sell, and at the time episodic tales full of adventure and strange new worlds was what was putting coins in his purse.[3] Unfortunately, his death in 1936 brought the first wave of sword and sorcery mostly to an end.[4]

What happened next was interesting. From the 1930s to the 1950s "Planetary Romance" or what we might call "Sword & Planet" stories grew in popularity in the SF magazines of the day.[5] These were SF set in secondary Fantasy worlds, such as the John Carter of Mars stories by Edgar Rice Burroughs, where manly men with great pecs and huge swords, who definitely weren't overcompensating for anything, fought "primitive" alien hordes in stories that nowadays read a lot like unexamined colonial propaganda. The popularity of this SF version of sword and sorcery would wane after the space program reached its goal of the moon in the late 1960s and we began to realise that other celestial bodies were not lush mysterious jungle worlds. Thus, sword-and-sorcery tales—definitely set in fantastic rather than in SF realms (planets) that we now know are empty worlds of dust—began to experience a revival.[6] The publication and popularity of J.R.R. Tolkien's *The Lord of the Rings* (1956–'55) in mass-market paperback form, which didn't happen until 1965, convinced publishers that there was a wide readership for Fantasy stories. A company called Lancer Books took up the challenge and published Howard's Conan tales in novel form in the second half of the 1960s, something which in turn generated newer sword-and-sorcery tales and writers, as well as a growing number of parodies.[7] The popularity, speed, and inexpensive publication materials (pulp) meant that, unfortunately, a "large amount of hackwork came to be published in the genre".[8] However, in 1970, Leiber won a Hugo and a Nebula for his Fafhrd and the Gray Mouser novella *Ill-Met in Lankhmar*, further cementing sword and sorcery's renewed vitality among readers and critics.

Anthologies too—in many ways the cultural memory of SFF/H— played a significant role. Author Lin Carter, who was also an editor of the hugely influential Ballantine Adult Fantasy series in the 1970s, created the Swordsmen and Sorcerers' Guild of America (SAGA), active from the 1960s–'80s. The group, though informal, put out a collection of anthologies

---

2. Nicholls, 2021, n.p.
3. Thomas, 2020, n.p.
4. Thomas, 2020, n.p.
5. Dozois, 2017, p. xiv.
6. Dozois, 2017, pp. xiv–xv.
7. Thomas, 2020, n.p.
8. Nicholls, 2021, n.p.

titled *Flashing Swords!* (Dell Books paperbacks, 1973–'81), edited by Carter.[9] The development of the tabletop role-playing game *Dungeons & Dragons* in 1974 also helped the subgenre survive when it gave players the opportunity to take on the role of a fighter with a sword hacking down monsters. The game exhibits a kind of symbiotic relationship with sword and sorcery. Author Joe Abercrombie, for instance, has discussed how the subgenre clearly influenced *Dungeons & Dragons*, which, played by so many current fantasy authors as they grew up, has in turn clearly influenced the revival of sword and sorcery![10] Nonetheless, the real boon for the subgenre, arguably its second coming, occurred with the emergence of home video in the 1970s and cable television in the 1980s, along with the creation of action figures by various toy companies (many of which are now collectors' items, so check your attics!). In 1982, Arnold Schwarzenegger donned a horned helmet in *Conan the Barbarian* (dir. John Milius). Schwarzenegger "transformed the blood-soaked, half-naked demeanour of Howard's originals into the blood-soaked, half-naked demeanour of a man fighting against the odds of a foreign landscape" (the classic "narrative of American success").[11] The film was followed by a sequel, *Conan the Destroyer* (dir. Richard Fleischer) in 1984 and the spin-off *Red Sonja* (dir. Richard Fleischer, 1985). Since then, Conan has been a fixture of comics, video games, and a number of table-top role-playing games, though it remains to be seen whether Schwarzenegger et al. will ever deliver the long-hinted-at third film, *King Conan*.

Another film of the time that really stands out as being a crucial part of the 1980's resurgence of sword and sorcery, and one that benefited from these new modes of film consumption, was *The Beastmaster* (dir. Don Coscarelli, 1982), based on Andre Norton's 1959 novel *The Beast Master* (though Norton was, to put it mildly, not pleased that the story in her novel was changed so much).[12] The film follows a man, bent on revenge, with the power to communicate telepathically with animals. It ticks many of the core sword-and-sorcery boxes, even including a sexy love interest played by Tanya Roberts, who promoted the film with a pictorial feature in October 1982's issue of *Playboy*. The film might not have been a box-office hit, but it found new life on television. One station that aired it, the American cable station TBS (Turner Broadcasting System), did so a lot. Like, *a whole lot*. A bit of internet searching will bring up jokes about how at one point TBS stood for The *Beastmaster* Station, though finding a credible source for that is difficult (all roads lead back to Wikipedia). That said, one of the present authors can confirm that in 1982/83 she saw the film on television at least a

---

9. Swordsmen and Sorcerers' Guild of America (SAGA), 2010, n.p.
10. Abercrombie, 2010, n.p.
11. Bailey, 2022, n.p.
12. Crispin, 1989, pp. 54–57.

dozen times and remembers it fondly, though suspects that a viewing now as a mature adult would not create quite the same effect! Rumours that HBO (Home Box Office) really stood for "Hey, *Beastmaster*'s On!" are equally, if delightfully, apocryphal.

As the Fantasy genre transformed further in the twenty-first century, so, too, did sword and sorcery. According to the late multi-Hugo-award-winning SFF editor Gardner Dozois, one significant moment was George R.R. Martin's publication of *A Game of Thrones* (1996), which offered "a grittier, more realistic, harder-edged kind of Epic Fantasy, one with characters who were often so morally ambiguous that it was impossible to tell the good guys from the bad guys".[13] Martin's work, which melds elements of both sword and sorcery as well as **High Fantasy** with a cynical, amoral perspective on Fantasy themes and characters, opened the floodgates for an even more recent, darker, and philosophically messier subgenre: **Grimdark**.

Yet one thing that this history might indicate is that this is a subgenre by and for White cis-het men, but that's not the case anymore. For example, C.J. Cherryh's Morgaine Cycle series (1976–'79), features a female lead and mixes sword and sorcery with SF; Jen Williams's Copper Cat trilogy (2014–'16) stars a female thief, a gay mercenary, and a Brown nobleman with a disability; while Elizabeth Bear's *The Stone in the Skull* (2017) follows a unique mercenary on a journey through dangerous lands. Saladin Ahmed's *Throne of the Crescent Moon* (2012) is set in a Fantasy world inspired by the Middle East, while African-American author Charles R. Saunders's Imaro trilogy (1981–'85) features a Black protagonist's adventures in a secondary world based on Africa. Saunders also coined the term "Sword and Soul" to describe this new subgenre of sword-and-sorcery tales with an African influence.[14] Following on from Saunders is Milton J. Davis, who's written several novels, edited several anthologies, and runs the publishing house MVmedia, which specialises in Science Fiction, Fantasy, and Sword and Soul.[15]

Element Spotlight: Making Characters *Do* Things

The best way to keep a reader up until three a.m. turning pages is to give them a compelling character to follow, and the journey-like narratives of sword and sorcery are a great opportunity to practice this. We don't just love characters because of how they look (in our imaginations) or what they say, but because of what makes them tick. Their motivation is what jump starts the story and keeps it going until the very end. One of the best—and

---

13. Dozois, 2017, p. xviii.
14. Vredenburgh, 2014, n.p.
15. Davis, 2018.

easiest—ways of creating a captivating tale is to know what your character wants and what your character needs:

- **Wants:** This is the character's end goal. It can be something as simple as vanquishing the villain or finding the treasure.
- **Needs:** This is a bit more complicated because there are two types of needs, and they aren't always obvious:
    - **What the character needs to get what they want:** This is everything from a sword to a magical amulet to a trusty steed to get them to the volcano to find the treasure, or even a sidekick who can read ancient carvings and translate the clues. Usually, the character knows what they need when they set out on the adventure; sometimes new needs will pop up, but they are usually obvious or tangible.
    - **What the character needs that they *don't know* they need:** We sometimes call this the "soul need". This is the thing that the character needs to fulfil something within themselves that they don't know—or won't admit—is missing or needs changing. Say your sword-wielding mercenary keeps on moving forward, from adventure to adventure, seemingly for money. As we peel away the layers of that particular onion, though, we discover that she lost her family because she didn't win a battle against a dragon that was more dangerous than she was led to believe. The guilt of losing that fight, and her family dying as a result, spurs her forward, and leads to, say, a drinking problem. She thinks she needs money to bankroll a cushy life in a peaceful kingdom, but what she really needs—"soul needs"—is to forgive herself for something that wasn't her fault and to go back home to her village and find closure. This realisation takes some time for a character, but it helps you create a story with much more depth than a series of battles with various monsters, and it helps you develop your theme.

Things That are Cool About Sword and Sorcery

Because this subgenre has evolved and changed so much over the years, it doesn't have strict delineations, which means that you can have fun with it. Humour is one element that attracts readers: we all love a snarky, sneaky, and clever hero (or anti-hero) who slings one-liners, rolls their eyes, and fights with the best of them! Another link between this subgenre and our daily pop-culture intake is the fact that you can use your *Dungeons & Dragons* characters or quests as inspiration. A final aspect of the subgenre that makes it fun to play with is the lack of hard-and-fast rules about where or when in the world the stories are set, so you can take advantage of the wealth of historical material as inspiration: highwaymen/women, con artists, strongmen/women, gods. And, because the subgenre lends itself to short stories much more easily than novels, the worldbuilding doesn't have to be as extensive as it does for high fantasy. So, you can dabble with the subgenre without having to commit to weeks/months/years of writing and rewriting!

Watch Out for That Sharp Pointy End!

- **Keep it focused:** Though the subgenre itself has changed over the decades, sword and sorcery usually only has one main character. This means you don't need to populate a whole world or create intricate maps. It also means that your focus should be on what that character wants and needs, even if the immediate motivation changes from adventure to adventure.
- **Find inspiration:** There's a lot of secondary-world Fantasy out there, and it's easy to fall into the trap of re-inventing the wheel and writing the same old same old. Sword and sorcery's evolution means there's opportunity to play with older tropes and come up with your own take on things. And remember, just because it's an old subgenre doesn't mean we shouldn't be making it more diverse and inclusive for modern readerships!
- **Sorcery needs rules:** We've mostly focused here on the sword-wielding hero, but sorcery is the other side of the subgenre, which means dealing with magic. The hero might have powers, or there might be a sorcerer (good or evil) to contend with. Be sure to consider magic systems (see **Witches** and **Folktales and Fairy Tales**) when conjuring up your spells.

ACTIVITIES

Howdy, sword-wielding pardner!: The Western was a popular literature and film genre from the 1950s to the '70s (even Robert Howard wrote Westerns!) and these usually feature the stoic loner goodie ("white hat") who, with his trusty horse and guns, travels the frontier righting wrongs and bringing the baddies ("black hats") to justice. We also have a tradition of television programmes featuring the lone cop/private investigator/lawyer/etc. doling out their own brand of justice. Take one of these as your inspiration, set the character in an imaginary land/secondary world (even one inspired by the original source material), give them a sword, and turn the villain into a supernatural monster. And, *voilà*, you have a starting point for a new sword-and-sorcery story.

All good adventures start with a list: You are a magician/sorcerer who has lost your magic, but you've kept the receipts and know who's who in your world. What you want is to get your magic back from the evil sorcerer who stole it without rousing the menagerie of creatures they use as guards. List the tangibles that you need to help you find the evil sorcerer and their minions (transportation, information, helpers, certain cursed or enchanted items, etc.). Then, decide what you need that you don't know you need (your "soul-need"); this will be related to how you lost the magic in the first place (a betrayal? A fear? Something else?). Then, try writing a draft of a story following the quest to reclaim what is yours!

GRIMDARK

When **High Fantasy** breaks bad, or **Sword and Sorcery** focuses on the pointy end, then you get grimdark. Here are cynical stories where you won't find any happily ever afters. Here are amoral antiheroes who are just in it for themselves. Here are tales in which might is right and the brutish violence of sellswords is portrayed as more "realistic" than the honourable combat of noble knight errands. It's an ugly, merciless world; here's hoping we survive it.

A Short History of Grimdark

The origins of the term "grimdark" are contested, though it's most often attributed to the tagline of the Warhammer 40K table-top gaming universe: "In the grim darkness of the far future, there is only war".[1] In practice, the subgenre is best envisioned as secondary-world Fantasy that's "anti-Tolkien" in terms of attitude and atmosphere.[2] Grimdark combines elements from across both Fantasy and Horror, with the stories here often physically filthy, with muddy characters and settings, as well as grubby philosophically, with dark moods, darker morals, and nothing much to hope for. These are worlds in which "clothes get dirty [and] Food tastes bad (and is prepared by angry peasants). Monarchs are useless. Justice is uneven. And, most importantly, the heroes and heroines are flawed human beings in understandable ways".[3]

Violence is commonplace in these tales and so the subgenre isn't for everyone. Yet grimdark's true definition is, fitting, squabbled over in the squalid taverns of internet comments sections and the spiteful knife-fights of literary criticism. One of the easiest ways to define it is to contrast it with the more readily understood high fantasy:

- High fantasy has heroes and villains (clear protagonists and antagonists) whereas grimdark has morally ambiguous antiheroes with character arcs that can't easily be guessed. If anything, it seems to actively punish "good" characters for their naivety.
- High fantasy often contains the belief that certain outcomes are predestined or a matter of fighting on the "right" side whereas grimdark features storylines that are more "real" (like in our primary world) in the sense that the best decision isn't always clear because what's right isn't always cut and dry. There's little in the way of high fantasy's

---

1. Games Workshop Limited, n.d.
2. Roberts, 2014, p. 42.
3. Shurin, 2015, n.p.

grand plans to how things play out in grimdark. Bad things just happen, sometimes randomly, to its characters. Some writers might even agree that the more shocking these events, the more impact they have on the reader.

The subgenre is relatively new, with a history that's difficult to lay out in a linear fashion. One of the earliest progenitor work we can identify with it is Michael Moorcock's novella *The Dreaming City* (1961), which introduces the character Elric of Melniboné and contains its fair share of battles, a soul-eating sword, and magic, but ends unhappily. From his inception until 2022, the Elric character has featured in various stories in different media, including games and comics. Stephen R. Donaldson's Chronicles of Thomas Covenant (1977–2013) also serves as an important ancestor text. The first book, exhibiting the violence associated with the subgenre, introduces us to a protagonist who's diagnosed with leprosy and finds himself in a fantasy world where he commits a violent sexual assault because he believes he's hallucinating his reality. In this case, the question of morality is at the forefront, with readers asking themselves whether his crime was something that he always had an urge to do but was kept from committing because of the primary world's rules and expectations.

Throughout the 1990s and early twenty-first century, the tone of the subgenre has become ever more prevalent within Fantasy as a whole. One series in particular, George R.R. Martin's Song of Ice and Fire (the first book of which, *A Game of Thrones*, was released in 1996) gave the violent, often misogynistic world of grimdark a prominence that it has retained ever since. Though marketed initially towards a high-fantasy readership, the casual violence of the characters and events in *A Game of Thrones*, as well as its debatably realistic depiction of mediaeval-style society and brutality, marked the book out as something new. Martin's willingness to remove "the idealism, cut out the pastoral myth and infallible heroes" and replace them with "mud, blood, shit, and a focus on the darker aspects of human nature" remains one of the yardsticks for grimdark today.[4]

More recent representative examples of grimdark include The First Law series by Joe Abercrombie (2006–'21)—who, embracing his association with the genre, goes by the handle @LordGrimdark on social media!—as well as Jonathan French's Lot Lands series (2018–'21), the first instalment of which, *The Grey Bastards*, is described as "*Mad Max* set in Tolkien's Middle-earth."[5] However, lest you think the subgenre is only populated by dudes, two of its most popular authors are Kameron Hurley and Anna Smith Spark, both of whom use grimdark to connect on a deep level with

---

4. Fultz, 2018, n.p.
5. Kirkus, 2018, n.p.

the reality of human existence. Hurley has produced the Worldbreaker Saga (2014–'19), a trilogy for which she offers a content warning on her website that serves as an encapsulation of grimdark as a whole:

> This series contains adult themes and situations, including: self-harm, genocide, murdered children, abuse, kidnapping, blood, PTSD, sexual assault against men, racial and religious discrimination/slavery, violence, vomiting, physical abuse, abusive relationships, war, torture, gore, mutilation, bullying, death of parent, death by fire, alcohol/drunkenness, smoking, body horror, cannibalism.[6]

Smith Spark, dubbed the Queen of Grimdark in a book blurb, is the author of the Empires of Dust series (2017–'19). When asked about the subgenre and its connection to real life, she says that "dividing the world into good and evil and agreeing that we are on the side of good is both too easy and far, far too dangerous. […] In the end, deep down, we're all walking on other's suffering. […] Hold those you love close to you. Recognise that the world's a cruel place. Grimdark is that awareness".[7] In this way, grimdark, like some other subgenres, attempts to approach our real life from an oblique angle. What makes it different is its focus on human nature's darker urges and its interest in illustrating that rules can't always protect you, that power and leadership aren't always wielded by those with your best interests at heart, and that the world can be a very, very cruel place indeed.

Element Spotlight: Putting the Grim and the Dark in Grimdark

Because it shares tropes and motifs with high fantasy and sword and sorcery, grimdark can be difficult to differentiate sometimes from other subgenres. The difference can be one of tone or mood. Sometimes newer writers will use these terms interchangeably, but there *are* important nuances. Both terms are about how the writer wants the reader to *feel*, and grimdark is known for its negative, even oppressive qualities. Both also depend on word choice, but they're opposite sides of the same coin:

- **Tone** is the author's attitude toward the character/subject or even reader that comes out on the page. Does a story have an overall sarcastic edge or a nostalgic feel? That's tone, and it usually lasts throughout the whole story or novel. This is to say that grimdark "does not prohibit any certain styles or author voices […] Grimdark simply implies a certain approach toward the Fantasy world and its inhabitants".[8]

---

6. Hurley, n.d., n.p.
7. Spark, 2019, n.p.
8. Fultz, 2018, n.p.

- **Mood**, on the other hand, is like good lighting, plush seats, and fancy serviettes in a restaurant: it's the ambience of a story or even just a scene. A single story can have a consistent mood, but a novel can shift in mood from scene to scene depending on how the author wants the reader to feel at that moment. This is why, for example, a grimdark novel can include humorous scenes in between the shocks and violence.

Things That are Cool About Grimdark

Fiction gives us a chance to explore human behaviour and beliefs, but grimdark grants you the opportunity to explore the philosophy of aspects of life that we often want to avoid or deal with quickly because of uncomfortable feelings or even pain. Because the settings are secondary worlds, we can at least partially separate ourselves from the questions (from readers, friends, and even family) of what's going on in our own heads that would lead us to write such reprehensible characters and actions. This takes the "What if?" question inherent in all speculative-fiction stories to an extreme, giving you the opportunity to play out scenarios you wouldn't consider in real life.

Sometimes the Dark Can Overtake You

- **A necessary evil:** Despite Hurley's content warning, grimdark, while violent and containing adult themes and situations, still needs to have some thought behind it. Your readers are there for the gore, yes, but they're smart and expect more than just a bloodbath for the sake of being explicit (if they want something in that direction, they can always try **Splatterpunk**). Think of the film *American Psycho* (dir. Mary Harron, 2000; based on the 1991 novel of the same name by Bret Easton Ellis); the abundant bloodshed in the film isn't necessarily there to drive home the point that the main character is a serial killer but to underscore the film's commentary on the mass consumerism of the 1980s. Yes, you can have fun and create as much havoc as possible but, like with sex scenes, this should contribute to characterisation or move the narrative forward in some way (and it can do both at the same time).
- **One-dimensional characters:** Think of the last bad choice you made, little or big, and how you justified it to yourself (the reasons you told yourself that it was the right decision). We humans do this all the time, whether we're talking ourselves into telling a little white lie to a co-worker or having unprotected sex with a one-night stand. Those decisions and the justifications make you a complex entity; you want to do the same for the characters you create. Your side and background characters can be one-dimensional or flat because the story isn't about

them, but the main characters, especially in grimdark, need to be three-dimensional and "just as lost as we are" to engage your readers.[9] So, give them choices, be clear on their wants and needs, and follow through with consequences. Compelling characters are what keep readers up late at night, telling themselves they'll go to bed after just one more chapter.

- **The villains can be the stars:** A further key aspect of grimdark is villainy: in much fiction, the protagonist is the "hero" of the story, with the antagonist sometimes relegated to being a cardboard cut-out villain who's just evil for the sake of being evil, or a more rounded character who, though jumping off the page, is still playing second fiddle to the hero. In real life, though, *everyone* is the hero of their own story regardless of how they're labelled by others. Grimdark, however, is a subgenre of antiheroes. It lets you inhabit the person we would normally consider the antagonist (the "bad guy") and make them the protagonist, the star of the story, and give them centre stage. It allows you to flip the script on more traditional Fantasy while you find reasons for the character's decisions and better understand how they justify those decisions to themselves and those around them.

---

9. Shurin, 2015, n.p.

ACTIVITIES

Flip the script: Take your favourite high-fantasy or sword-and-sorcery story—one that has a happy ending and where the heroes know that to win the day they need to defeat the evil entity—and turn it on its head. Your main character is now morally ambiguous, faced with the choice of possibly not doing the right thing, and the "right thing" might not be as clear cut anymore. What are the pros and cons for doing each? What does the character want that, perhaps, the "wrong" choice would get them? This is Frodo deciding to keep the One Ring because he believes he can keep it safer than if he undertakes the journey to Mordor. The tone—your attitude towards the protagonist or cast of characters—will also change (imagine if Tolkien wrote Frodo as weak and useless rather than someone, though small, containing great possibilities). Write a scene from this new story, and don't forget to create a mood to match the grimdark subgenre.

Allegory: The closest thing we have to real world grimdark is probably politics! So, take a political event from the real world—maybe infighting amongst a political party or a contentious election—and use this as the basis of a Fantasy plot: who is the royalty in this world and how have they failed their subjects? Who are the usurpers and how do they go about undermining their rivals? Who are the cynical opportunists in the grey spaces in between and what are they prepared to do to turn events to their advantage? Draw your inspiration from real events and manoeuvrings; you'll be surprised to see how readily they map onto the disillusioned world of grimdark!

HISTORICAL FANTASY

Got a Fantasy story with people riding horses and using swords set in 1400s Germany? How about one with those things but set in the seventh realm of King Loquacious of Redheath? Or a story in which the European conquest of the Americas encountered magical resistance? In all these cases, what you've got is historical fantasy. This is one of those subgenres that ties itself into knots with its own sub-subgenres! So, let's start by stepping back in time to look at the linked history of Fantasy fiction and historical fiction so we can better understand how the mash-up took place!

A Short History of Historical Fantasy

Early in the history of "literature" in the West, before the printing press, books were made by hand and the stories inside them based on tales passed down orally or based on whatever written records the author could lay his hands on (yes, usually *his* because women's literacy rates were low until relatively recently). One such book is Geoffrey of Monmouth's *Historia Regum Britanniae* (*The History of the Kings of Britain*) written around 1136.[1] At the time, it was presented as history, but the veracity of its contents is questionable when you consider, for example, that not only does it mention giants and magic but that large sections are dedicated to telling the story of the wizard Merlin and the rise and reign of King Arthur, whose existence has never been proven beyond the belief that he might have been a sixth-century warrior.[2] But for centuries, Monmouth's work was believed to be historical fact. This helps explain why and how the King Arthur myth developed when Sir Thomas Malory's *Le Morte d'Arthur* (1485) coincided with the Tudor victory of the War of the Roses (1487), which necessitated Henry VII's attempt to further cement his claim to the throne, including name his firstborn Arthur; furthermore, Henry VIII had an already old round table, which now hangs in the Great Hall at Winchester, painted to depict the legendary round table, with the red Tudor rose in the centre, himself (possibly) placed as Arthur and the remaining places named after the other Knights of the Round Table.[3] You can already see how history and fantasy became entangled in the evolution of literature in the Western world.

In later centuries, as literature began to develop into the now-familiar forms of novels and short stories, the split between history and fantasy was still wiggly. One example is the *Roman a clef* of seventeenth-century

---
1. Brain, n.d., n.p.
2. Editors of Encyclopaedia Britannica, 2021, n.p.
3. Moore, 2012, n.p.

France, which was thinly veiled fiction about real people, something that writers still do now (though do be careful about using real people as your characters, especially if there are descendants who remember them when they were alive!). This was followed by Daniel Defoe's *Robinson Crusoe* (1719), which was published as "true history" and readers believed it (!); a modern equivalent is the film *The Blair Witch Project* (dirs. Eduardo Sánchez and Daniel Myrick, 1999), which, because it was filmed with hand-held cameras, some viewers believed was real. A century after Defoe, Sir Walter Scott published what we now consider to be the first historical fiction, including *Waverly* (1814) and *Ivanhoe* (1820), based on research but including fake events to make the stories more exciting. So even two hundred years ago, way before the internet, writers were doing research for their stories! Though by now, of course, historical fiction has become such a popular genre that larger bookshops will have whole sections dedicated to it.

Meanwhile, the Fantasy genre, from early days, gave writers the opportunity to tell tales about the past. **Folktales and Fairy Tales** traditionally begin with "Once upon a time..." And some stories use **Time Travel** as a means of linking the present with the past to give writers a chance to try out historical fiction via fantastic methods. Two examples are *A Connecticut Yankee in King Arthur's Court* by Mark Twain (1889), with a contemporary protagonist who, via a bump on the head, travels back in time to the mediaeval past where he introduces people to modern inventions, and Alison Uttley's *A Traveller in Time* (1939), also with a contemporary protagonist, who time slips via a magical door back to sixteenth-century England where she tries to help rescue Mary, Queen of Scots.

Historical fantasy is a popular subgenre because of the freedom it gives writers who want to play in a historical sandbox. While many examples adhere closely to the traditional mediaeval Western Europe setting of much popular **High Fantasy**, the historical fantasy subgenre has experienced a renaissance of expansion into the history of other places and cultures. Some recent examples include *The Lions of Al-Rassan* by Guy Gavriel Kay (1995: based on Moorish Spain), *The City of Brass* by S.A. Chakraborty (2017; partly set in eighteenth-century Cairo), *The Poppy War* by R.F. Kuang (2018; set in an alternate early-twentieth-century China), *Dread Nation* by Justina Ireland (2018; **Zombies** in the post-Civil War American South), and *She Who Became the Sun* by Shelley Parker-Chan (2021; set in an alternate fourteenth-century China).

A Spotter's Guide: Fictional Worlds Collide

Historical fantasy as we know it now can be different things, but the most generic definition describes it as historical settings containing fantastical elements. The setting in particular is where the differences between types of historical fantasy become clear:

- **Primary world:** This is the world as we know it outside our doors. Historical fantasy set in our primary world's history sometimes uses time travel as the device, moving the protagonist back to a historical moment that itself contains no fantastical elements (Diana Gabaldon's Outlander series, 1991–present, is one example). Other types of primary-world historical fantasy lean more on the side of Fantasy but are set in our past, sometimes resulting in the description of the world as, for example, an "alternate nineteenth-century England" because the world looks and feels just like the past but contains fantastical elements that have slightly changed the historical record; Susanna Clarke's *Jonathan Strange & Mr Norrell* (2004) is one of these, set in an alternate early nineteenth century in which magic exists. Other examples of primary-world historical fantasy include King Arthur stories (based on mediaeval Western European history but including magic, sorceresses, etc.), and even Gaslamp stories (like **Steampunk**, as these are often set in nineteenth-century Britain but include more magic or Fantasy elements than science).
    - A sub-type of primary-world historical fantasy is known as Alternate History. These stories use a real historical event from our past (our primary world) and change an outcome, such as having the Allies lose World War II (one of the most popular alternate history timelines asks, "What if the Nazis won?"). The fantastical element is this change to history and the subsequent consequences of that change. There might not be anything else fantastical about it, such as magic or certain creatures, but the alteration of our primary-world history takes this type of story out of the realm of "regular" historical fiction. Alternate history isn't a new subgenre. Philip K. Dick's *The Man in the High Castle* (1962) is generally considered the granddaddy of the form, but author Harry Turtledove is the undisputed master: examples include his Southern Victory series (1997–2007), in which he speculates on the ramifications up to the mid-1940s of a world in which the South wins the American Civil War, and *Ruled Brittania* (2002), in which the Spanish Armada defeats the English in 1588..
- **Secondary world:** Coined by J.R.R. Tolkien, the secondary world is one that we humans create and that "your mind can enter"[4]. Historical fantasy set in a secondary world contains fantastical elements, which strongly affect the worldbuilding you'll have to do (see **High Fantasy** for more on that task). Sometimes, however, secondary-world historical

---
4. Tolkien, 1988, p. 37.

fantasy is loosely based on our primary world's history (or even myth and legends) but with different names for places and people so that the world isn't immediately recognisable. George R.R. Martin's A Song of Ice and Fire series (1996–present) is an example; the battling factions in that epic series are based, Martin has said, on the fifteenth-century War of the Roses, but we know that the lands in the story are not in our primary world, and the stories contain dragons and some magic, identifying this novel series as secondary-world historical fantasy.[5]

Things That are Cool About Historical Fantasy

This subgenre gives you the chance to question the historical record. Without going into too much detail about the development of historical fiction, suffice it to say that a *lot* of historical "fact" contains biases, and in recent decades historians have uncovered new information about how people in the past lived, including information about how women, People of Colour, and LGBTQ+ people lived in certain times and places. These discoveries have led to writers exploring the past with a different perspective. We've seen this approach inspire more mainstream pop culture, enjoyed by audiences that might find themselves surprised that what they've been consuming would be considered Fantasy: namely, the "colour-blind casting" of the multi-award-winning *Hamilton* and the Netflix sensation *Bridgerton*, among others. While exploring the past from a more modern standpoint with the new information we've discovered, historical fantasy allows us the opportunity to explore the human condition without writing mimetic fiction (that is, fiction that "mimics" a version of real life outside our own front doors). Despite being set on far-away planets or in imagined secondary worlds, SFF/H is still about people now, but approached "from the side" so to speak. For example, in Ireland's *Dread Nation*, young African-American girls, previously enslaved, are trained in weaponry and etiquette as "Attendants" for wealthy white girls to protect them not just from the danger of the undead horde that threatens the country but also the etiquette mishap of a mismatched place setting, and one of the protagonist's frenemies is light enough to "pass" as white; exploring racism during a zombie uprising in the later nineteenth century gives the author—and readers—the opportunity use historical fantasy to explore the continuing scourge of racism instead of "head on" using literary fiction, which can sometimes put off readers who are feeling overwhelmed by our 24-hour news cycle.

---

5. Tharoor, 2015, n.p.

The Challenge of Bringing the Past Alive

- **Accuracy vs authenticity:** The historian has a responsibility to be accurate, and the novelist to be "authentic". A historian must get dates and names and places right, but a writer of historical fantasy must set the scene so that the reader believes that they are reading about the time period or place; it has to "feel right" to the reader.
- **Verisimilitude:** One way to make the story feel right to the reader is to focus on the details of the historical time period. This means giving the reader the feeling that the world in the story is true and based on fact. Verisimilitude is built by clothing historical people correctly for the time and place, giving them the right food, the right building materials, the right clothes, the right words, etc. And, yes, this requires research (more on that in a moment!).
- **Suspension of disbelief:** Suspension of disbelief is getting a reader so entrenched in a story that they won't stop and question the existence of whichever SFF/H element you have introduced. In historical fantasy, if you use verisimilitude to help suspend a reader's disbelief about the historical veracity of a setting, you're one step closer to getting them on your side to suspending disbelief for the fantastical element(s) you will add.
- **Avoid writing a book report:** Meeting these challenges—authenticity, verisimilitude, suspension of disbelief—depend on research. One important caveat: writing historical fantasy (or even historical fiction) is not about showing off all the cool historical details you discover while doing research. The research you do will inform your writing; this means that the details you find out about the time and place of your story will affect how your characters act and how the world itself works. But if 100% informs your writing, only about 10% should end up on the page. You're not writing a non-fiction book about your historical time period, and you're not writing a book report. You're writing fiction and have a responsibility to entertain your reader.

Research Methods for Historical Fantasy

Instead of having to come up with an idea for a story and then doing research, you can use various methods of research to find ideas for historical fantasy stories:

- **Books:** Books and magazines and journals have been our go-to source for all the topics we study, but books themselves are historical objects. If you're lucky enough to have access to a library that has antique books, you can hold books that your characters might have used. There are also ways to access these books online, such as via *Internet Archive* (www.archive.org). The book itself—what the paper is made of, how it's bound, the typeface used, the ink used, the syntax and vocabulary of the information, and even how widely available it was—can tell you a lot about the time period and the people who lived then.

- **Museums:** We often think of museums as only containing art, which itself is a great way to find historical fantasy ideas (for mythological stories, check out the paintings done during the Renaissance, for example). But they also contain *things*. You can find armour, housewares such as tapestries and spoons and *bric a brac*, clothing, ceramics and porcelain, toys, and all manner of other things in some museums, and it was all made by people, so you can think of both sides of the equation: the maker as well as the user. Don't forget to read the little description cards displayed with each item; sometimes they'll include details about the person who made or owned the item, and that can lead you to new story ideas. Some museums even contain people themselves, such as the bog bodies—the preserved remains of humans sacrificed thousands of years ago—on display in the archaeology section of Dublin's National Museum.
- **Living museums:** Look online at local historical spots—houses, gardens, forts, castles, farms, etc.—to see if they have special "living history" days. These events often include people dressed in historical costumes, speaking as accurately as possible, and living as if they were in a certain time period. They're a fun way to experience history and watch possible characters walk and talk.
- **Television shows:** Much like living museums, some television programmes give us a behind-the-scenes look at historical people and events, and some are even hosted by historians, making them more trustworthy sources. Our favourites are specials hosted by Lucy Worsley and the historical farm series that includes *Tales from the Green Valley* in 2005, *Victorian Farm* in 2009, *Edwardian Farm* from 2010–'11, and *Wartime Farm* in 2012 hosted by domestic historian Ruth Goodman with archaeologists Alex Langlands and Peter Ginn.
- **Online sources:** Luckily, we have the internet to bring history right to us. We can look at websites for museums when we can't visit in person, or other sites such as Instagram and Pinterest for historical costumes; furthermore, sites such as the Historical Thesaurus of English, created by the University of Glasgow, provides historical terms for all sorts of things.

ACTIVITIES

A curiosity workshop:
1. Read this interesting historical fact we found:
"No one in a coastal town is safe. You come across women who do not know whether they are widows or not—all they know is that their husbands went to sea and never came back. Such women are in a terrible plight for they cannot presume their husbands are dead until seven years have passed; only then can they remarry. In the meantime they have to fend for themselves".[6]
2. Next, spend three to four minutes answering the following:
   - What questions can you ask to start to dig into this idea? About the culture that believes this? About the women stuck in this situation?
   - What questions might lead you to a fantastic element for a possible story?
   - What would you research on the heels of this to develop it more?
3. Take the ideas gathered and see if you can start to plot out a new historical fantasy story.

Grab Bag: A time, an event, a creature: Follow the steps below to begin a new story.
1. Choose one of these numbers: 15, 16, 17, 18, 19.
2. Add your age to the back of it to make a 4-digit number: this is your year.
3. Search for that year on Wikipedia and read the events (give yourself just a few minutes so you don't get too bogged down). Choose an event that you find interesting.
4. Now, choose a creature: Vampire, Mermaid, Ghost, Zombie, Orc, Wizard, Witch, Dragon, Selkie, Bigfoot, Yeti, Banshee, Chimaera, Elf, Giant, Goblin, Troll, or Siren.
5. Insert your creature into the event you chose.
6. Now, spend about three to four minutes listing what questions you can ask about the layering together of the history and the fantasy to get you started.
7. Finally, think about what story about our world or our "human condition" or even life now you can possibly explore via this overlap of ideas.

---

6. Mortimer, 2013, p. 215.

STEAMPUNK

Steampunk is all about how the past saw the future. It's a Fantasy version of Science Fiction, closely related to **Historical Fantasy** (often influenced by the Victorian era), but with a twist! This is a subgenre that's as much to do with fashion and cosplay as with storytelling. So, fire up your dirigible, holster your ray gun, grab your octopus, and let's get retro….

A Short History of Steampunk

Early SFF in the nineteenth century includes tales by Jules Verne (*20,000 Leagues Under the Sea*, 1872), H.G. Wells (*The Time Machine*, 1895) and others that feature amazing inventions and their adventurous creators. The stories are set in the air, under the sea, in the American (wild) West, and even on other planets (often supporting "exploitative capitalism"[1]). Most of these took advantage of technology powered by steam and, later, electricity, that didn't widely exist at the time. The continuing love of modern writers and fans for this material eventually saw this tradition evolve into what we now call steampunk. The movement first developed in the late 1970s and early '80s and came to the height of its popularity in the '90s and early 2000s. The term itself was coined in 1987 by author K.W. Jeter.[2] (Other ~punk subgenres explored in this book include **Cyberpunk** and **Solarpunk**, both SF, as well as **Splatterpunk**, which is Horror and so very different in its focus.) Interestingly, steampunk's early history was mainly American, with authors whose works see nineteenth-century London as "at once deeply alien and intimately familiar", a fantasy Victorian London that twentieth-century American authors created from their imaginations inspired by the world in Charles Dickens's work.[3] Included in this group are Jeter's *Morlock Night* (1979; the morlocks from Wells's *The Time Machine* time travel to Victorian London), Tim Powers's *The Anubis Gates* (1983; time travel, magicians, and werewolves), and James P. Blaylock's *Homunculus* (1986; dirigibles, aliens, and corpse reanimation).

Steampunk was initially a ~punk subgenre because it had something to say about society. Mainly set in Victorian England, a place and time that "is an excellent mirror for the modern period", steampunk used its trappings—"the social, economic, and political structures of the Victorian era"—to comment on our own, which are arguably "essentially the same".[4] William Gibson's and Bruce Sterling's *The Difference Engine* (1990), for example,

---

1. Nevins, 2008, p. 8.
2. Nicholls and Langford, 2022, n.p.
3. Nicholls and Langford, 2022, n.p.
4. Nevins, 2008, p. 9.

comments on unchecked technological progress and the **Dystopia** it can create. But in the past couple of decades steampunk has lost some of its social commentary and turned towards being more of an aesthetic entity. Critics have even called this "second generation steampunk", "steam sci-fi" or even "gaslight romance" because of its loss of bite.[5] A lot of steampunk now is full of the motifs and tropes—elaborate Victorian clothing (corsets, bustles, parasols, top hats, etc.), ray guns, copper gears, octopi symbols, vampires, werewolves, zeppelins, and on and on—that make it look *amazing*, but the stories themselves are sometimes just an amalgam of these images and not much else beyond an adventurous plot. The subgenre has arguably lost some of the edge that a movement requires to earn the ~punk moniker. One argument is that YA books such as Philip Pullman's *His Dark Materials* series (1995–2000) and Philip Reeve's *Mortal Engines* series (2001–'06), along with the ~punk label, caught the attention of younger people in the early 2000s, leading to the popularity of the aesthetic and the rise of cosplay and steampunk conventions.[6]

In our primary world, of course, steam engines were invented and in development from the late 1700s and then, starting in the early 1800s, used to power trains, boats, some farm machinery, and some factory machinery. Steampunk takes this idea and runs with it, setting stories in our nineteenth-century primary world with steam technology doing things it didn't do, such as power flying machines that had the capacity to carry passengers and cargo long before the Wright brothers flew their first rather rickety plane in 1904; there were hot-air balloons and various types of early dirigibles, even a steam-powered one, in the nineteenth century, but none as robust or powerful as those created on the pages of steampunk stories.[7] Tweaking this technology to do more earlier means that the steampunk world would be different in many ways from our own real past. For example, air flight would move people and goods across bodies of water or mountain ranges more quickly, which would have changed society in several ways, such as making once-costly cargo (fabrics, building materials, etc.) much cheaper and easier to get. But steampunk takes the speculative further by introducing fantasy elements, such as supernatural events; for example, in some stories inventors harness the "aether" from the air to power flying ships, while in other stories **Vampires** are present and acknowledged and part of society, or clockwork automatons are much more robust and complex than they ever were in our primary world and seemingly run on magic. So, while steampunk is SF in its use of technology that's advanced for its time, it's also Fantasy with its imagined past and magical elements.

---

5. Nevins, 2008, p. 10.
6. Nicholls and Langford, 2022, n.p.
7. Bellis, 2019, n.p.

Changing the past by inserting technology that wasn't there and adding ray guns and other inventions is fun, but steampunk is mainly set during the height of the British empire, and that's where things can be problematic (and, indeed, where it has lost some of its sharpness). The technology we had then in our primary world depended on large amounts of resources—steel, rubber, etc.—that often came from countries colonised and ruled by Britain, with the materials mined or grown by people who were either enslaved or exploited and paid very little. The effects of colonisation and empire are still being felt over a century later, so ignoring them when writing steampunk is ignoring one of the great things about SFF/H: approaching real-life issues "from the side".

A Spotter's Guide: "Goggles, people…"

- **The tech:** The research methods here are very similar to those described in the **Historical Fantasy** section because it's so important to capture the verisimilitude of the time period and setting. If you're going for steampunk that only uses steam power, for example, it's important to know a bit about how a steam engine works. But, beyond that, having some information about the world-changing importance of the steam engine and the connected and subsequent scientific discoveries can help you elevate your work in the subgenre. One of the best sources for this—and one that will inspire no end of great story ideas—is pretty much anything by science historian James Burke, who hosted a series of television shows that linked scientific inventions across time. Especially great are the episodes 'Thunder in the Skies' (from the 1970s, *Connections*), 'Revolutions' and 'Separate Ways' (from the 1994 *Connections²*), and 'Feedback' (from *Connections³* in 1997). You can look these up and view them online!
- **The look:** The steampunk aesthetic is one of its calling cards, and for that you'll need to know a bit about the clothing, etiquette, transportation, and décor of the era. But this isn't just about what things looked like. Remember, SF is about science and progress and technology, and the Victorian era was a watershed moment when it comes to everything from fabrics to glass to steel to paper to so many other materials and what they were used for. Researching the bustle, for example, isn't just about what it looked like but also about the story that this particular piece of clothing tells us about the materials it's made from and about how women's bodies were viewed at that time, as well as the expectations for women of the class who could afford dresses that required a bustle and how they moved, sat, and got around town. One great source for the trappings of the time is the Victoria & Albert Museum (aka, the V&A).

If you can't get to London to see it in real life, you can visit its galleries online. Another great online source is from the Smithsonian (do you sense a theme, with our attention on museums?), via their magazine and online site. Their search engine will take you to articles on all manner of fascinating historical subjects.

Things That are Cool About Steampunk

This subgenre has a beautiful aesthetic and a clear brand that makes it fun to dabble in because, as a newer writer, you can feel secure in the paddling pool before you take on the ocean. One author who's leaned into the aesthetic is Gail Carriger with her Parasol Protectorate series (2009–'12); the first book, *Soulless*, a comedy of manners, introduces us to Alexia Tarabotti, who's quickly embroiled in a murder mystery in an alternate Victorian London complete with vampires, werewolves, and a best friend who has questionable taste in hats. While this is a pretty subgenre, it does provide an opportunity to explore another world with more substance (as pastiched by heavyweight writers such as Thomas Pynchon in 2006's *Against the Day*). With steampunk, we think the question "What's your story really *about*?" is especially important because of the subgenre's historical setting. It's ripe for further examination for what it can tell us about the world in the late nineteenth century from the point of view of those who've been deprived of an historical voice to tell their story: those on the other side of empire building and colonialism (see historical fantasy for more on this approach). So, ask yourself what you might want to say about our world today through the lens of those issues in the nineteenth century, via steampunk and its fun tropes and motifs.

Be Careful: Steam Can Burn!

- **Being a mad scientist:** This genre, at its most basic, uses steam to power inventions much earlier than they existed in our primary world (basically, flying machines and other modes of transportation, although several stories are obsessed with Charles Babbage's Difference Engine). There are plenty of steampunk stories with zeppelins, proto-automobiles, etc., so consider how you can use steam technology to do something different. Many steampunk stories use other technologies, such as electricity, to power elaborate but make-believe machines that didn't exist over a hundred years ago. Do a bit of research into when certain machines were actually invented (for example, did you know that there were proto-zeppelins much earlier than you might have thought? Or that the punch cards used to run looms in the eighteenth century were the forerunner of computers?). This will help you better understand the science of the time and how to approach creating your new inventions.

- **Following the (social) rules:** Because steampunk is so often set in late-Victorian Britain, we can't neglect the strict social regime of that time period. Comportment, etiquette, and social hierarchy were all vitally important to keeping the status quo, well, the status quo, and for the continuation of established social relationships. These rules helped people feel secure because they knew where they belonged in the social hierarchy, or, seen in a different way, ensured people felt safe by keeping *others* in their place. This is another example of how exploring uncomfortable aspects of this time period and world can help you cook up themes for story ideas. So, while the Industrial Revolution was mechanising daily life, the rules of how people interacted were still rather complex, especially if you compare them to how we act nowadays. Consider how this might affect your characters' actions and behaviours, and what this says about human nature then and now.

ACTIVITIES

Around the world in steampunk fashion: You and your steampunk companions need to travel a great distance, possibly across the ocean, possibly across a continent. Do you travel by zeppelin and tangle with sky pirates, by a steamship that is a microcosm of pseudo-Victorian society, or even by a submarine created by a mad scientist? Perhaps you travel on clockwork camels across the desert or along some vast and secret rail network? Write a short scene detailing part of your adventure. Be sure to emphasise the steampunk aesthetic throughout!

Something can't come from nothing: Your steampunk inventor has come up with a new invention that requires a resource that doesn't come from their own country but is imported. Come up with the new invention and the required material (this might be an improvement on a traditional steampunk machine, such as a zeppelin, and the materials can be as common as copper or rubber). Do a bit of research on the item to have a better idea of where it's from and what was involved in making it. To have more control over the quality of the basic components, the inventor travels to where the material originates. While there, they discover the toil involved in mining/growing/attaining the resource. How will your inventor react to the situation? How might your inventor use their skills and know-how to build an invention there, and how might that invention benefit the local people?

URBAN FANTASY

When we think Fantasy fiction, we often think "traditional" secondary worlds, those with a quasi-mediaeval and heavily European aesthetic, an agrarian population, maybe dragons, and a wizard or two. But as our own primary-world population has moved from the countryside to cities, so too has the genre. Here dark alleys can be as scary as any cave full of orcs; here finance bros can be as evil as any necromancer. For this is Fantasy with a contemporary twist. This is urban fantasy.

A Short History of Urban Fantasy

Urban fantasy is just that: Fantasy set in a modern city rather than in the countryside (whether that be a real/primary world or an imagined/secondary world). In this subgenre, setting (which includes not just the place but the time period) is key, influencing how the characters act. It contains magic and the supernatural rubbing up against electricity and the internet, cars, and fast food! We can think of some historical tales, such as the London-set *A Christmas Carol* (1843) by Charles Dickens, as being a precursor to urban fantasy, written when the modern, industrialised city was growing faster than people were used to; at the time, "capturing the essence of a city" strained writers' imaginations, turning them to flights of fancy.[1] Moreover, the pursuit of progress and money—the capitalist system—left urban populations thinking they had a hold of something only to see things become old and outdated in a flash, which led to considerable anxiety.

The urban fantasy subgenre began to develop in the twentieth century, when the SFF/H-writing and -reading population that lived in cities grew. Early forays in which the reader can find an urban setting and supernatural elements, but that aren't as solidly urban fantasy as later examples, include Thorne Smith's *Topper* books (1920s), about a bank president's run-in with ghosts, which were popular for their commentary on modern life pre-Great Depression; Gustav Meyrink's *The Golem* (translated into English in 1928), set in the Prague ghetto, which illustrates the beginnings of the subgenre's growth in non-US/UK areas; and Ray Bradbury's *Something Wicked This Way Comes* (1962), which brings the subgenre to a small American Midwest town. It was later, though, in the 1980s and 1990s, that urban fantasy became a weightier—and commercially *very* successful—subgenre label.

The most popular urban settings for this subgenre have been major "old" cities such as London or Paris, with locations frequently presented

---
1. March-Russell, 2020, n.p.

as characters in their own right because of their complexity: they contain neighbourhoods that are "separate" from the main city, hidden doorways and alleys, various layers from basements to penthouses, and are ripe for research relating to urban legends and other mysteries. An old city's history is also layered, with new builds abutting homes or businesses that are centuries old. London, often the setting for **Steampunk** stories (related to urban fantasy but even more specific in its focus), has starred in Neil Gaiman's *Neverwhere* (1996; about a mysterious girl named Door; includes London Below, a Floating Market, actual Black Friars and an Angel of Islington, as well as many magical beings and items), Mike Carey's Felix Castor series (2006–'09; Castor is a freelance exorcist working to rid London of its ghost problem), Vivian Shaw's Dr Greta Van Helsing series (London, 2017–'19; the good doctor treats vampires, mummies, banshees and other supernatural patients and must try to stop a murderous monk), and Ben Aaronovich's Rivers of London series (2011–present; a cop is recruited to be part of the Metropolitan Police's supernatural unit; also, the gods of London's rivers are feuding!). More "modern" cities that have featured include New York in Mark Helprin's *Winter's Tale* (1983; a love story in an alternate NYC complete with a consumption-suffering woman and a possibly immortal man with his magical horse), Chicago in Jim Butcher's Dresden Files series (2000–present; private investigator and wizard Harry Dresden has to deal with demons, faeries, vampires, spirits, and werewolves), Los Angeles in Mishell Baker's Borderline series (2016–'18; disabled Millie works for the Arcadia Project, which polices the border between faerie and Hollywood), and various smaller US cities in Gaiman's *American Gods* (2001; manifestations of the old gods go to battle with new-world American gods). Some urban fantasies are also set in imaginary cities, such as Ankh-Morpork in Terry Pratchett's City Guard/Night Watch books (1989–2011); Bordertown, a town on the border between Elfland and the human world, in the Borderlands series (1986–2011), initially developed by editor Terri Windling and featuring some of the most popular Fantasy writers in English from Charles de Lint to Ellen Kushner to Holly Black; and Crescent City in Sarah J. Maas's series of the same name (2020–present). You notice a lot of these are series; it's easy to see how a city the size of LA or London can't be contained in just one volume!

Element Spotlight: Incorporating Crime Genres into Fantasy

Just as any real-life city is full of people from all over the world and contains various cultures, different businesses, types of housing, and on and on, urban fantasy lends itself well to cross-over fiction. One of the most popular combinations is urban fantasy mixed with crime and detective fiction because cities where people from all social classes, religions, and ethnic backgrounds live in close proximity obviously have their share of crime. Of course, stories and novels contained mysteries to be solved long before crime fiction became a named genre, but the growth of our modern cities changed the literary landscape. In the early days of our big cities, there were no official police departments; volunteers kept watch, with sheriffs and courts of a sort in place to judge and punish those who were caught committing crimes. The birth of law enforcement in America as we know it can trace its beginnings to the "Slave Patrols" of the early-eighteenth-century American colonies[2]; in Britain, a police force was established in 1829 as a reaction against the high crime in London[3], and American cities soon followed suit with the first official force established in NYC in 1844, with other big cities replicating the practice soon after.[4] The first detective department was established in London in 1846.[5]

This rise of official, organised police forces coincided with changes to, of all things, paper making, transport, and education systems; paper got cheaper to make with the shift from rag to wood[6], trains became more widespread and could move people and goods much more quickly and cheaply than coaches or ships, and literacy rates were rising[7]. This resulted in an explosion of reading materials (books, periodicals, newspapers) that could be quickly shipped across distances to get into the hands of a growing urban reading public (one now often looking for something to pass the time on their commutes!). And how to sell all those newspapers? Why, by printing stories that titillated and shocked: namely, stories about robberies, murders, and other crimes, the natural extension of the broadsheets and pamphlets carrying gossip or warning about notorious criminals that had come before (for more, see 2009's *Get Me a Murder a Day!* by Kevin Williams or 2013's *A Very British Murder* by Lucy Worsley). The study of human behaviour—psychology—was also advancing at the same time, followed by sociology and criminology, all of which contributed to the development of crime fiction. So, you can see how nothing ever exists in a vacuum! All this inspired fiction writers to churn out crime and detective stories, from Edgar Allen Poe's 'The Murders in the Rue Morgue' (1841), considered to be the first modern detective story[8], to Arthur Conan Doyle's Sherlock Holmes solving his first mystery in 'A Study in Scarlet' in 1887. It wasn't long before Agatha Christie's Hercule Poirot showed up in 1920

---

2. Hassett-Walker, 2021, n.p.
3. Banton, 2021, n.p.
4. Brodeur, et.al., 2021, n.p.
5. Evans, 2009, pp. 20–22.
6. Britt, 2020, n.p.
7. Lloyd, 2007, n.p.
8. History.com, 2020, n.p.

and her Miss Marple in 1927, followed by Patricia Highsmith and Patricia Cornwell, Val McDermid and Ann Cleeves, and many more, all contributing to crime fiction becoming one of the highest selling genres.

So, what does this have to do with urban fantasy, you ask? Well, crime and detective fiction are about solving mysteries, and urban fantasy is all about uncovering the secrets in a city containing more than is initially expected or shown (namely, supernatural creatures and events). Take a look back at the list of urban fantasy titles we've provided, and you'll notice a majority of them contain some sort of crime or even feature a detective, making this a natural stomping ground for sexy, broody David Boreanaz types and feisty, flirty Laurell K. Hamilton heroines. Driven detectives with shady pasts share the page—and sometimes a lot more, **#ParanormalRomance**—with vampires and succubi. Movies such as *Bright* (dir. David Ayrer, 2017) sometimes pair cops with supernatural creatures, but the real meat of urban fantasy has long been stories about private investigators.

Things That are Cool About Urban Fantasy

We can't travel to the (imagined) past, and many of us aren't able to visit castles or other fantasy-adjacent places, but urban fantasy offers a way to bring the fantasy to us. It's a means of mixing the folklore that we love, such as faeries and werewolves, with our own familiar surroundings. This subgenre treats cities as a magical landscape ripe for exploration. Because beyond what we see as tourists when visiting a city, or even beyond what we habitually notice when we live in one, cities have their secrets and layers—not just geographically but also historically—and this gives a writer a *lot* of material to draw from!

Watch Out for Dark Alleys

- **Be specific with your setting:** Urban fantasy is focused on the characters' lives (and sometimes afterlives) in the big city, so consider your reasons for choosing a particular city. If your city is generic, you aren't fully embracing the urban part of urban fantasy: the particular city needs to be central to the story. For example, in Gaiman's *Neverwhere*, certain elements of London such as the British Museum and various Underground stations are key. So do a bit of investigating yourself! Read guidebooks and interviews with people who live in your chosen city. Use Google Image Search and Google Maps because they let you "see" places you perhaps can't visit so you can gather details you might not have imagined, and generally help make your setting more realistic. Remember, it's not cheating, it's research!

- **Explore a theme along with a place:** Just like with all SFF/H, knowing what it is that you want to explore or say with a story is important for creating a story that resonates with readers, and with urban fantasy you have the opportunity to use your daily experiences of a place to do just that. But ask yourself why it's important for you to insert fantastical elements into a real place instead of just telling a non-Fantasy story about that place. What do the fae add to stories about, say, gentrification (our advice? Don't build apartments on their ringforts!). What can vampires say about social stratification? How can ghosts symbolise or literalise the long history of a city?
- **Your knowledge of the city:** There's no rule that says that you must visit a place before using it as a setting in a story but take it from someone who's tried: it's better to write about a place you've visited so that you know about not just the buildings you choose to feature but also little details that inhabitants take for granted. For example, one of us wrote about London before ever visiting, but moving there taught your author that you stand on the left on an Underground escalator at your own peril, every street corner has a slope with little bumps on it to warn those with low or no sight that they're near the road, and there's no such thing as a water fountain to drink from! Those little details might not make it into a final draft of a story, but they're things that a city's population just "knows" about and will affect a character who lives there. If all else fails, there's no shame in crowd-sourcing details online from people who live there.

ACTIVITIES

Map the fantastical: Either use an already drawn map of a neighbourhood in your town/city or draw one (a fun exercise is to place one map on top of another and map out the "secret" intersections!). Find the out-of-the way spots such as alleyways, boarded-up buildings, or dark streets that seem to go nowhere (though please be careful and never go alone if you're exploring on foot). Check for any particularly old and historical place of interest, then insert a supernatural creature along with their particular characteristics. For instance, if you place a fairy into a setting with a lot of old iron fences, the iron will have a very negative effect on the fairy's ability to do any magic. How would this, in turn, affect any sort of connection between the fairy and humans? This is just a simple example, but you get the idea that there will be consequences for the supernatural beings and the humans in these situations.

The rule of three: Earlier in our education as SFF/H writers, we learned from a very smart author that to get a story idea she wouldn't just try to combine two ideas together but would add another so that she had three ideas crashing together, trying to make something whole. Doing this pushes your brain to solve the puzzle, and that's what gets your creativity flowing. Below is a table of elements: a place, a type of fantastical creature, and a third column of other "stuff"; for the "third thing" we have provided a list of general ideas, but it's up to you to come up with a specific example. Choose one from each column and see how mashing them together jump-starts ideas for you. Then, start a new story with a scene set in your chosen city, with the chosen creature as your protagonist, and the "third thing" an immediate situation.

CITY	CREATURE	THIRD THING
Liverpool	Vampire	Art (Your favourite painting?)
Vienna	Werewolf	Crime (An unsolved historical mystery?)
Nairobi	Mermaid	Underground societies / groups (the Mob?)
San Francisco	Faerie	A natural disaster (earthquake, etc.)
Cape Town	Succubus	A reality TV show

Rome	Big Foot	A hobby, handicraft, or physical skill
Ho Chi Minh City	Ghost	A corrupt politician
Lagos	Centaur	A beauty pageant
Austin, Texas	Demon	Education (any level or institue)
Add your favourite city here:	Add another creature here:	Add another "third thing" here:

PARANORMAL ROMANCE

Adding Romance to Fantasy is lots of fun (and, sometimes, can lead to serious sexytimes!). The resulting subgenre, paranormal romance, embraces both sides of its family line and runs the gamut from chaste to smutty with the twist of including fantastical species such as **Vampires** and werewolves. So, swipe right and let's get this date started….

A Short History of Paranormal Romance

Paranormal romance is a flavour of **Urban Fantasy** in which the relationship between the human and the not-human (or special human) is the focus; that is, if you took the relationship out of the story there wouldn't be any story left! The material is usually set in our primary world (or a variation thereof) rather than a secondary world, and often in a city or urban setting, with the protagonist traditionally a woman or female-identifying character whose love interest is either a supernatural being, such as a vampire or werewolf, or a human with supernatural abilities. These empowered female characters, often but not always detectives or monster hunters of some variety, are generations away from their ancestors, the "damsels in distress" running around at night in a white shift in the **Gothic** subgenre. Instead of fleeing from something they fear, the protagonists of paranormal romance run toward what they want. Considering the lasting popularity of the Romance genre, it would seem that adding fantastic elements to the genre would be old hat by now, but it's relatively new: *The Ivory Key* by Rita Clay Estrada (1987), from Harlequin Books, with its inclusion of **Time Travel**, is considered one of the first paranormal romance books.[1] Indeed, the use of time travel in paranormal romance found cult-like popularity with Diana Gabaldon's Outlander series (1991–present); her story about the World War Two nurse Claire who falls in love with the dashing highlander Jamie in the 1740s spawned its own sub-sub-genre of Scotland-based time-travel romance novels.[2] But most paranormal romance is going to feature a character who isn't human, which twists the usual romantic expectations—and experiences—of readers, leading to writers sometimes having to pursue new heights of titillation.

Like the traditional Romance genre, paranormal romances can run the gamut from the more innocent, in which maybe there is kissing and the lights go dark when anything more happens, all the way to full-on sexytimes, in which the lights stay on and it's all described (what people in the industry

---

[1]. Romance Writers of America, n.d., n.p.
[2]. Stefanie, 2021, n.p.

like to call a "one-handed read"!). In recent years, following changes to the traditional Romance genre, the hetero-normative set-up has been subverted and newer paranormal romance stories includes relationships that aren't just hetero and combinations beyond the more traditional "pair". Recent popular paranormal romance books include Laurell K. Hamilton's Merry Gentry series (2000–'14; a human-looking faerie gets down and dirty with faeries and goblins, sometimes with several at once); Charlaine Harris's True Blood series (2001–'13; the telepathic heroine falls in love with a vampire, and there are shapeshifters and faeries, too); J.R. Ward's Black Dagger Brotherhood series (2005–present; a human female and a vampire male become life mates, while he fights threats with his gang of vampire "brothers"); Deborah Harkness's All Souls trilogy (2011–'14; vampires and magic, some time travel, as well as demons, with more focus on love than full-on sex); and Cassie Alexander's Dark Ink Tattoo series (2022; vampires and werewolves and *lots* of sex, of all kinds of different combinations!). On the lighter side is Gail Carriger's Parasol Protectorate series (2009–'19; a **Steampunk** crossover that includes vampires and werewolves). And, of course, there's a definite argument to be made that the vampire Twilight series by Stephenie Meyer (2005–'08) jump started the subgenre's popularity with YA readers; a quick internet search will bring up dozens, if not hundreds, more YA paranormal romance titles, as well as much fanfiction taking place in established series.

Element Spotlight: Writing Sex Scenes

Just like with writing anything else, be it dialogue, exposition, or even a non-prose form such as poetry, writing a sex scene takes practice. A caveat to that, however: sometimes, for some people, it just will never happen, and that's okay. There are plenty of great writers out there who either write awful, awkward sex scenes (and don't know it), or who know they're bad at it and just avoid writing it at all costs (hey, play to your strengths!). Writing sex scenes is a bit different from writing other elements because while we all converse with people (dialogue), we don't all like or have sex, or care about it at all, or have much of it, or have sex that includes various kinks, and that's okay, too. You can still write paranormal romance, but it just might be heavy on the romance and light(er) on the naked. Remember, the subgenre is called paranormal romance, not paranormal hook-up! But, if you want to write steamy stories, try practicing writing sex scenes to get comfortable with how to describe things that lots of people can't discuss without blushing and giggling. Let's look at some suggestions:

- **Do your homework:** There's a lot of erotica out there, and if you haven't dipped in, now's the time. To write in a genre, you need to read it (time spent reading is never wasted!). You should be reading paranormal romance, of course, but also erotica. Just as writing a novel is very different from writing a screenplay, prose erotica is going to be very different from visual (video) porn. There are plenty of anthologies out there with stories by various authors that'll give you a wide variety of perspectives as well as writing styles.

- **Let it go:** The number one tip about writing a sex scene: let yourself go. Tell that voice in your head that sounds like your mum or grandfather or parent/guardian to shut it. This also goes for what you believe your significant other will think, too! If necessary, come up with a penname and allow yourself to write sex as someone else who isn't related to whoever you hear shaming you in your head. You also do NOT have to share any of this writing with anyone you're related to or are friends with; this can be just for you, and if you do decide to publish one day you've already got a penname handy (Chuck Tingle, anyone?).
- **Get in touch (with yourself):** As with writing scenes outside our comfort zones in **Body Horror** and **Psychological Horror**, writing anything sexual is going to require that you tap into (pun not intended!) what makes you hot or not. Even this can be scary because we've been socialised to think some practices are "icky" or even "immoral". Remember, though, you're following the number one rule of sex: consenting adults. Plus, your consenting adults are imaginary! This means that they're allowed to have practices or habits or kinks that you don't have (but that maybe your secret side has always wanted to try).
- **Variety is the spice of life:** To expand on the previous point, remember that you're also writing for an audience that has various tastes and attractions, and paranormal romance has non-humans in it. So, learning more about various practices and kinks, as well as thinking about how a human and non-human will get freaky within the parameters of the rules of that paranormal character's life, will require some thought (and research). For example, if you want to write about a human and a vampire, read other stories with this same combination to know what's already out there and, perhaps, what you don't want to do with the relationship. A warning: be careful when doing internet research about sex; you don't want to end up with a really weird computer virus that will kill your hard drive! A few safe (and informative) sources include *Scarleteen.com* and *Sexetc.org*, which both might teach you a thing or two while giving you some insight into what the YA world is thinking, as well as *Salty* (*saltyworld.net*) for more adult-focused information. Another way to learn more, aside from reading, as instructed in "Do your homework" above, is to talk to trusted friends (although this might require a few glasses of wine!). Having a chat about someone else's

experiences will not only add to your well of information but also give you a first-person point of view, a vital element of good writing (just be sure to change names and details if you end up using some of the good stuff!).

- **This is not *Gray's Anatomy* (and no, we don't mean that television show!):** Remember, you're not writing a science manual. If there's one thing us humans are good at, it's being creative with language as well as behaviours and actions. In the heat of the moment, you're very unlikely to hear anyone utter "penis" or "vagina" because we have other, better words (and there are even sources out there where you can find historical slang for body parts to use if you're looking to add to the verisimilitude of some historical paranormal romance!). Remember the episode of *Friends* in which Monica and Rachel give Chandler a list of how to please his girlfriend that includes the seven erogenous zones?[3] Monica doesn't say what they all are, but we can guess, and she instructs him to mix things up because nothing is less sexy than sex that follows an instruction manual. People have quirks, techniques, inside jokes, things they've heard about or seen that they want to try (sometimes these don't work out, but characters laughing together during a sex scene can be super adorable).

- **Poetry in motion:** One challenge in making a sex scene realistic and hot is trying to avoid making it sound like a transcript from a porno. (And again, we definitely *don't* suggest you watch porn to learn to write sex! It's created in a certain way for a certain audience and is a completely different animal from written sex scenes.) For instance, in 1922, James Joyce scandalised readers with his experimental novel *Ulysses*, especially the unapologetic sexuality of the character Molly Bloom:

> ...when I put the rose in my hair like the Andalusian girls used or shall I wear a red yes and how he kissed me under the Moorish wall and I thought well as well him as another and then I asked him with my eyes to ask again yes and then he asked me would I yes to say yes my mountain flower and first I put my arms around him yes and drew him down to me so he could feel my breasts all perfume yes and his heart was going like mad and yes I said yes I will Yes.[4]

The way Molly expresses herself is poetic and elicits a reaction in readers without any real specific sexual detail. Some modern paranormal romance readers will expect a bit more (okay, a lot more!

---

3. Steinberg, 1998.
4. Joyce, 1922, (excerpt available online).

That excerpt is a hundred years old!) but giving them what they want without it being clinical or "put tab A into slot B, oh baby" will help you create a world—and a relationship—that'll resonate. Remember, this subgenre is about relationships, which means intimacy even if it's a one-night stand, and intimacy is built on the page with your words, images, figurative language, dialogue, etc.

- **Actions lead to reactions:** To boil down the laws of motion, when thing A crashes into thing B, thing B will move. Bodies in a sexual situation will be the same: when person A touches person B right there, person B will sigh or moan or laugh or react in some other way that shows person A that they have done just the right—or wrong!—thing. A sex scene (usually) isn't one party doing things to another party (or parties) mindlessly without any concern for anyone else and with the reader only being provided with the do-er's thoughts/actions/etc. unless the receiver is a sex doll. It's those reactions, from a little sigh and flinch to a big moan and surge that help a sex scene encompass the experience of all the characters in the scene, and help the reader be part of things.
- **Turn us inside out:** We are both physical and mental animals. A character in a sexual situation is going to feel bodily urges and reactions while simultaneously having thoughts, even if those thoughts are so instinctual as to defy simple words or vocalisation. But reading prose is a mental act; readers depend on words that provide insight into a character's thoughts to identify with them, even if the character is another gender or, in the case of paranormal romance, species. Molly Bloom's "yes" moment above is an extreme—and, again, very poetic—version of this, with her internal thoughts a litany of visual images while her physical self is reacting positively to whatever is going on in the moment. So, remember to express the internal (mental) while describing the external (physical) during a sexual encounter.

Things That are Cool About Paranormal Romance

No matter what genre you write in, fiction is about characters, and characters have relationships—romantic and non-romantic—with each other. Usually the characters are human, but (cue some philosophy here) even if the character is a non-human it was created by a human, which means it's going to have human-like or human-understood actions and reactions because as humans we can only create that which we understand. Confused yet? Simplified: Paranormal romance is a way to explore how romantic and sexual relationships develop between characters who are very dissimilar, against all sorts of odds and risks, like how in real life we say, "Opposites attract"! And part of that attraction includes the sexy kind, which is how this subgenre gives you, with its use of vampires, shapeshifters, ghosts, magic, and other fantastical elements, the opportunity to explore whatever kink your imagination can make up outside of "vanilla" reality. Just imagine the fun you could have playing with that toybox!

Bow-Chicka-Wow-Wow

- **How comfortable are you with writing sex?** While not all paranormal romance crosses into full-on erotica or even pornography, readers buy the subgenre because they want to read about relationships, and that means writing about physical intimacy. This can be a whole new writing experience for some of you; if you feel weird writing it, that awkwardness will show on the page. And that awkwardness might be a clue that you want to stick to handholding, kissing, expressions of love, and then maybe "dim the lights" on anything beyond that. And that's okay. You can practice your sex-writing skills until you feel more comfortable
- **Where's the line on what I'm "allowed" to write?** You as an individual are allowed to write anything you please, but publishing it is another matter. Paranormal romance pushes the envelope by combining humans and non-humans in relationships, including sexual situations. This subgenre has hugely benefited from the growth of self-publishing, but a publishing platform's rules will be the final word on whether your work sees the light of day. For example, Amazon's KDP (Kindle Direct Publishing) platform has rules, and what they term "Offensive content" is not allowed.[5] Writers of paranormal romance and other erotica discovered about a decade ago that this had an effect on their stories because, while contact is okay between humans (consenting adults), it isn't allowed between, for example, a human and a shapeshifter when that shifter is in animal or non-human form because the platform deems that bestiality, which is not just considered offensive but is also illegal because an animal cannot consent to sex (and non-consensual sex of any type is a no-no). This is an issue not just for self-publishing but for most traditional and independent/small publishing houses, which have their own rules about pornographic content. So, keep this in mind when writing your paranormal romance: keep it innocent & sweet or keep it hot & steamy, but don't make it illegal.

---

5. Amazon.com, 'Content Guidelines for Books', n.d., n.p.

ACTIVITIES

Tweak a couple: Take a popular romance novel or film and make one of the love interest characters into a supernatural creature: a vampire, werewolf, ghost, demon, dragon, etc. How would this change the story? Would it mean that the protagonist would only find their love interest at a certain time of day/month or in a certain place? Consider all the implications and make a list. This will then help you set up some of the rules before starting a story because the changes you make should be enough to make your story separate from the original (for example, *Pride & Prejudice & Zombies* by Seth Grahame-Smith, 2009, did much the same thing!).

Dip your toe in: If you've never written a love/sex scene, here is your chance to try it out. Take a supernatural being—we'll use a vampire as an example—and consider how you could use the figurative language associated with that being to describe a sexual situation. That is, what similes and metaphors and motifs can you use that are related to vampires to describe sex? In our example, we thought of descriptive words related to teeth and skin: sharp teeth against soft skin; the puncture wounds throbbed with pain; his skin was cold like marble; an icy embrace; her blood-red lips glowed against her snow-white skin. You get the picture. Now you try it with a different being (or continue the vampire example) and write a scene keeping in mind the images and terms. Also don't forget the "rules" of the paranormal creature and how it can be used in the scene: for example, vampires don't cast reflections, so what effect would this have in a kink/sex room with lots of mirrors?

TIME TRAVEL

Time travel is here in the Fantasy section because someone went back to the Cretaceous Period and stepped on a butterfly. Seriously though, time travel is a subgenre/element that's common to *both* Fantasy and Science Fiction. Who among us hasn't wished for a time machine or a magical doorway that moves us from now to then? You could return to your junior prom and leg it out of there before the embarrassment that still haunts you today, or you could go back to fix the misunderstanding that led to the worst break-up of your life. You know, important things! So, who wants to go on a little trip....

A Short History of Time Travel

Time as a concept has intrigued philosophers for millennia. But it's only fairly recently—in the last few hundred years—that smarter people than us have seriously tried to understand how time passes. In 1655, Thomas Hobbes argued that "time is a phantasm of motion".[1] He connected time to movement, but for movement of anything you need it to exist in space. A little later, in his *Principia Mathematica*, Sir Isaac Newton "created an inevitable analogy between time and space" with his mathematics (cue the development of the TARDIS!).[2] Fast forward to the early 1800s (which you can do because, you know, time travel), and we find German philosopher Arthur Schopenhauer claiming that "in mere Time, all things follow one another, and in mere Space all things are side by side; it is accordingly only by the combination of Time and Space that the representation of coexistence arises".[3] By this, Schopenhauer meant that a thing cannot exist in space without time and vice versa. But we still have difficulty really understanding what time is. Here's a challenge: *Define time without using the word "time"*! We'll wait.

The nineteenth century is when our concept of time started to shift even more. Suddenly, we had trains, and they had to be on time, which meant the creation of the train timetable, which had the knock-on effect of making everyone pay attention to their schedules. Telegraphs connected people across space. And archaeology—yes, that thing Indiana Jones does!—was developing into a serious discipline, with museums beginning to give regular people a peek into the distant past. Enter time-travel literature. First up, we had outright fantastical tales in which the protagonist sleeps into the future, such as 'Rip Van Winkle' by Washington Irving (1819), and similar stories in other cultures. Then, we got stories in which time travel

---
1. Hobbes, quoted in Gleick. 2019, p.10.
2. Gleick, 2019, p. 11.
3. Gleick, 2019, p. 11.

might just be the result of the protagonist dreaming, such as *A Connecticut Yankee in King Arthur's Court* by Mark Twain (1889). But the big one of course, and the one most responsible for introducing SF elements, was H.G. Wells's novella *The Time Machine* (1895), based in part on an earlier story he called 'The Chronic Argonauts' (1888). This novella introduced a figure of a time traveller and coined the term "time machine" (the term "time travel" first appeared in the *Oxford English Dictionary* in 1914[4]). Because of Wells, readers and viewers now automatically accept the concept of a time machine; we don't really question the science or how it works, which is great for us as writers!

After Wells, and as we move into the twentieth century, time-travel stories began to change. Travel with a time machine becomes more SF at this point because it depends on technology we don't (yet) have, but the original strand of Fantasy time travel remains a huge part of the subgenre. In such stories the travel happens by accident or via more "magical" reasons. In the early and mid-twentieth century, a lot of time travel like this could be found in children's literature. Books by E. Nesbit (*The House of Arden*, 1908), Alison Uttley (*A Traveller in Time*, 1939), Edward Eager (*The Time Garden*, 1958), Philippa Pearce (*Tom's Midnight Garden*, 1958), Antonia Barber (*The Ghosts*, 1969), Helen Cresswell (*Moondial*, 1987), and others had child protagonists travelling through time, often via something such as a sundial or a doorway or herbs (so, via magic!). These books gave kids history lessons by introducing them to important historical figures or showing them decisive historical moments (much as *Doctor Who* did in its early years). Other Fantasy time-travel stories—often for adults—have characters meeting their own ancestors or even someone they come to love but who exists in a different time; *The Lake House* (dir. Alejandro Agresti, 2006), starring Keanu Reeves (showing his softer side in contrast to his performances as Neo or John Wick!) and using a magic mailbox to move letters through time, is one of our romantic favourites.

On the SF side, though, time travel has evolved to become more complex, and more attuned to scientific hypotheses. Recent work in this vein includes Annalee Newitz's *Future of Another Timeline* (2019) and the utterly brilliant *This is How You Lose the Time War* by Amar El-Mohtar and Max Gladstone (2019). Television has tackled it many times in *Star Trek*—via intentional journeys, spacetime rifts, the intervention of god-like aliens, time loops, and more—as well as on more recent shows such as *Timeless* (2016–'18). You can also find a plethora of semi-scientific explanations in movies such as the stone-cold classic *Back to the Future* (dir. Robert Zemeckis, 1985); the brain-melting *Primer* (dir. Shane Carruth, 2004), in which two men invent time travel and discover the terrible consequences; along with no end of

---

4. Gleik, 2019, p. 23 (footnote).

time-travel films that try to get the science right but are mostly action heavy such as *Looper* (dir. Rian Johnson, 2012) and the Terminator franchise (various directors, 1984–2019).

A Spotter's Guide: The Dummy's Guide to Temporal Mechanics

Time travel can be a nightmare of logical pitfalls and paradoxes! Fun, right? A paradox as it relates to time travel is an idea that seems sound—the time travel seems logical—that falls apart once you begin to question it. Basically, you have created a scientific or narrative problem that cannot hold, and the story will fall apart. Let's look at some common examples:

- **The grandfather paradox:** This is a consistency paradox based on the idea that time travel to the past will cause an insurmountable inconsistency in the present. For example, killing your grandfather in the past means you'll never be born; so, if you kill your grandfather (or father, etc.), you won't be born, and you won't be around to build the time machine or use the time machine to go back and kill him. This same argument can be used in cases in which the character goes back and talks to their younger self: if they don't remember it happening when they were a kid, then it didn't happen. *The Big Bang Theory* addresses this in the 2010 episode 'The Staircase Implementation' (dir. Mark Cendrowski) when Leonard and Sheldon agree that if one of them invents time travel in the future, they will come back to this moment (plus five seconds) to tell their now-selves; not surprisingly, their future selves don't appear.
- **The predestination paradox:** In this paradox, the time traveller goes to the past and causes something to happen that sends them into the past, or they inadvertently cause whatever event they are trying to prevent. Therefore, they were destined to go into the past (this brings up the question of free will again!). Robert A. Heinlein's classic 1958 story 'All You Zombies' (released as the film *Predestination*, dirs. Michael and Peter Spierig, 2014) is a wonderful example of this: [spoiler alert!] everyone in the story is the same character (female in the early part of their life but male in the later years) who tries to go back in time and stop herself from getting pregnant but inadvertently gets herself pregnant with their now male body. The characters in *12 Monkeys* (dir. Terry Gilliam, 1995) also discover that, despite time travel, they can't stop the pandemic that ravaged the world forty years in their past.
- **The bootstrap paradox:** This paradox is named after Heinlein's 1941 novella *By His Bootstraps*, which, in turn, takes its name from the fact that pulling oneself up by their bootstraps is actually impossible. In this paradox, something (a character, a piece of information, an object) gets

trapped in an infinite cause-and-effect loop with no point of origin. For example, if you travel to the past and give someone a watch, and then in their future they give it to you, and then you travel to the past and give it back to them, the watch never came from anywhere but only exists inside this constant loop. There's a small example of this paradox in *Bill & Ted's Excellent Adventure* (dir. Stephen Herek, 1989) in which the future B&T go back and meet the past B&T and refer to Rufus by his name, but Rufus never introduces himself to either of them at any time: the fact of his name is the paradox because it has no source.

- **The "Let's kill Hitler" paradox:** Taking on Adolf has been a popular trope for decades, but despite the attraction of wiping him off the planet and out of history books—even if just in fiction—the paradox, which is related to the Grandfather Paradox, stands in your way. Going back and killing Hitler erases the reason why you went back to kill him in the first place, so in the future you would not have travelled back to the past. This is such a popular storyline—and one that, at this point in the history of SFF is nearly impossible to undertake because it's been done to death—that there are even meta references to it such as a 2011 *Doctor Who* episode titled 'Let's Kill Hitler' (dir. Richard Senior) though, unfortunately, he survives.

Even More Time-Travel Hypotheses Straddle the Line Between SF and Fantasy:

- **Course-correcting hypothesis:** This is the idea that if we alter events in the past we'll set off another set of events that will cause the present to remain the same.[5] This is used to explain how travelling into the past and doing *anything*, no matter how big, won't affect the future; history will basically heal itself. The latter seasons of television's *Lost* (2004–'10) played heavily with this idea, as, to an extent, did the 2009 *Star Trek* reboot (dir. J.J. Abrams).
- **The multiverse or "many-worlds" hypothesis:** In this one, an alternate parallel universe or timeline is created each time an event is altered in the past.[6] The science of this hypothesis is complex, but if you watch *Back to the Future Part II* (dir. Robert Zemeckis, 1989) there's a great scene during which Marty and Doc use a chalkboard to illustrate the split timelines they have created and discuss how they'll fix things! Recent examples include *This is How You Lose the Time War* by El-Mohtar and Gladstone, and the final season of Marvel's *Agents of SHIELD* (2013-'20).

---

5. Del Monte, 2013, n.p.
6. Del Monte, 2013, n.p.

- **Erased-timeline hypothesis:** With this hypothesis a person travelling to the past would exist in the new timeline, but have their own timeline erased.[7] It's like opening a magical door into a new timeline, but when you close the door behind you everything on the other side of it—your old life—is gone. A short five-minute film titled *One-Minute Time Machine* (dir. Devon Avery, 2014), available on YouTube, hilariously deals with an alternate version of this.

Things That are Cool About Time Travel

Time-travel stories allow us a chance—in fiction at least—to get a "do over", to have a second chance to go back and fix something in our lives. This is where, even if the travel is done via a machine (so is SF), we are exploring Fantasy as "a literature of desire".[8] Oddly, very few protagonists travel to the future; this is partially because imagining a future world—and then building it—takes so much speculative work (though kudos to *Futurama*, 1999–2013, for sending a twentieth-century delivery boy into the thirty-first century as its central premise). On a practical level, this is often because we have historical records, as well as television- and movie-studio warehouses full of historical props, to help us more easily recreate the past; narratively too, the past is easier to create because we know what happened and where events lead. Time-travel stories also offer us a way to explore the concept of free will. Often a character will travel to the past to right a wrong (to get their "do over"), but then, when they return to their present, they discover that they've inadvertently messed things up even more, sending them back to "unfix" the thing they changed. This provides the writer a way to deepen the theme, especially when a character goes back to undo something only to find that they were the one who did it in the first place, leading to the question whether our actions are already planned out.

Beware the Scientific Pretzels

Time-travel narratives are a philosophical minefield, but they're also a goldmine for writers! When Wells gave us the time machine that he didn't have to explain, he also sprinkled pixie dust over other elements of time travel that twenty-first-century writers need to consider. Some of the questions can be ignored, especially in Fantasy stories in which time travel happens via some sort of magic; but in SF stories, with the sophisticated readership we now have, you'll have to consider how to address them:

---
7. Miller, 2014, n.p.
8. Jackson, 1981, pp. 3–4.

- **How the time machine gets its power:** Wells didn't explain this, but some recent time-travel stories have addressed the omission. In the *Back to the Future* films, Doc Brown first uses plutonium to power his Delorean's flux capacitor; the second film shows he's "gone green" and has altered the machine to use garbage instead. In Fantasy time travel, how a character travels is just magical in and of itself, such as via the time-turner in *Harry Potter and the Prisoner of Azkaban* (1999), or via a mysterious portal as in the British sitcom *Goodnight Sweetheart* (1993–'99) in which Gary Sparrow travels back and forth from the 1990s to the 1940s by walking along an old alley in London's East End.
- **Moving in time and space (spatial precision):** In Wells's time, flight hadn't yet been invented, so no one questioned the science of moving through space and time in his outlandish story. Now, however, we all know that the earth spins and travels along its orbit (and the solar system in turn orbits the centre of the galaxy), so if you travel forward or backward in time you'll pop up in the past or future in a different spot on the map, or even end up floating in space as in early episodes of the television show *Seven Days* (1998–2001)![9] *Doctor Who* deals with this by inventing the TARDIS (Time and Relative Dimension in Space), a time machine that is also a **Spaceship**.
- **Being visible as you move through time:** If you travel from this Monday to next Friday via time machine, how come no one sees you from Tuesday through Thursday? In *The Time Machine*, the Psychologist explains that it's because the time machine is like the spokes on a bicycle wheel, spinning so fast no one can see it.[10] But scientifically we must assume that you and your time machine would be visible, and possibly even in the way, as you experienced time at a completely different rate to everyone else.
- **Taking up space when you "land":** In Wells's novella, the Time Traveller explains that he didn't appear in the new time inside a table or a wall or even a living creature because as the time machine travelled it "'was slipping like a vapour through interstices of intervening substances'" and that stopping "inside" another object would result in an explosion.[11] So, it was dangerous, but possible. But if you move through space as well as time then your departure spot is going to be different than your arrival spot, so you're taking a big risk of landing your time machine in the same space as something—or some*one*—else!

---

9. Diodati, 2020, n.p.
10. Wells, 1895, Chapter 2.
11. Wells, 1895, Chapter 4.

ACTIVITIES

Course correcting timeline "ruins" your story: Your protagonist has travelled to the past (magically or with a scientific machine) to right a wrong, but when they come back to their original timeline they discover that everything has reverted back to the original situation. How would a protagonist feel if whatever they tried to change just unchanged itself? Would they go back again and try something new? What theme could you explore in this situation?

Travelling into the future: Moving into the future is more of a challenge than re-creating the past because you must tackle worldbuilding as well as consider how our now will affect our future. Choose a time period 20 years from now, 50 years from now, 100 years from now, or 1,000 years from now (in fact, comics writer Jonathan Hickmann did a variation on multiple future destinations *all* at once at once in *Fantastic Four* #605, 1998). Your choice might depend on whether you want your character to be able to see their future self or to move beyond their own life span. Choose either an unfortunate thing about the present you want to eradicate or a good thing you want to see become more important. This can be something personal to the protagonist or something bigger about your world. Using a SF time machine or a Fantasy-based means of time travel, your character travels forward in time to discover how our current world has affected the future.

CHAPTER THREE

HORROR

What is Horror?

The Horror genre is about what scares you. Sure, unexplained sounds in a dark house late at night are scary, as are unfamiliar creatures that come out of the forest or from under the ground or even down from the sky, and bloody and gory injuries are definitely scary because *ew*! But the question for us as writers is *why* are these things scary? On the surface, we can explain that we, as a society, are conditioned to be afraid of these things because of the cultural belief in the scariness of what, say, Halloween represents. We can say it's because ads or reviews of books we've read, shows we've watched, and films we've seen all *tell us* that these narratives are scary. Our parents were scared of certain things, and so are we, often unconsciously by learning the fear from them. But, really, *why*?

It has to do with order.

When something happens out of order, when something happens when it wasn't supposed to—or expected to—happen, when something appears that doesn't belong here, order is being upended. The status quo is subverted. What we think the world is like is completely undermined when it has just shown itself to not be that way. That's when we're frightened. Order has become disorder, and we, as adults or kids, don't know how to make things go "back to normal". And that scares us, sometimes just a bit and sometimes to the point of completely freaking the f*ck out. Horror is a peek to the other side: "It is an essential, troubling accompaniment to the complacencies of the everyday, reminding us that behind artifices of comfort and rules, order and stability, wholeness and righteousness, lie the flip sides of these: discomfort, terror, violence, disgust".[1] It's the wardrobe out of which the knife-wielding lunatic lurches. It's the phone call coming from *inside* the house.

So why do we love the blood and guts and screams and wide-eyed terror of the Horror genre? Isn't that, well, kinda messed up?

It depends on who you ask. Stephen King, who's basically our Grand Poobah of Horror and has been for nearly five decades, argues that we like

---

1. Wisker, 2015, p. 130.

being scared: "We love and need the concept of monstrosity because it is a reaffirmation of the order we all crave as human beings ... and let me further suggest that it is not the physical or mental aberration in itself which horrifies us, but rather the lack of order which these aberrations seem to imply".[2] He's telling us that we crave frights—and this is presumably why so much horror, such as **Vampires**, has an eroticised touch—because it shows us what a lack of order looks like, and this in turn solidifies for us the order we work to create and keep.

More than a fear of what's "out there", though, Horror also brings home to us that *we're* the ones creating the make-believe monsters (or sometimes very real, in the case of serial killers), be they alien or insect or human. Horror holds up a cracked mirror that allows us to live out whatever fantasy or dream we might have that we're afraid to share even with our daily go-to-work and pay-the-bills selves. King, for instance, is often asked why he would choose to spend his life creating such horrible stories when real life contains so much awfulness. He explains that "we make up horrors to help us cope with the real ones" as a means of catharsis: "The dream of horror is in itself an out-letting and a lancing" and "the mass-media dream of horror can sometimes become a nationwide analyst's couch".[3] There's a common aphorism, "Don't say it or it might come true"; here, though, King is twisting that and claiming that we *need* to say a horrible thing or to create it in fiction in order to practice for when it—or something horrible in our personal lives—inevitably happens; only by rehearsing how to deal with life's terror can we be ready for the alarm. Horror, says King, is, "in a symbolic way, things we would be afraid to say right out straight. It offers us a chance to exercise (that's right; not *exorcise* but *exercise*) emotions which society demands we keep closely to hand".[4] It's a way of processing our fears—be they of monsters, machetes, or machines—and thus regaining some kind of control over them, even if that's just closing the novel's cover or switching off the television late at night.

Throughout this book we delve into Science Fiction and Fantasy's evolution. Yet many of humankind's earliest stories also contain elements of Horror (revisit **Folktales and Fairy Tales** or **Historical Fantasy**), and SF got started literally because of a group of friends trying to out-scare each other in the early nineteenth century. Horror overlaps in all sorts of ways with SF and Fantasy, which makes sense when you consider that Fantasy often contains monsters, ghosts, and the unexplained, and Science Fiction contains robots or other human-like creations (see **Robots**... for more about the uncanny valley) and is often about exploring worlds and entities so vast

---

2. King, 2006, Loc. 761.
3. King, 2006, Locations 309–311.
4. King, 2006, Loc. 629.

and strange that puny humans cannot even fully comprehend them (see **Big Dumb Objects**).

Horror is in fact everywhere in literature.

It has always been in here in the dark with us.

GOTHIC HORROR

Something stirs on a stormy night. You thought you were alone, but you aren't. A shadow moves through a castle hallway and in that moment you become disorientated. An eerie double of your own face smiles back from an old oil painting. A withered hand beckons you into the darkness. This is a world of fear. These are stories of chaos versus order. This is gothic horror.

A Short History of Gothic Horror

The first gothic novel was Horace Walpole's *Castle of Otranto* (1764), which set the stage for an adaptable subgenre defined by a particular balance of psychological and supernatural elements. "At once escapist and conformist," explains critic Clive Bloom, "the Gothic speaks to the dark side of domestic fiction: erotic, violent, perverse, bizarre and obsessionally connected with contemporary fears".[1] A parade of examples refined the form throughout the late 1700s. Among the most important are Ann Radcliffe's contribution to eerie castle fiction *The Mysteries of Udolpho* (1794; later spoofed by Jane Austen in 1817's *Northanger Abbey*), and Matthew Lewis's then-scandalous *The Monk* (1796). The burst of gothic horror at the time may be, as *The Encyclopedia of Science Fiction* puts it, "a reaction to the emphasis on reason which prevailed in the Enlightenment, the intellectual world of the eighteenth century".[2] Indeed, this rejection of reason—often manifesting as inexplicable events or perverse character motivations—would go on to be a hallmark of gothic horror for centuries.

In the 1800s, however, writers sought to add more psychological depth to the subgenre and its protagonists. Influential works in this period include Mary Shelley's *Frankenstein* (1818), which swapped out the overtly supernatural for a literal embodiment of human hubris; Charles Maturin's classic *Melmoth the Wanderer* (1820), a variation on the Wandering Jew myth in which a man sells his soul to the Devil in exchange for a longer life; Edgar Allan Poe's 1839 story 'The Fall of the House of Usher', which links madness and physical disintegration; and, of course, Bram Stoker's *Dracula* (1897), which once more cemented the supernatural as one of the two poles—the other being good, old-fashioned human irrationality—that continue to define the subgenre.

In the twentieth century, gothic horror became ubiquitous, arguably threatening to subsume all of Horror beneath its cloak. Nonetheless, the

---

1. Bloom, 1998, p. 2.
2. Nicholls and Clute, 2021, n.p.

resulting familiarity with the tropes of crumbling castles and flocks of bats and rainy moorlands dulled some of gothic horror's energy for several decades. Gone were the "strong images or instances of voyeuristic gore" that defined the work of Lewis or Maturin (at least until the coming of low-budget sensationalist cinema in the latter part of the century).[3] The subgenre would find its rudder again in the postwar era when writers began to concern themselves with the grotesque violence of families and communities. A case in point is the writing of Shirley Jackson, nearly all of which is classifiable as gothic horror. Special attention should be paid to her novel *The Haunting of Hill House* (1959), one of the finest examples of literary terror to be found (and an excellent instance of a queer character in the genre), as well as to her brilliant story 'The Lottery' (1948), a slow-burning exemplar of small-town gothic horror that builds to a terrifying conclusion.

Modern gothic horror continues to be a rich source of frights and fiction for readers across all mediums. Significant examples include *The Shining* (1977) by Stephen King, *The Woman in Black* (1983) by Susan Hill, and, throughout the 1990s, *The X-Files* (1993–2002), which brought the grotesque into audiences' living room on an almost weekly basis. More recently again, Sarah Perry's *Melmoth* (2018) revisits the transmitted narrative structure of Maturin's novel for a modern take on the material that hooked audiences anew, while Silvia Moreno-Garcia's bestselling *Mexican Gothic* (2020) offers exactly what the title promises, brilliantly linking the subgenre to the unfortunately immortal themes of colonialism, settler violence, and classism.

A Spotter's Guide: Things That Go Bump in the Night

Beyond the prototypical castles and mansions, gothic horror comes in many macabre flavours:

- **Schoolhouse gothic:** Gothic horror lends itself to school stories (and certainly television shows such as *Buffy the Vampire Slayer*, 1997–2003, got significant milage out of this). This corner of the subgenre comprises vast buildings filled with claustrophobic classrooms (even more unsettling again after hours), power imbalances between students and staff, as well as curious histories and hierarchies that frequently veer into the occult (see *The Chilling Adventures of Sabrina*, 2018–'20). At their worst, schools—and for that matter, universities—lend themselves to paranoia and obsession.[4] In schoolhouse gothic, a term coined by academic Sherry R. Truffin, educational opportunities become pressures, students become competitors rather than classmates,

---
3. Reyes, 2014, p. 2.
4. Truffin, 2008.

and teachers become monsters rather than mentors. The hallways, classrooms, offices, and grounds are frequently places of violence, not just via the half-truths of indoctrination, but also physical violence (see, for instance, the crimes against indigenous children in Canadian state-funded Christian boarding schools). The classic fictional example is, of course, King's *Carrie* (1974).

- **American gothic:** Sometimes called southern gothic, this is a particular blend of culture and characters informed by the history of the southern United States. It combines Horror tropes with unsettling scenarios drawn from the economic and racial inequalities of that region. It's usually set in a small town or countryside, and only rarely in a big city (though New Orleans gothic could probably be its own subgenre!). A typical backdrop includes a Spanish-moss-draped swamp, an abandoned farm, or a plantation, already deeply disturbing places on account of their brutal history of slavery. Indeed, the historical stain of slavery on the South is American gothic's defining aspect. These stories acknowledge that terrible things happened in these places: violent transgressions are quick and common; irrationality and repression are customary; racism and patriarchy remain powerful forces, often exercising control through secret societies; and physical decay is everywhere in a powerful metaphor for moral decay (see the first season of *True Detective*, 2014, itself influenced by the 1895 horror classic *The King in Yellow* by Robert W. Chambers). Some terrific work from African-American writers exists in this subgenre, including that of Zora Neale Hurston (see 1924's 'Drenched in Light' or 1921's 'Black Death'), who transformed the hurtful absurdities and supernatural strains of Southern life into vivid art.
- **Rural gothic:** A cousin of American gothic, the rural gothic plays on the usually urban protagonist's clear unease in, and unfamiliarity with, the countryside. It can, of course, be set anywhere, with significant potential for stories about repression and the struggle for empowerment set against African, Asian, or South American rural backdrops. Often these stories follow a newcomer who either runs up against tradition and prejudice ("This is how we have always done things") or discovers some hidden horror the locals have chosen to ignore (see, in a real-life example, the mass burial of infants in a septic tank at the religious-run Tuam Mother and Baby Home in Ireland). Anyone who's lived in a rural area will tell you that these are places of secrets. Abandoned houses (frequently associated with locally infamous crimes), strange carvings, graves, and folk practices are regular imagery. A further recurring element is "the rural poor as monstrous other", playing on economic inequalities between urban and rural communities.[5] Examples of rural

---

5. Murphy, 2013, p. 133.

gothic on screen include *The Wicker Man* (dir. Robin Hardy, 1973) or the very violent *Midsommar* (dir. Ari Aster, 2019).
- **Body gothic:** Our bodies are beautiful but, let's face it, they're also prone to a lot of squishy, moist, weird stuff! Body gothic, which is closely related to both **Body Horror** and mad scientist stories, contains tales of bodily integrity and the violation thereof. For as much as ruined towers or haunted houses are a key to this subgenre, so too is the human body a site "of Gothic fear—sexual, injured, dismembered and," occasionally, even "celebrated".[6] Body gothic often involves transformation, mutation, or the imprisonment or subjugation of others, such as in *The Human Centipede* (dir. Tom Six, 2010), or even abduction narratives on the SF continuum (such as Whitley Strieber's *Communion* (1987). Characters held prisoner in attics or dungeons predominate here, as do descriptions of examinations or surgeries, often with outdated or rusty instruments. As violation is a traumatic experience, these stories are often at the more unsettling end of the gothic horror spectrum. What we as writers need to remember is that, as academic Xavier Aldana Reyes cautions, "effective viscerality" is "complicated to achieve".[7] It requires practiced use of detail and experiential language to ensure that it serves character and doesn't become gratuitous or exploitative (as in **Splatterpunk**).
- **Eco gothic:** One relatively recent development is the so-called eco gothic (see: the Andrew Smith and William Hughes edited *EcoGothic*, 2013). These stories examine how nature itself is an agent of the monstrous and the terrifying. Where traditional gothic horror is predicated on a tension between the human and the uncanny non-human, eco gothic capitalises on that between the animal and the faunal. Motivated by contemporary climate collapse, these are tales in which plants and landforms themselves—the body of the Earth, if you will—take centre stage and reject the human. Untended gardens and overgrown estates offer some of the obvious settings, especially in terms of their liminality between the wild and the cultivated. Strong examples are found in the comic book character Swamp Thing (created by Len Wein in 1972), in Margaret Atwood's *Oryx and Crake* (2003), and in Aliya Whiteley's novella *The Beauty* (2014).

Things That are Cool About Gothic Horror

Gothic horror is a *great* way to tell scary stories! It offers a palette of classic tropes from which a writer can assemble a compelling sense of atmosphere. The subgenre lends itself to baroque description and memorable antagonists.

---

6. Smith, A., and Hughes, W., 2013, p. 8.
7. Reyes, 2014, p. 2.

These are stories where the rules no longer seem to fully apply. They play on our innate sense of unease in the world. They never go out of style.

Creatures Crawl in Search of Blood

- **Setting:** Traditional gothic horror is often set in isolated places, such as mansions on the moors or empty hotels high in the mountains. Occasionally, as in *Rosemary's Baby* (Ira Levin, 1968) they take place in urban areas such as apartment buildings that are framed as oppressively as any castle. These are eerie spaces defined by an aesthetic of unease that leave the characters feeling off balance. Their vastness, remoteness, or restrictiveness are emphasised by their deserted nature; there might be a caretaker present, or perhaps an eccentric aristocrat glimpsed in the distance. But your protagonist will likely be alone, and when shadows flicker, colonies of bats burst out of the darkness, and unexplained noises shatter the silence, their imaginations runs away with them. Settings in gothic horror are essentially characters, often antagonists, so use plenty of sensory detail!
- **Weather:** A crucial and highly symbolic aspect of gothic horror's whole vibe is weather. It is frequently cold and gloomy like the emotional life of our troubled characters (and here, as writers, we have the opportunity to deploy what is called a "pathetic fallacy", that being the attribution of human feelings and responses to non-human things). In classic examples, writers regularly use thunder and lightning as shorthand for a threatening ambience (echoed in modern stories when lightning causes electrical outages). Storms force our protagonists to stay inside and come face to face with their inner fears or, if they're caught outside in the wind and driving rain, can denote how lost they are. Fog is a particular signature element of the subgenre. It obscures people and objects as much as it does truth, and its arrival often heralds that of a supernatural force or a message containing bad news.
- **Doubles:** Like the evil-twin trope used in so many television soap operas, many stories in this vein include a dark or twisted double to the protagonist. Oftentimes this is a metaphorical or philosophical opposite, but the supernatural elements allow for literal doppelgängers to be present (Neil Jordan plays with this trope in both his Stoker-influenced realist novel *Mistaken*, 2011, and its own fantastical double *Carnivalesque*, 2017). Such doubles can serve several functions within a story: they immediately destabilise certainty and generate ambiguity—often sexual—for both characters and readers (though this can easily become weird-for-the-sake-of-weird); they're frequently depicted as the embodiment of a protagonist's hidden or sinister self; and, equally,

doubles and their actions can represent a split aspect of a character, without the acceptance of which they can never be whole.
- **Guest starring:** The strong emphasis on setting in gothic horror makes it a powerful vehicle for other genre stalwarts such as **Vampires**, werewolves, ghosts, and sundry immortals. The subgenre's ability to accommodate any supernatural figure that causes unease ensures a smooth rhetorical meshing of material because readers *expect* to meet Dracula or the Wolfman or the unquiet dead. Successful stories can result both by rewarding this anticipation with a monstrous appearance or by denying it. The latter cases, hewing close to **Psychological Horror**, leave the reader wondering what was really out there....
- **The sense of an ending:** There's no one way to conclude a gothic horror story; however, a writer ought to be aware of the different effects created by different *types* of endings. The subgenre is stereotyped as a tragic one concluding on notes of violence and disintegration; that being said, happy endings weren't uncommon in early examples (and, indeed, persist today in much of the Gothic Romance field). A greater difference is found between so-called closed endings and open endings.
    - **Closed endings** bring about resolution for the characters and for crucial elements of the storyworld. Though somewhat formulaic (and, in that way, straightforward to write), closed endings satisfy reader expectations of a story to be tied up neatly (for examples, a ghost finds peace and moves on, or a monster is finally accepted by their community).
    - By contrast, **open endings** leave unresolved elements (the vampire escapes, the evil castle vanishes). In gothic horror, these can be quite unsettling and ominous. They can be more difficult to accomplish without causing confusion, but they have the potential to stay longer with the reader.

ACTIVITIES

An epistolary story: An epistolary narrative is one composed of letters or other written paraphernalia. Stoker's *Dracula* did this, with a narrative that comprises Mina's letters, Jonathan's journal, a ship's log, and other pieces. This narrative form gives readers a character's own words; though, in the case of letters, what is told is often curated for the recipient. Take this idea and write a gothic horror story set in our own time using our own methods of communication: email, text, blog posts, etc. You've gone on a trip to house-sit a cousin's cat in another city or country, but when you arrive there is no cat and the house/apartment/loft isn't at all what was expected, so you must reach out to find out what's going on while simultaneously living in the place.

A picture is worth a thousand words: Let's take this adage literally and write a thousand words about an imaginary painting hanging on the wall in a gothic manor. The picture is of a lady or a lord from hundreds of years ago, one who vanished in mysterious circumstances. Describe their face, their clothing and stance, and the backdrop they're posing against. Use detail and descriptive language to unnerve the reader (maybe, for instance, the artist has included an insect crawling on the subject's skin?). Convey the idea that there is something unnatural or even supernatural about them.

SUPERNATURAL HORROR

Supernatural horror is what we traditionally think of as scary stories about things that go bump in the night. It explores the paranormal, the weird, and the scary with a buffet of recognisable threats and monsters. It speaks to the tendency of all cultures to believe that there's more to this world than meets the eye. So come with us now if you dare and let's see if the truth is indeed really out there....

A Short History of Supernatural Horror

The words "supernatural" and "paranormal" have both come to mean 'beyond what is natural', 'beyond the rules of nature', or refer to an event or entity that cannot be explained scientifically. As (mostly) rational adults in the modern world, we depend on science to create our medicines and help protect food and water supplies, among many other things. But as humans with imaginations, we can't help but wonder whether that one time we played "Light as a Feather, Stiff as a Board" at a slumber party when we were twelve years old was *real*; the same with playing "Bloody Mary" in the mirror in a bathroom with the light turned off, or experimenting with a Ouija board, or even that time we could *swear* we heard whispering in the basement. These supernatural games are part of your authors' Gen X and Millennial "heritage", a sort of evolution of our ancestors' superstitions (some of which we've inherited) about not whistling in a graveyard (it can summon the Devil!)[1], avoiding certain cursed objects[2], not walking under ladders, and on and on. All cultures have stories, legends, and superstitions like these that include elements of the supernatural.

Supernatural horror is the first kind of horror story we have on a cultural level. It is, in fact, difficult to separate it from our first written stories here in the West (also our first Fantasy narratives) such as *Beowulf* and *Sir Gawain and the Green Knight*, most of which contain Horror elements including ghosts and spirits, demons and monsters (over in **Folktales and Fairy Tales** you can read more about the evolution of oral tales to written tales and their contents, which include Horror elements and supernatural beings). Many supernatural horror stories also include religious elements (even the Bible contains supernatural horror) such as demons, devils, and possession, and all these elements have frequently made it to popular fiction and films.

Some of our culture's first published short stories were also supernatural

---

1. Haddad, n.d., n.p.
2. Dagnall and Drinkwater, 2018, n.p.

horror; most short fiction was published in newspapers or other journals during the expansion of the industry due to cheap materials, faster shipping, and an increase in literacy (as described in **Urban Fantasy**), and stories about supernatural events would attract buyers, just like they do now. These early supernatural works include Edgar Allen Poe's first published story, 'Metzengerstein: A Tale in Imitation of the German' (1832 in the *Saturday Courier*), about a feud between two families, a mysterious horse, and an even more mysterious fire; 'The Ghost in the Garden Room' (1859) by Elizabeth Gaskell, published as part of Charles Dickens's 'The Haunted House' series in his periodical *All the Year Round*; and Ambrose Bierce's 'An Inhabitant of Carcosa' (1886 published in the *San Francisco Newsletter*), in which a wandering man discovers he's actually dead (a story trope that has reappeared countless times since). There were also early collections of supernatural horror, such as those by one of the masters of the ghost story, M.R. James, who published four collections from 1904 to 1925. It's said that he wrote many of the stories to tell his friends on Christmas Eve, continuing the British tradition of ghost stories being for Christmas, and this oral heritage has led to James's tales being mainstays of radio and other audio formats (as well as television). James is still popular enough that performance storyteller Robert Lloyd Parry has delivered his one-man show 'The M.R. James Project' since 2005, in which he sits in costume as the author/narrator, lit only by candlelight, telling his stories to enthralled audiences.

With the advent of film, supernatural horror benefited from costumes, lighting, special effects, and other elements used to bring the paranormal "to life" and so enhance the audience's terror. No longer did they have to just imagine; viewers could now see the ghosts, ghouls, and demons up close. The Hammer Film Production company pretty much dominated the Horror film market for decades, churning out films from the 1950s through the 1970s and even in the early 2000s. Their list contains dozens of horror classics from various subgenres, with several supernatural titles such as *The Mummy* (dir. Terence Fisher, 1959), in which a titular baddie is resurrected and all hell breaks loose; *The Gorgon* (dir. Terence Fisher, 1964), in which something is turning people to stone; and *Hands of the Ripper* (dir. Peter Sasdy, 1971), in which Jack the Ripper's daughter is seemingly possessed by his spirit and goes on a murder spree. Many of these films aren't super scary to modern audiences due to their low budgets and the propensity for sequels that rendered the materials stale; however, some supernatural horror films of that time still provoke terror. These include *Rosemary's Baby* (dir. Roman Polanski, 1968, based on Ira Levin's 1967 novel) about a demonic infant, *The Exorcist* (dir. William Friedkin, 1973, based on William Peter Blatty's 1971 novel), about a little girl possessed by the devil, and *The

Omen (dir. Richard Donner, 1976), about, you guessed it, a demonic child (what is it with these kids?).

A Spotter's Guide: Who's Who and What's What

- **Ghosts and spirits:** From the ancient Egyptian practice of placing food and other goods into tombs so the dead could enjoy the afterlife, to the current swathe of ghost-hunting reality teleivision, we've always been curious about what happens to us after we die. In Britain, ghost stories are a Christmas tradition (think of Dickens's *A Christmas Carol*, 1843), while they are more strongly connected to Halloween in the US, where this holiday is most popular. While we often link ruinous houses with **Gothic** literature, there are hauntings connected to more contemporary abodes (check out David Mitchell's *Slade House*, 2015; see **Suburban Horror** for more) and even people themselves (*Paranormal Activity*, dir. Oren Peli, 2007). The novel *Hex* (2013) by Thomas Olde Heuvelt brings this further into the present with the ghost of a witch that's tracked in a small town via an app.
- **Demonic possession:** Demons are evil entities found across many religions, and it's believed that they can possess a human and act maliciously through it. Blatty's *The Exorcist*, the most famous horror novel about demonic possession, was turned into one of the most famous horror films about demonic possession, complete with a young girl saying seriously shocking things in a gravelly voice while doing the unspeakable with a crucifix before spewing copious amounts of green vomit. The trope is still a popular one, with Grady Hendrix's *My Best Friend's Exorcism* (2016) a more recent addition.
- **UFOs and aliens:** While scientists have been trying to find evidence of life out in the solar system, there are lay people who believe that unidentified flying objects (UFOs) are spaceships from other planets containing beings (aliens) that have abilities beyond our terrestrial human ones. Some have even claimed to have had contact with aliens; this phenomenon began in earnest in 1961 with the widely reported case of Betty and Barney Hill's claimed abduction.[3] If you want more about this trope in SF, be sure to read the **Aliens** section. But aliens can also be a Horror element because they aren't human; that is, they undermine the control and order that we expect in the real world. Examples include the otherworldly "greys" that show up in abduction reports and some popular culture, the sinister xenomorphs from *Alien* (dir. Ridley Scott, 1979), and the creepy aliens in the film *Signs* (dir. M. Night Shyamalan, 2002), especially the jump scare when one walks out of a cornfield. But

---
3. Lacina, 2020, n.p.

it isn't just the visual medium of film where supernatural horror with aliens works; Stephen King's book *Insomnia* (1994) is about beings on another plane of existence, but the supernatural characters come across as aliens of a sort and reading that book late at night in a quiet house is definitely scary because the idea of beings in a parallel plane of existence spying on you is hard to shake.

- **Cryptids:** Like ghosts and spirits, magical or unexplainable creatures have been a feature of folklore from all cultures around the world. For example, sea sirens (closely related to our idea of mermaids) that lure men to their deaths come from Greek mythology; in Norse folklore, trolls live in the forest and attack humans; and Irish folklore contains ethereal creatures such as the banshee whose piercing scream warns that death is coming. We know the rules about werewolves and silver bullets, we still search for the Loch Ness monster, and Big Foot sightings still happen every now and again. The television show *Grimm* (2011–'17) ran with this idea and featured cryptids from various cultures and folklores. The resurgence of folktale references and fairy tale retellings (see **Folklore and Fairy Tales**) has also shown up in Horror: for example, Adam Neville's *The Ritual* (2011) is a terrifying story about a group of friends who get lost while hiking in Sweden and run afoul of people performing supposed-Viking rituals; oh, and there's an actual monster!

- **Psychic powers:** These include extra sensory perception (ESP), clairvoyance, astral projection, precognition, telekinesis, and other supposed "skills". Many SF stories feature characters who have psychic powers, following the idea that in the future we will have tapped in and be able to control these powers of the mind. In some Fantasy stories, psychic abilities are part of the magic system (see **Witches** for more). But in the horror genre, psychic powers undermine the status quo; we live life chronologically and believe in the here and now, but someone being able to move items with their mind, know the future, read minds, and be in two places at once isn't part of the natural order and can be a bit scary for some, absolutely terrifying for others. What's experienced by characters with these skills can also be horrifying. King has used psychic powers in many of his books: *Carrie* (1974), *The Shining* (1977) and its sequel *Doctor Sleep* (2013), *The Dead Zone* (1979), *Firestarter* (1980), *Pet Sematary* (1983), *Dreamcatcher* (2001), and *The Institute* (2019), among others.

- Then there are those things that aren't supposed to be scary but are. This brings us to King's *It* (1986): there's a clown. Even if it wasn't a completely bonkers and scary-as-we-don't-know-what clown, it's still a clown. And clowns are terrifying. End of discussion.

Element Spotlight: Adding Thrills Through Suspense

Throughout this book, we explore some related genres/subgenres to give you a quick idea of where they sit in the SFF/H matrix. Yet one genre designation that's difficult to pin down is Thrillers. You've likely heard of crime thrillers (you can read more about crime fiction in **Urban Fantasy**) as well as supernatural thrillers, but crime and supernatural horror books are going to be shelved in different places in a bookstore, so what gives? Thriller, sometimes called suspense, is more about the *feeling* it generates in the reader (or viewer) than about specific elements or tropes in the story. Think about the heightened feelings that make your pulse race or make you lean way forward in your seat when there's a chase scene or even a slow build to a jump scare. That's thriller material (oh, and you're welcome for the Michael Jackson earworm!).

Thrillers depend on elements such as pacing and suspense to build that feeling, elements that some newer writers can struggle with. For example, pacing is the speed at which your story moves; this can be adjusted in various ways, such as by shortening sentences in a fight scene or adding punchy dialogue to make readers move along at a good clip, even inserting longer descriptive passages to slow readers down a bit. Suspense, though, is much more difficult to pin down. Too often, newer writers think that keeping things *from* the reader, what one of your present authors likes to call "being coy with information", is how to build suspense, when the truth is actually more nuanced. Suspense can be built by the characters keeping information *from each other*; so, the reader knows—or suspects—what is going on and is on the edge of their seat waiting for the characters to discover the truth. You can see, then, how a supernatural thriller might use this technique to build suspense when Characters A and B are separated in a haunted house: they've each discovered clues about the ghost that the other hasn't, and maybe they're both trying desperately to meet back up but are being chased by various ghouls and spirits, while you—the reader—keep turning pages to find out what happens when they finally find each other near the front door (the only escape) where a pair of red eyes pierce the gloom.

Things That are Cool About Supernatural Horror

There is so much material out there! We (your authors) grew up in the generation that cut their teeth on the Reader's Digest books about mysteries of the unexplained; while we fully believed that the Bermuda Triangle and quicksand were threats we'd have to watch out for our whole life, we also got an education on just how many strange phenomena are out there, from the clearly fake (spirit rapping during Victorian-era seances) to the bizarrely curious (spontaneous human combustion, anyone?). Even these debunked events and phenomena are ripe for turning into fiction. And all these phenomena make supernatural horror the "easiest" way to scare readers. We say easiest because we humans have a very long history of being frightened by stories about monsters and ghosts, etc. So, it's sort of built-in that we're scared of the unexplainable!

Earn Those Screams

- **Join the conversation:** As with all SFF/Horror, you're joining conversations that are ongoing. But you aren't expected to know all of what has come before (nobody has time to read *everything*). So, if you want to write about a mythical being or about ghosts or any of these other elements, maybe do a little poking around to see where it's been used most recently. With such a long history, there's bound to be a lot of material out there; your task is to write *your* story, even if you're using similar elements to other fiction.
- **Consider cultural appropriation:** This is taking traditional clothing or a ritual from a culture not your own and using it for either entertainment or decoration. There's a fine line between homage and appropriation that shows a lack of respect. If you decide to use folklore or a story from a culture not your own, be sure to do some research and check that in your depiction you aren't further disenfranchising the culture and people to whom the tale belongs (see **Zombies** for a bit more about how the original source of a cultural belief can be lost).

ACTIVITIES

Mash up: Choose two of the previously mentioned types of supernatural elements: for example, werewolves and telekinesis. By choosing two—or even three—elements, you'll force your brain to try to solve the problem of how to make them fit together (creativity is problem solving!), which means that it'll come up with creative solutions. This is one of the best ways to jump-start a story idea. Take those two elements and put them in one of the following scenarios: waiting on a train or bus; getting stuck at the side of the road with a flat tyre; preparing for a twelfth birthday party; walking into a new school for the first time; proposing to your significant other. On the surface, none of these are particularly scary environments or situations (okay, maybe the school thing is), but adding in the supernatural elements will undermine the mundanity of the situation and interrupt the order/status quo, helping you get started making things scary.

Improvisation rules: The trick to improv is to always say "yes" to whatever your partner says to keep the activity going. One bugbear we have with some Horror stories is when a character just won't accept that something inexplicable has happened and they keep on saying, "It can't be' or "No, this isn't happening." After a while, you want to smack them in the back of the head and say, "Yes, it is happening. Now deal with it!" This drafting activity will give you practise writing quickly and not falling down the trap of thinking too much about consequences. The set-up: two frenemies go into a supposed haunted house and see a ghost. But they never deny what they see or say, "It can't be." Where will you take the story? Will it be scary or maybe funny?

VAMPIRES

From *Dracula* to *Nosferatu* to *Interview with the Vampire* to *Twilight* to *What We Do in the Shadows* the vampire mesmerises us with its hypnotic gaze. We stare into its eyes and see our own obsession with outliving death; we see our own erotic hunger reflected back at us. Come with us now as the sun goes down, the fangs come out, and sexy vampires in your area hunger for blood....

A Short History of Vampires

The vampire as we know it today emerges from a deep past of folktales about undead or semi-alive creatures who feed, or perhaps subsist, on the blood of human beings. Legends around various historical personages, such as the infamous mediaeval Romanian ruler Vlad the Impaler, have also been incorporated into these narratives with grisly effect. In practice, however, this hodgepodge of origin stories matters very little to readers who have taken on their own version of the vampire (often inspired by modern film) as a dark and ominous figure repurposed by writers again and again.

Although from the middle of the nineteenth century onwards the vampire was mostly a prose figure, its literary origins might better be seen in the brooding, mysterious, threatening subjects of Romantic poets such as Lord Byron (in 'The Giaour', 1813) and Samuel Taylor Coleridge (in 'Christabel', 1816). Yet while Byron and Coleridge were invested in the literary merit of their work, we would be remiss if we didn't point out that the author of the first popular vampire story was using the figure as biting satire (pun intended). 'The Vampyre', published anonymously in 1819, and initially taken to be the work of Byron, was written by Byron's personal physician and hanger-on Dr. John Polidori. He developed the story from a plot nugget that the poet proposed during the same story competition that Mary Shelly won with what became *Frankenstein* during that fateful 1816 Italian summer when Byron, Mary Shelly, Percy Shelley, and Polidori hung out and told each other scary stories: *Love Island*, Regency house party style! Polidori modelled his vampire on Byron: he's a mysterious aristocrat, a black-clad bored-of-the-world cad with a hypnotic gaze, and a bloodthirsty predator set loose in high society.[1] Thought subsequently unfriended by Byron, Polidori started a vampire craze that included plays, an opera, unauthorised sequels, and a lurid penny dreadful chronicling *Varney the Vampire* (1845–'47; the first to describe a vampire with fangs), variously attributed to Messrs. James

---

1. Clute, 1997, 'John Polidori', n.p.

Malcolm Rymer and Thomas Peckett Prest.

Vampire stories found a ready readership among the Victorians who lived under hefty etiquette rules related to death and funerals. Irish author Joseph Sheridan Le Fanu was the first significant writer to address this with *Carmilla* (1872), which added several key characteristics to the figure of the vampire (in this case a pale, passive-aggressive young woman who latches on to a series of well-off families and drains their daughters of their energy and blood), playing up the sexually transgressive nature of the figure. Le Fanu added the idea of killing a vampire with a stake through the heart (though likely borrowed this from Eastern European folklore). All this, however, was prologue to the most famous vampire story of them all: Bram Stoker's *Dracula* (1897), which forever cemented the notions that vampires need to drink blood to keep up their strength, can be repelled by crucifixes, holy water, and garlic, don't show a reflection in mirrors, and have to be invited to enter a home, though the no-sunlight rule wasn't accepted until the novel's unauthorised film adaptation, 1922's *Nosferatu* (dir. F.W. Murnau).[2] *Dracula* further contributed animalistic figures and supernatural powers to the vampire repertoire. Nonetheless, Stoker's great innovation was perhaps adding a crucial element of foreignness to the vampire, giving readers not just a proto-techno-thriller with a supernatural twist, but an insightful story about immigration and English racism (something Stoker, another Irishman, knew a little about). Count Dracula is in many ways portrayed as a barbarian who crawls out of this middle-European-mediaeval fastness and takes up residence on the street next door. He's depicted as a threat to home, to English society, and to English womanhood. The sexual transgressions of earlier vampire figures are here crystalised as violations against the morals of decent English society at the time. Consider, if you will, the structure of the novel: a series of stories *about* Dracula, a series of self-exonerating accounts to justify the murder of a foreigner who endangers the social, sexual, and economic structures of Victorian society ("No, of course we weren't threatened by the swarthy foreigner's sexual prowess; he was a *Vampire*, we *had* to kill him!"). The central character is in fact not Dracula, who rarely gets to tell his own story in the novel, but instead a lawyer or, if you prefer, someone who lies for a living. *Dracula* is perhaps one of the most influential Horror stories ever written, and the rules of vampirism that Stoker laid out were mostly adhered to by writers throughout the following century.

In particular, the way *Dracula* pretzels death and sex is key to understanding the development of modern vampire lore despite our awareness of these as opposites: death as an end, sex as a generative act. Stoker's novel hit bookstores at a time when social mores required chastity and modesty from women, as well as respectful manners from men. Britain

---

2. Cole, 2017, n.p.

was also decades into Queen Victoria's unending mourning period for her husband Prince Albert, who had died in 1861; the etiquette around death and mourning was thus extremely complex at this time, with a guide listing details including the lengths of mourning, the household-in-mourning set-up, and the costs of funeral arrangements.[3] Victorians were so wrapped up in the spectre of death that they took steps to avoid accidentally being buried alive or being purposely exhumed by grave robbers (such as using "*mortsafes*", cages built over their graves to protect their corpses[4]), as well as taking photographs of family members after their deaths.[5] Basically, death and funerals were a national sport, so a novel about a man who cannot die but is dead was right up their street!

How a laced-up society that was so obsessed with death got turned on by vampires is a bit murkier. How are vampires, well, *sexy*, beyond the cool clothes and accents? Traditionally, vampires become undead when bitten by another vampire (but not fully killed) and then by drinking that vampire's blood to take in whatever makes it a vampire. This is an intimate act requiring body-to-body contact, penetration, and fluid exchange; it's usually described as something painful that then *transcends* pain to become a moment of slaking a hunger or a thirst (like how girls are traditionally taught about the pain and blood involved in "losing their virginity" via heterosexual intercourse). In this way a vampire story allows a reader or viewer to skirt the edges of death and sex. All of which, of course, is teased out by Stoker who has the beautiful young Lucy Westenra, on the verge of marriage, bitten by Dracula. Dr Seward tries to heal her, even giving her a transfusion of her fiancé's blood (a stand-in for sex in this case). She dies but soon rises again as a vampire, the image of human virginity, never having been to her honeymoon bed, but insatiable in her attacks on humans. Back in his castle, Dracula's three brides are further sexualised with a nod to succubus mythology, trying to seduce the dowdy Jonathan Harker. After the popularity of Stoker's novel, writers and filmmakers repeatedly layered sex and death in this fashion, often pitting a black-tuxedoed and caped vampire (the image of high-class manliness) against a white-nightgown-clad woman (unlaced, so open to suggestion, and either in or adjacent to her bed) to increase the sex appeal.

Yet before modern audiences were tempted to swipe right on an undead hook-up app, popular culture further remixed the growing vampire mythos. Richard Matheson's *I Am Legend* (1954), deemed the best vampire novel of the century by the Horror Writers Association[6] (you will note that this was

---

3. *Cassells Household Guide*, c.1880s, Vol 3, Death in the Household.
4. Emery, 2021, n.p.
5. FuneralBasics.org, 2022, n.p.
6. Horror Writers Association, 2012, n.p.

only halfway through the century!), offered readers a SF approach to the material, explaining vampirism as a blood disease, and a vampire's fears of garlic, crucifixes, and so on as succumbing to cultural hang-ups. Vampires also emerged on the small screen with the goth soap opera *Dark Shadows* (1966–'71). Shortly thereafter, Stephen King's novel *Salem's Lot* (1975) updated the setting to suburban America, setting up Stephenie Meyer's subsequent take on the vampire figure; though her Twilight series (2005–'08) went atmospheric it also attracted its share of criticism for a storyline that saw a 90-year-old vampire seducing a teenage girl.

When it comes to screen vampires with real bite, many will still point to the iconic television series *Buffy the Vampire Slayer* (1997–2003) and its spinoff *Angel* (1999–2004). Buffy and Angel, though, would likely not have existed without the ground-breaking novel *Interview with the Vampire* (1976) by Anne Rice, a revolutionary book that turned vampire lore on its head because it allowed her 200-year-old vampire to tell his own story in a way that Stoker never permitted Dracula. In *Interview*, Louise, Lestat, and Claudia travel to Eastern Europe where they find other vampires that are nothing more than shambling corpses, brilliantly bringing the early folktale vampires and our pop-culture vampires face to face; while in Paris they meet up with a theatre troop that perform their kills on stage, titillating an audience that believes it's watching a play, a clever comment on the intersection of snuff films and pornography. The film version of *Interview* (dir. Neil Jordan, 1994) also played with the homoerotic undertones of the book, putting hetero pretty boys Tom Cruise and Brad Pitt, along with Antonio Banderas, into *very* close contact. Two years earlier, *Bram Stoker's Dracula* (dir. Francis Ford Coppola, 1992), starring Gary Oldman, Winona Ryder, and Keanu Reeves, brought our Victorian-era great-grandparents' preoccupations with death, sexual mores, and even technology back to life. Suddenly, vampires were seriously and unapologetically sexy again. Enter **Paranormal Romance** and the shift from vampires as monstrous killers to boyfriends and girlfriends with special dietary needs. Kinda like dating the opposite of a vegan.

After that, it seemed that we couldn't get enough of vampire fiction and films, from the Vampire Diaries series (1991–2014) by L.J. Smith and its subsequent television adaptation, to the Idris Elba-starring, high-tech vamp-hunting *Ultraviolet* (1998), to the *Underworld* film series (various directors, 2003–'16) pitting sexy vampires against werewolves. The trope went back to basics with *Penny Dreadful* (2014–'16), featuring Eva Green in all her goth glory alongside a cast of characters picked from Horror classics such as *Frankenstein* and *Jekyll and Hyde*. Rounding out our trip down memory lane is cult favourite *What We Do in the Shadows*. The 2014 film (dirs. Taika Waititi and Jemaine Clement) charmed audiences with a mockumentary following a set of vampire roommates in New Zealand, each from different time periods, while the television series (2019–present) is a spin-off of set in New York that finds the Old World undead navigating a confusing modern existence. Honestly, we sometimes know how they feel....

A Spotter's Guide: Blood Types

- **The standard vampire:** The idea of a vampire today is a collection of tropes, tics, powers, and vulnerabilities that have accrued for several centuries: pop culture tells us they're immortal, gaunt, and pale, burned by holy water, repelled by garlic and crucifixes, and destroyed by sunlight. They bite people with their fangs and drink blood; can sometimes transform into animals or even mist; might need to be buried in soil in order to cross water; maybe cannot enter your home without an invitation; and tend to have a human servant to do their bidding in daylight hours. All that said, please remember that *your* vampire can do whatever you want it to do as long as you're consistent within your story.
- **Subtypes of vampires:** Writing in 2019, Lauren James identified a series of vampire "types" that includes "Seductive Sinners" (seen in everything from Classical myth to *From Dusk Till Dawn*, dir. Robert Rodriguez, 1996), "Aristocratic Romantics" (*Interview with the Vampire* or "Lady Gaga as Elizabeth in *American Horror Story*"), "Castle-Dwelling Drama Queens" (Dracula!), "Nocturnal Party Animals" (David Bowie and Tilda Swinton; not their characters, mind, just themselves), "Weapon-Wielding Goths" (the badass Selene in *Underworld*, dir. Len Wiseman, 2003) and "Emotionally Unavailable Hunks" (*Buffy*'s Angel and Spike).[7] The important takeaway from this is that despite the well-known traits listed above, there's still a lot of distinctiveness to be found in writing vampires. Always remember that character counts!
- **Reformed vampires:** Sometimes vampires have had enough of their lethal ways (or, like Angel, have been cursed with a soul) and attempt to become heroic characters. These bad fangs gone good can be intriguing to write about in terms of both practicalities (do they drink from black market blood bags?) and emotional considerations (how do they justify or make up for the sins of their past?). A relevant example is 2009's *The Reformed Vampire Support Group* by Catherine Jinks.
- **Emotional vampires:** *What We Do in the Shadows* has some fun with the idea of vampires who drain humans of their energy and enthusiasm (I think we all know people like that!). These vampires are the *least*

---

7. James, L., 2019, n.p.

sexy variety. They sulk around water coolers rather than cool nightclubs and bore us to near death! What they're successful at, however, is demonstrating the form's ability to transcend Horror and reach into comedy.
- **Daywalkers:** Everyone knows that vampires can't go out in daylight without bursting into flames or experiencing enormous pain, but it may surprise you to learn that this "rule" was only added in the film *Nosferatu*. If earlier vampires slept during the day, it was a consequence of their decadence and all-night partying! Modern vampire stories occasionally play with the idea of "Daywalkers" (such as the Marvel Comics character Blade), often with a reason or explanation provided for readers only familiar with the nocturnal variety.

Things That are Cool About Vampires

Sex and death are perpetual elements of literature, always attracting readers. More than that, they're contradictory themes that offer a creative tension that's *fascinating* to write about. Vampires are obviously the poster children of both. They're titillating to readers, so why not have fun with them? Though if your story isn't selling now, don't worry! Vampire fiction goes through cycles: it's in fashion and nobody can get enough of it, then it's out and no one wants it. But then, like an actual vampire, it rises from the dead and is asking for entry again.

Things That Bite

- **The drought of the damned:** Let's flip the coin of vampire popularity for a moment and consider that when vampire fiction is hot, you don't necessarily want to chase that gilded carriage because by the time you finish your own vampire novel, most publishers won't be buying it. It's impossible to predict the future, so you either need an original take on the mythos (such as Kim Newman's alternate history *Anno Dracula*, 1992) or be willing to be patient with a "trunkable" novel until the inevitable next wave of bloodsucking.
- **Historical research:** If you're like us and love to do research, vampire fiction lets you lean right in. This includes the settings, cities, food, events, etc. Old photographs and paintings can be fabulous sources of descriptive detail, as can any newspapers or published diaries you can lay your hands on. Remember, the more real you can make the everyday elements of your story (verisimilitude!), the more your reader will trust you and believe the fantastical parts. You can nerd out on this more in **Historical Fantasy**.

- **Costume porn:** Vampires in fiction tend to be wealthy, young, attractive, and often originally from our historic past, represented by clothing that we find "romantic", as myriad Instagram accounts or that *Buffy* episode with the vampire groupies remind us. In all actuality corsets were a bit of a faff and the upper classes had to have help getting dressed, but when you've spent two years wearing sweats (we can only imagine how the COVID-19 era will be represented in the sartorial record) the idea of donning yards of velvets and ribbons and lace feeds our Disney royalty daydreams. Vampires mostly go out at night, when humans are all dressed up and flashy for going to shows or clubs, so vampires need to fit in and attract prey. Whatever era you set your story in, your vampires will cut a striking figure.

ACTIVITIES

Reinvention: Like the proverbial undead, readerships get bored and need something new to interest them, but that can be a difficult challenge when dealing with reader expectations. Vampire rules are tried and true, and when someone tweaks them, even slightly, they run the risk of censure (*Twilight*'s sparkly vampires, anyone?) but can potentially reap enormous rewards (*Twilight*'s huge sales!). So, junk some of the aspects of the traditional vampire. Think about new ways of depicting traditional wants or hungers. What would a vampire be in the here and now? What do they do for a living? Who are their friends? What are their weaknesses?

Become the willing victim: Instead of writing about someone who's attacked, or a vampire who's out for blood, turn the tables and write about someone who wants the kiss of the undead. What motivates someone to seek a "sire" and be turned, like Guillermo in the *What We Do in the Shadows* series, and potentially lose their own identity and humanity in the process? Do they do it for eternal youth? For glamour? For power, be that supernatural or political? Perhaps it's a way to deal with personal trauma or loss, or perhaps it's a deal with a demon or devil? Considering the motivation of your (once) human characters will really help them to stand out against a cast of paranormal beings.

PSYCHOLOGICAL HORROR

Many Horror subgenres are about scary things *out there*: ghosts, vampires, haunted houses and the like. But sometimes, what's scary is what's inside us. This is psychological horror, and to grasp its potential, as well as to gain a better sense of how the subgenre has developed, let's visit the history of our understanding of psychology. Just relax and tell us all about it....

A Short History of How our Brains Work and How They've Been Treated

The history of mental health as a mostly separate thing from physical health has heavily contributed to some of the images and tropes we still see in the Horror genre. Early in our history, people believed that someone displaying mental-health illnesses was guilty of a crime or other trespass and being punished or even possessed by demons (obviously they were very wrong). In ancient Greece, "father of medicine" Hippocrates believed that a patient was depressed because their four fluids or "humours" (blood, phlegm, black bile, and yellow bile) were out of balance.[1] In seventeenth-century Europe, physicians still believed in the four humours and used "bleeding, purging, and even vomiting" as treatments; needless to say, success rates were likely very low.[2] Other early treatments included trepanning (as far back as 7,000 years ago), exorcism, and isolating patients. In 1676, London's Royal Bethlem Hospital, soon known as Bedlam (a word that we still use today to mean chaos), opened to treat patients exhibiting symptoms of mental-health issues; unfortunately, the treatments could be very inhumane, and the hospital was open to visitors who paid to see the patients, much like visiting a zoo.[3] In the late nineteenth and early twentieth centuries treatments included putting patients into induced comas, isolating or restraining them, shocking them, and giving them fevers and even seizures as a way to counteract whatever was happening in their minds.[4]

It isn't difficult to see how the fear of such treatments could lead to a worsening of any symptoms and even avoidance of finding help. Believing that if anyone finds out what's going on in your head means you'll immediately be put in a straitjacket and locked in a cell is difficult to overcome when those images proliferate in our fiction. All this contributes to our continuing stigmatisation of mental-health issues.

---

1. Fornaro, Clementi, and Fornaro, 2009, n.p.
2. Vann, 2014, n.p.
3. Ruggeri, 2016, n.p.
4. Vann, 2014, n.p.

Of course, the evolution of modern psychology as a science is a history too complex to fully outline here, but what's important to note is that our understanding of how the mind works, and the creation of theories to describe various mental-health issues, is relatively recent, traced in some form to William Battie's "Treatise on Madness" (1758) and more solidly established with Sigmund Freud's "examination of psychopathology" and Carl Jung's "analytic psychology" in the early twentieth century.[5] It wasn't until 1952 that the first *Diagnostic and Statistical Manual of Mental Disorders* was published; the *DSM* is still in use today, being updated often as our knowledge grows.

A Short History of Psychological Horror

The adjective *psychological* has been attached to "thriller" and "horror" to describe subgenres that focus on the effects of the situation on the protagonist's mental state and—at a remove—on the reader's state. Psychological thrillers are a crime subgenre because they contain a mystery/crime to be solved. But in psychological horror, there isn't (usually) a crime; instead, the story is less about the terror that an external event or thing creates—a supernatural being, for example—than about internal feelings of uncomfortableness, instability, paranoia, and even insanity that the character experiences. In psychological horror, the monsters are often manifestations of fears that readers themselves have. So, as we read, we identify with the protagonist, and that connection creates a heightened feeling of unease and even terror: we're not only afraid *for* the character but also *of* ourselves because we recognise the human behaviours on display. Some creators will use this fear of mental instability in a more realistic way by introducing an outside character that has a mental-health issue; unfortunately, as humans we're often afraid of anything we deem "other", and people who act in unpredictable or erratic ways in public—or private—make us uncomfortable and even scare us. There's no lack of horror out there that features psychotic or otherwise unstable characters; but again, it's often our fear of losing our own faculties and finding ourselves in that state that adds to our sense of unease and horror at the situation while we read a story or watch a television show or film.

Early Horror novels, those eighteenth-century **Gothic** tales such as *The Castle of Otranto* (1764) by Horace Walpole, cemented the connection between the present and the past (haunted houses!). In particular, they forged the connection between place and emotional mood. Edgar Allen Poe pushed this envelope further in the early nineteenth century with stories that explored our emotional extremes, such as 'The Tell-Tale Heart' (1843), in which the

---
5. Cherry, 2022, n.p.

protagonist is going mad thinking that the heart of a man he murdered is still beating under the floorboards and that other people can hear it. Henry James's *The Turn of the Screw* (1898) is still subject to questions about whether the ghosts are real or figments of the governess's imagination. In these stories, the characters are suspicious of their own senses or of other people, they aren't sure who to trust, and their paranoia often gets the better of them.

In the twentieth century, psychological horror became an established subgenre, enhanced by the popularity of the film medium. Many of the most popular films took a chilling book and made it truly unsettling, even in a crowded cinema:

- *Psycho* by Robert Bloch (1959), quickly filmed in 1960 (dir. Alfred Hitchcock): Norman Bates runs a motel, which becomes a true house of horrors when the effects of his relationship with his mother, whose mummified body he keeps in the house, pushes him to commit numerous murders. Readers and viewers are kept unbalanced, not knowing whether his mother is truly alive or dead until the end.
- *The Haunting of Hill House* by Shirley Jackson (1959), filmed in 1963 (dir. Robert Wise) and again for a Netflix mini-series in 2018 (dir. Mike Flanagan): on the one hand, this is a **Supernatural Horror** story about a group of people investigating a haunted house, but on the other it's about the characters' experiences in the house, their mental states, and whether at least one is going mad.
- *The Shining* (1977) by Stephen King, filmed in 1980 (dir. Stanley Kubrick): Jack Torrance's unbalanced mental state brought about by his frustration over being unable to write, his alcoholism, and the weird goings-on at the Overlook Hotel lead to his violence and unpredictability; his son Danny's ability to read minds (to "shine") contributes to the growing sense of horror as the Torrance family falls apart.
- *Misery* (1987) also by Stephen King, filmed in 1990 (dir. Rob Reiner): there are no supernatural elements, and only a little **Body Horror** when Annie hobbles Paul, but her unbalanced-ness is the centre of all the terror because he doesn't know what she'll do next, and neither do we, which leads to feelings of paranoia.
- *The Silence of the Lambs* (1988) by Thomas Harris, filmed in 1991 (dir. Jonathan Demme): though this novel is a crime thriller about the FBI trying to find a serial killer, it's psychological horror when Clarice Starling has to match wits with killer and cannibal Hannibal Lecter. We have no idea whether he can be trusted and whether he's manipulating Clarice to escape or if he's truly helping her.
- *The Last House on Needless Street* (2021) by Catriona Ward and currently being adapted by Andy Serkis's film-production company:

this is about the effect that abuse can have on a person's psyche and how memory plays tricks on us. The use of multiple points of view, including a cat and a child, means that readers don't know who to trust or what's really happening.

Element Spotlight: Setting the Scene in Psychological Horror

Setting is a sibling to worldbuilding. With worldbuilding (see **High Fantasy**) your job is to create all the various elements of a secondary world. Setting, though, can be found in all genres of fiction, and is mostly limited to the place and time period during which a story happens. The place is the physical geography of the outside, the architecture of the inside, and the things—or props—surrounding the characters as well as the related sensory details. When writing in your current time, you don't have to worry about the time period aspect of setting as much (see **Gothic** for more) but writing about the past will require some research (see **Historical Fantasy** for more). In psychological horror, the source of fear is due to what's going on inside the character, but setting can be used to affect the reader's reaction, especially if you pay attention to sensory descriptions:

- **Mental institution:** It's no wonder this is one of the most used tropes in psychological horror, considering the importance of Bedlam on our cultural memory and the elements that we automatically relate to these places. It's populated with other patients who make noise or look disturbing in some way; there are silent solitary rooms and mysterious corridors with flickering lights; and clothing includes white uniforms, aprons, masks, gloves, and straitjackets, all of which can create variable levels of disturbance in a reader or viewer.
- **Hospital:** Second to a mental institution, a hospital is going to affect a character's mental state as well as that of the reader/viewer depending on their feelings about what they find there. Elements include bodily injuries, blood and unfamiliar smells, masked doctors and nurses, and even a morgue.
- **Church or other religious building:** As noted earlier, people in the past often believed that someone exhibiting certain behaviours was possessed by demons or being punished for sins. It isn't a stretch to see how, in psychological horror, characters might believe that what they hear inside their head is coming directly from their god. This setting (in a Western/Christian church) can include colours from stained-glass windows, the smell of incense, relics such as the bones of saints, severe crucifixes, images of blood, and paintings or carvings of demonic creatures (see Hieronymus Bosch's 'The Garden of Earthly Delights', from 1490–1510, and other religious paintings of the mediaeval and

Renaissance periods for some ideas of what the faithful believed). Note that the elements will depend on the denomination.
- **Home:** We spend most of our time at home, and home—whether it be a flat or a mansion—is where family is. Unfortunately, family dynamics are sometimes the source of mental illnesses, so the home can be a fraught setting (see Brian De Palma's 1976 film version of *Carrie* for a good example). The house as setting will have items specific to your character, but some elements that pop up in this subgenre include "hidden spaces" such as closets, basements, and attics.

Things That are Cool About Psychological Horror

Human beings are messy, yes, but fascinating. And learning more about how our brains work adds to your writing arsenal. One challenge of good writing is creating believable characters that your readers want to learn more about, and so practising writing about how we react to things, both externally and internally, can help improve your writing. Furthermore, a lot of people don't enjoy stories about ghosts or werewolves or other supernatural elements (yes, we know: what fun is that?). But these readers do enjoy stories about humans they can relate to, and writing psychological horror means that you don't have to make up outlandish creatures or events; you just use what's right in front of us and what's inside our own heads.

Brains are Tricksy

- **The unreliable narrator:** There are many reasons that a narrator could be unreliable or untrustworthy: age (very young children won't understand things that adults will; the flip side of that is someone older with dementia or memory loss); mind-altering substances such as drugs or alcohol; language or cultural differences; the side effects of trauma or PTSD; and other mental illnesses such as schizophrenia. Sometimes the protagonist is the unreliable one and sometimes it's another character, which can still increase the questions about what's real and what's not. As humans we relate to other humans, and in psychological horror, the depths of human behaviour and mental somersaults are laid bare. We must ask ourselves how close we are to tipping over the edge into paranoia and even madness. And that's what makes psychological horror so scary: we know vampires and ghosts don't exist, but we do, and we're the scariest monsters there are.
- **Do your research:** When dealing with anything relating to psychological matters, it's important to do some research into mental-health issues. We're often too quick to judge and diagnose people we barely or don't

even know as being "crazy" or "a lunatic", but these are coarse, indeed offensive judgments. We've all had moments in our own lives when, looking back, an outsider could've watched our behaviour and made an uninformed mental-health diagnosis. To create believable characters, you always want to do research, and that goes double in this case. Before we go any further, let's clear up one thing: not all psychological horror is going to be about someone with a diagnosable mental-health issue. Often, the horror in the story is an effect of the situation on the character (and even the reader). But, because some terms get bandied about, let's break down two of the most often used diagnoses in this subgenre: psychopath and sociopath. Both are diagnoses under the header of antisocial personality disorder. People with either have issues with empathy as well as understanding the difference between right and wrong; they're not necessarily violent and tend to use manipulation more than force to get what they want.[6]

    o **Psychopath:** has no conscience and can be very "calculating"; they're very good at hiding their manipulation beneath a veneer of pretend morality.[7]

    o **Sociopath:** has a weak conscience but makes wrong choices anyway; they aren't as good as psychopaths at hiding their manipulation because they "act without thinking".[8]

You can, and should, consult the *DSM* and other trusted sources for information on whatever illness you plan to use in your fiction.

- **Remember not to forget:** One thing to consider avoiding is amnesia, especially from the first page. Starting a story with a character who can't remember what happened to them is starting your reader off in a blank room with no anchor. Reading a character say "I can't remember X" for pages gets boring very quickly. However, if you have an established character experience a blow to the head or other trauma that results in temporary amnesia later in a story, you'll already have the reader on your side, and they'll want to see what happens as the character slowly remembers important details and events.

---

6. Robinson, 2022, n.p.
7. Robinson, 2022, n.p.
8. Robinson, 2022, n.p.

ACTIVITIES

Self-analysis: The easiest place to start is with your own mind. This is going to be one of those activities that require you to be honest with yourself while remembering that no one else will see this. What mental health diagnosis would you be most afraid of getting? Ask yourself why you're afraid of this, what you think it would mean for your future, and what you think it would mean for your relationships with others. After you answer those questions, pair the idea up with one of the following: waking up in a vacant house; experiencing a plane crash; being lost at sea or in the wilderness; finding yourself in an abandoned office building; being dropped into the middle of a war zone. Then, write a scene in which the protagonist is experiencing the mental-health issue at the same time as experiencing one of the scary situations or environments. This pairing will give you forward momentum for a story idea because you won't be concentrating just on the character's mental-health. When you're finished with a first draft, see if you can edit it so that the reader can't be completely sure whether the narrator is reliable and actually experiencing this situation or is having a mental break.

Harvey **redux:** *Harvey* is a film (dir. Henry Koster, 1950) in which a man is deemed insane because he talks to an invisible six-foot-tall rabbit; it was filmed as a comedy, but we're going to take this to a darker place. Pretend there's an animal of some sort in your room that is as tall as the ceiling. You get to pick the animal; make it something you're scared of. When you try to escape the building, you either can't open the door or (if you can open the door) you physically can't walk out, and it's the same with windows or any other means of escape. You're stuck in the building with this enormous animal. Write a scene in which you discover that no one else can see or hear or even smell the animal. How do your family members or housemates (or even workmates) react to your claims? How does that make you feel? How do you know that the animal is real and not a figment of your imagination?

BODY HORROR

Bodily integrity is a crucial part of what makes us feel safe and secure. When something goes awry with flesh or blood or bone, when our physical self is violated either by violence from the outside or changes from the inside, it can be deeply disturbing. Body horror thus derives its power from how we, as gooey meatbags, relate to our own images of ourselves and to the world around us. So, let's place this subgenre on the table and slice it open for a closer look....

A Short History of Body Horror

This is a subgenre of invasion, alteration, or mutilation on an intimate level. A frequent aspect of it is a traumatic transformation of the human body (that being said, it could also be about a non-human body undergoing the same, but to truly connect with a reader keep in mind that humans more closely relate to humans). Body horror doubles down on its parent genre's overall anxiety about a lack of control and things going wrong; it isn't about facts but about feelings. Consider how your own meatspace is all about feelings, both emotional and physical. Violations of the body thus bring about a physical and/or psychological reaction in the reader. Horror that deals with the body runs the gamut from introspective, atmospheric, or seductive in its weirdness, to gory, repulsive, or even pornographic (in the sense that everything is shown). For this subgenre, we'll stick more to the former and let **Splatterpunk** tackle fiction on the latter end of the spectrum,
 As detailed in **Historical Fantasy** and **Folktales and Fairy Tales**, our earliest stories have always contained fantastical and often horrific elements. Even proto-horror included the first inklings of what we now call body horror, because being hurt—or killed—is, obviously, one of the biggest causes of terror on a personal level. One of Western literature's earliest heroic epics is the Old English poem *Beowulf* (circa late 900s to early 1000s), set in sixth-century Scandinavia (so we can argue it is perhaps one of our earliest known Historical Fantasies).[1] In it, the monster Grendel attacks sleeping men in the great hall:

> No thought had the monster of deferring the matter,
> Grendel immediately seizes a sleeping warrior, and devours him.
> But on earliest occasion he quickly laid hold of
> A soldier asleep, suddenly tore him,
> Bit his bone-prison, the blood drank in currents,

---
1. The British Library website, "*Beowulf*", n.p.

Swallowed in mouthfuls: he soon had the dead man's
Feet and hands, too, eaten entirely.[2]

The audience listening to this tale, when it was told orally, would've found it terrifying because they believed in monsters, so being torn limb from limb by one wasn't outside the realm of possibility. As we moved from oral tales to written ones, authors began to adapt body horror ideas to generate powerful reader reactions: in Mary Shelley's *Frankenstein* (1818), cadaver body parts are sewn back together and the resulting being is brought back to life; in Edgar Allen Poe's 'The Tell-Tale Heart' (1843), a man murders another, dismembers him, and stores the pieces beneath his floor; in 'Who Goes There?' by John W. Campbell (1938), a shape-shifting alien terrorises a group of men in an Antarctic outpost by absorbing their bodies and imitating them; in 'The Fly' by George Langelaan (1957), a scientist accidentally combines himself with the body of a fly; and Stephen King's 'Survivor Type' (1982) toys with the gross-funny line with a character who survives a plane crash by slowly eating himself.

But body horror really found its footing when translated from the page to the screen, when special effects could show what had only previously been imagined from the words. Some of the stories mentioned above were made into seminal films such as *The Fly* (dir. Kurt Neumann, 1958; and again in 1986 by dir. David Cronenberg) and *The Thing* (dir. John Carpenter, 1982, based on Campbell's 'Who Goes There?'), but we have no end of new editions of the *Halloween*, *Nightmare on Elm Street*, *The Texas Chainsaw Massacre*, and *Saw* film franchises. Television shows such as *The X-Files* (1993–2002) traumatised a whole generation with iconic imagery such The Flukeman in 'The Host' (dir. Daniel Sackheim, 1994), the parasitic twin of 'Humbug' (dir. Kim Manners, 1995), and the deeply unsettling limbless mother of 'Home' (dir. Kim Manners, 1996). More recently, the anthology series *American Horror Story* (2011–present) has taken up the body-horror baton for a contemporary audience. The potency of body-horror has also found its way into a variety of successful music and theatrical performances, with musicians such as Marilyn Manson and Alice Cooper including body horror elements in their shows, and even magicians such as Penn & Teller who, in their early performances, included tricks that mimicked trauma to their own physical bodies. It's clear that seeing all manner of horrible things happening to bodies on screen or stage sells. The question is why.

On a macro level, body horror can help us better understand societal fears, such as a fear of the "other" that we see in **Zombie** stories. But more important is what body horror can do for us in our individual (micro) exploration of how our own bodies work—or don't—and how we deal with

---

2. Project Gutenberg, 2021 (1892 translation), n.p.

that. In some cases, this disconnect is related to the uncanny. This is the spot where what you think you see and what you actually see creates a weird frisson in you that can be frightening. For example, the newest robots are often modelled to look like humans: your brain initially recognises it as *human*, and then there is a shift when your brain realises, no, *not human*. But *almost* human. It's familiar but strange, right but *wrong* (see more in **Robots**... and **Gothic**). One way to consider how the uncanny relates to body horror is to think about what is or isn't there. Academic and author Mark Fisher explains, "the eerie concerns the most fundamental metaphysical questions one could post, questions to do with existence and non-existence: *Why is there something here when there should be nothing? Why is there nothing here when there should be something?*"[3] The idea of existence and non-existence rubs up against that need for control of the body.

A Spotter's Guide: It's Never Only Skin-deep

Brought down to our individual level, body horror can help us express and even try to explain that disconnect we feel between what the outside world sees and how we experience our own bodies as they change throughout our lives:

- **Disabilities:** Some readers and writers with disabilities relate to body horror—especially the subgenre's emphasis on augmentation and/or amputation—because they rarely see people like themselves being depicted in daily media. In this subgenre, says cinema critic Douglas Laman, "the vulnerabilities of all our bodies are reflected in the silver screen. These movies can be terrifying, but they can also be oddly comforting in how they normalise the nuances of our bodies".[4] That said, please keep in mind that characters with disabilities are avatars of a very real segment of society, one too often demeaned or cruelly misrepresented in literature. They should not be used to merely add freakishness to fiction. Always try to write them in a respectful and three-dimensional fashion.
- **Gender dysphoria:** Transgender people have also described finding body horror strangely comforting as they deal with gender dysphoria.[5] To one writer, the film *Possessor* (dir. Brandon Cronenberg, 2020), in which a woman assassin takes control of a host body to complete each job, is relatable because being closeted as trans is "literally wearing a new skin and trying to pass it off as your own".[6]

---

3. Fisher, 2016, Kindle Loc. 85 (his emphasis).
4. Laman, 2021, n.p.
5. Smith, Nadine, 2021, n.p.
6. Smith, Nadine, 2021, n.p.

- **Ageing:** Our bodies aren't static. They obviously change as we grow and age. When we're teenagers or in our early twenties, we think we'll always be strong, flexible, etc. (this is speaking about people without any physical disabilities or chronic illnesses). But ageing is inevitable and results in changes that we have no control over, altering our bodies from what they were to a new and unfamiliar state. In the real world, this can be disappointing or upsetting, even horrifying, and so is another emotional vulnerability for body-horror stories to poke at. One recent example is M. Night Shyamalan's 2021 film *Old*, in which the ageing happens in the blink of an eye.
- **Puberty:** Ah, yes, when that sweet summer child turns into a spot-ridden bag of hormones! King's *Carrie* (1974) doesn't so much encourage body horror in the reader (or viewer of the 1976 Brian De Palma film) as it shows the titular character's own horror at what her body does naturally. Body horror often takes puberty's effects to an extreme in this fashion to symbolise the resulting anxiety and distress: in *Ginger Snaps* (dir. John Fawcett, 2000), Ginger's first period attracts a werewolf, and the intense changes she experiences as puberty progresses intensifies as her wolf side takes over and she "snaps".
- **Pregnancy and childbirth:** Even when chosen, changes such as pregnancy and childbirth can contribute to psychological as well as physical trauma and even horror. Fiction and film have often used these in effective metaphorical fashion. In *Alien* (dir. Ridley Scott, 1979) John Hurt's character is impregnated with an alien "baby" that bursts out of his chest; the spectre of a man experiencing the trauma of "giving birth" brings home the ramifications of this body change—as well as the lack of control when something *inside* wants to get *outside right now*—to the whole audience. On the page, a writer must depend on the reader's imagination. In Josh Malerman's *Bird Box* (2014), pregnant Malorie is stuck with no professional medical care in an apocalyptic situation. She distracts herself from thinking about the actual birth, but when she and her housemate Olympia give birth on the same day, things go from bad to much worse when Olympia jumps out the window. Gary, another character, describes it all to Malorie: "'She hangs! She hangs by her cord!' *Don't. Please, God, don't let this man describe it to me.* 'She hangs by her cord!'".[7] Malorie can't see it—and we can't see it—but the description of the completely unexpected mangling of Olympia's body takes childbirth one step beyond the expected or anticipated horror.

Element Spotlight: Exploring POV (Whose Body is it?)

This shift from what a character experiences to what they describe happening to someone else brings up point of view (POV), one of the most important

---

7. Malerman, 2014, p. 350 (his emphasis).

narrative choices we make when writing any story of any length. For body horror, your choice is going to be determined by the effect you want:

- **First-person POV is "I":** Do you want your character to experience the trauma first-hand via a character in the story? Using first-person POV requires you as a writer to describe not just the feelings a body has but also the associated thoughts filtered through the character. This requires you to understand your character's experience of the world, of their own body, and of their relationships with other characters. For example, a fourteen-year-old first-person POV is going to describe the feelings of body trauma differently from a forty-year-old or an eighty-four-year-old character.
- **Second-person POV is "you":** Are you hoping for absolutely no distance between the narrative and the reader? Second-person POV places the reader *in* the story as a character. This POV choice can be gimmicky, and it can be difficult to pull off in a longer piece. Consider how you'll describe the body trauma in such a way that the reader, no matter their personal background or experience, will be able to *feel* the moment.
- **Third-person POV is "she/her", "he/him", or "they/them":** Do you want a slight remove between the reader and the situation? Third-person POV allows the reader to experience the trauma via one or more particular characters but from outside the first-person POV. Third-person POV is a bit finicky because there are two types:
    - **Limited third-person**, in which the POV is limited to one character. This allows for limited *alternating*, with the POV shifting to a new character in a new scene or chapter, which is one of the most popular choices out there.
    - **Third-person omniscient**, which means the POV is sort of "god-like" and can shift from character to character within a scene; however, these aren't "deep dives" into characters and are more of a shallow shift. This is a more old-fashioned mode, not used as much anymore because readers these days find limited alternating, in which we get to know more than one character intimately, more satisfying.

Things That are Cool About Body Horror

This subgenre is a way to push the envelope in your own writing by exploring the things about your own physical experience that make you uncomfortable or even freak you out the most in a safe and controlled way. It can even be darkly funny, such as King's aforementioned 'Survivor Type', a story that made us actually laugh out loud because it was so bonkers (some cases on the procedural television show *Bones*, 2005–'17, work similarly). By taking the time to consider how bodies work and relate to each other, and then describing bodily horror/trauma, you'll build a direct route to a reader's empathy. Whatever you're writing, you want your reader to identify in some way with the protagonist or antagonist and body horror is a way of meeting your readers where they live: in their imperfect fleshsuits. You might not be writing about whatever specific ailment or issue a reader is currently dealing with, but because your readers are real humans with all sorts of bodily experiences, they can imagine—and will react in some way to—the body trauma that you write.

Controlling the Body

- **Like with writing sex, there's a fine line:** As we explain in **Paranormal Romance**, you don't want your sex scenes to come across as medical/science manuals; think the same thing here because this isn't meant to be a "how to" guide or an autopsy report. Instead, you're trying to psychologically disturb your readers for a reason (remember, that thing we've been going on about: theme). What does the modification or disease or violence mean beyond "ouch"? What does the bodily transformation cost? What does the realisation that there's something malevolent inside our body do to us?
- **Consider where on the line you want to land:** Just as there are differences in levels of horror—and repulsion—in films, there are the same in stories and books. But in prose you must explain things in a way that the reader can relate to, and it's likely that very few of them will have experienced the body trauma you want to express. Here you use your words, you spell it out, you don't leave things unsaid. Here, telling is as important as showing. This doesn't mean you lay it all out on the first page, of course; you want to leave the reader guessing a bit, to amp up the feelings. But could you imagine 'The Fly' without the descriptive images of the man's head or hand if the author just said, "Something bad happened to his head"? It wouldn't work as well.
- **How you use style and language:** This type of fiction, as with most Horror writing, isn't about "facts" but about feelings. You might want to scare the reader, or you might want to make them slightly uncomfortable, but both are about making them *feel* something, even against their better judgement and despite the cognitive estrangement that's inherent in the experience of reading SFF/Horror.

ACTIVITIES

We eat with our mouths *and* eyes: Food is necessary for our bodies, and those of us who aren't vegetarians or vegans eat parts of formerly living bodies and things that come from other living bodies. Furthermore, the appearance of food is important: it's said we "eat first with our eyes". To start to edge towards writing about bodies gone awry, try at first to write about food in a visceral way. Imagine the bones, juices, textures, and colours. There's a fine line between food being beautiful and food being, well, gross. How can you brush right up against that line when writing about a sandwich, for example, before it turns the stomach?

Keep it to yourself: This one is personal, so you have our full permission to write about anything and then never show it to anyone. In order to get fully comfortable with writing body horror, you have to cross that invisible line that you perhaps didn't know you even had in regard to your own body. Find a spot in a quiet place and make yourself comfortable. You can sit or lie down but try not to fall asleep! Take two minutes—set a timer if you wish—and do an inventory of your body from your head to your feet, thinking about each and every part of it, from eyes to fingers to heart to stomach to knees, etc. As you take this inventory, imagine the outside and inside of each part, and take note of what you can feel and even hear: your heartbeat, your breathing, the food in your gut digesting. Then, flip that and consider what removing each piece would do to you, both physically and mentally. This all comes down to one big question: what about your body *scares* you? What about bodies grosses you out? And how would you react if something happened to that part of you? Then, write it down. Be as flowery or as clinical as you wish: this is just practice. To take it one step further, write a scene including a moment of trauma happening to a character (who isn't you—just to give you some distance) and imagine how they deal with it.

ZOMBIES

This subgenre is ... brains. No, what we mean to say is that this is one of the sections that is a character type instead of ... *brains* ... [stop it!] ... instead of a subgenre. Brains! Its creation is more *Brains!* ... more recent than some of the others here, but there is no lack of nuance BRAINS!

Fine, okay, let's get to it. *BRAINSBRAINSBRAINS!*

A Short History of Zombies

The spectre of the zombie is rooted in the basic fears and desires of enslaved peoples in the Caribbean during the seventeenth to nineteenth centuries. Specifically, the zombie's origins lie in Haitian folklore, heavily influenced by the practice of the Voodoo religion, a belief system combining rites and magical elements drawn from both Roman Catholicism and West- and Central-African traditions. From as far back as the late 1600s, enslaved people on Haiti believed that only in death could they return to their homes in Africa, but suicide, a quick way to escape the trauma of enslavement, would turn them into zombies "condemned to skulk the Hispaniola plantations for eternity, undead slaves at once denied their own bodies and yet trapped inside them".[1] Later the belief shifted to zombies as mindless creatures created by Voodoo witch doctors (called bokors[2]) for malicious purposes.[3] This incarnation of the zombie is still rooted in fear: the fear of being enslaved and having no agency over one's own body or mind. Indeed, *The Encyclopedia of Science Fiction* flags the "heavily loaded metaphorical association of Zombies and Slavery"[4] as key to the modern figure's origins, something academics such as Sarah Juliet Lauro have followed up on in great detail (see *The Transatlantic Zombie: Slavery, Rebellion, and Living Death*). As with many entities from the Fantasy and Horror genres, however, the story of the zombie has inevitably been "whitewashed" to downplay the lasting effects of slavery. This process became blatant in 1932 with the release of the first zombie film, *White Zombie* (dir. Victor Halperin), which centres on two men's desire to possess another man's wife, a far cry from the zombie's original form and its very real anxieties related to the living death of slavery. Once zombies made it to film, of course, the undead were out of the box and the fears—and fantasies—they embodied continued to shift as the world changed around them.

---

1. Mariani, 2015, n.p.
2. Mariani, 2015, n.p.
3. Mariani, 2015, n.p.
4. Langford, 2022, n.p.

The next significant evolution of the form occurred when Director George A. Romero cemented zombies into the popular Western/Northern/ *Blanc*[5] zeitgeist with his 1968 film *The Night of the Living Dead*. In it, an alien virus falls to Earth and transforms people into insatiable, flesh-eating zombies, a "horde" easily associated with American anxieties about the 1967 race riots as well as the Vietnam War (the first televised conflict) and fears among conservatives about changes to the social status quo.[6] These zombies, creatures whose hunger for flesh can never be satisfied, have also regularly been read as a stand-in for unrestrained American consumerism.[7] Romero continued the series with *Dawn of the Dead* (1978), which further emphasised fears about consumerism (zombies in a mall!) and race relations (dehumanised zombies attacking *en masse*, speaking to American fears of unregulated immigration), along with *Day of the Dead* (1985), in which surviving humans live in an underground bunker where scientists, protected by the military, try to find a cure. *Day of the Dead* in particular illustrates our fear of diseases, the conflict of science vs faith, and how easily communication can break down when different groups lack a common goal. The 1980s further saw the zombie hunger for brains (*braaaaaaains!*) becoming a central aspect of how the creatures were depicted.

Since Romero's films, the figure of the zombie has been firmly embedded in the spec-fic landscape, experiencing several notable revivals (see what we did there?) with themes relating to their established fears and fantasies repeatedly exhumed (okay, we'll stop!). In *28 Days Later* (dir. Danny Boyle, 2002), a virus that escapes an animal testing lab wipes out most of the UK in the titular timeframe, surprising a bike courier who wakes up from a coma to find the world permanently changed. Pop-cultural juggernaut *The Walking Dead* franchise follows groups of survivors trying to find a permanent home while dealing with human threats as well as the undead. It began as a comic by Robert Kirkman and Tony Moore (2003–'19), which led to a popular television series (2010–'22). Max Brooks's spectacular *World War Z: An Oral History of the Zombie War* (2006) followed his *Zombie Survival Guide* (2003) with various fictional interviewees recounting the events of a zombie war that started two decades earlier, a disaster that could have been avoided if not for government ineptness and our human ability to ignore what's right in front of us (*cough* the climate crisis *cough*). Seanan McGuire, writing as Mira Grant, released *Feed* (2010), *Deadline* (2011) and *Blackout* (2012), an engaging series presenting Zombification via the accidental result of mixing two viruses created to combat cancer and the common cold. Meanwhile, Sarah Davis-Goff's *Last Ones Left Alive* (2019) demonstrates

---

5. Term used by Haitians to refer to non-Haitians; in Lauro, 2015, p. xv.
6. Cassese, 2017, n.p.
7. Bradshaw, 2017, n.p.

the ongoing flexibility of the subgenre with a coming-of-age zombie story set against an Irish geographical and literary backdrop.

Zombie tales overlap organically with **Apocalyptic Fiction** because, well, once you have zombies, human civilisation is in very serious trouble. This elimination of most of the world's population feeds into fantasies that many people have of being able to start over: a small band of survivors is left behind; they are now "on top" as the only sentient beings; and, if they can avoid being eaten by the zombies that drastically outnumber them, they get to make decisions on how a new society will be built in this apocalypse of plenty.[8] On the one hand, we can see how this fantasy is tangentially related to "prepper" or survivalist thinking, with individuals and groups preparing for the end of the world, which they expect imminently. On the other hand, the US CDC (Centers for Disease Control and Prevention) has utilised the zombie metaphor as a means of educating people about real infectious disease scenarios, releasing a graphic novel titled *Preparedness 101: Zombie Pandemic*.[9]

While most zombie narratives pit humans against murderous hordes of the undead, some recent work has shifted the perspective again to showcase zombie characters with various levels of understanding about what they are. One of the first to tell the story from the zombie's point of view (POV) is *The Girl With All the Gifts* by M.R. Carey (2014), about a child who doesn't really know what she is or where she came from. The backstory grows around her, and readers are provided with the clues they need to put the various narrative pieces together, with the tale continued in *The Boy on the Bridge* (2017). This shift in POV further invigorates the stories available to readers, proving once again that the zombie is a figure that won't ever die.

A Spotter's Guide: Post-Mortem Examination

There are an extraordinary range of zombie depictions out there (with many websites devoted to their categorisation). We've provided you with a starter pack:

- **Classic zombies:** AKA Romero zombies or slow zombies. This is the one that probably shuffles to mind when you hear the word "zombie". They are a shambling, slow-moving, mindless but still somehow walking corpse. Classic zombies often move in herds (and can consequently *seem* to exhibit collective behaviour) but they don't know where they are or, indeed, why. Their defining characteristic is their cannibalistic hunger for human flesh. They're aggressive beings who'll bite and tear at their victims, passing on their affliction in the process. Nonetheless,

---
8. Mariani, 2015, n.p.
9. CDC, 2011.

classic zombies aren't the smartest adversaries (they are, in fact, pretty dumb). Their great strengths are their numbers (always increasing) and their ability to continue functioning despite decay and/or massive damage inflicted by human survivors. To combat them, your characters will need to be nimble, avoid being cornered or trapped (buildings or underground spaces can be tense settings!), and be armed with both projectile weapons and blunt objects. Rendering classic zombies inert usually requires a shot to the head or decapitation.

- **Fast zombies:** These are sometimes called "runners" and, while initially quite controversial among zombie purists, are now found everywhere in film and fiction (mainly because they're even scarier!). First featured prominently in *28 Days Later*, they're often stronger and faster than not just classic zombies but humans, too. Their behaviour is rabid and animalistic. They rush uninfected humans individually and in groups, scratching and clawing at their victims, giving characters little time to think and even less to outrun or escape their onslaught. They perhaps lose some of the distinctiveness of the zombie figure, becoming just another kinetic-but-generic monster (they are, after all, supposed to be the *walking* dead and not the parkouring dead), but if you want to write exciting chase sequences, then fast zombies are the best choice.
- **Smart zombies:** Speaking of losing some traditional zombicity, it can sometimes be useful in a story to have an antagonist who isn't entirely mindless. So-called smart zombies range from those whose human intelligence has not been *entirely* destroyed, so are capable of surmounting obstacles or using basic tools, to ordinary people who just happen to eat brains, to exceptionally smart (one might say brainy) but nonetheless bloodthirsty ghouls capable of organising and leading their horde in complicated ways (see 2021's *Army of the Dead*, dir. Zack Snyder). Sometimes these zombies may even be able to communicate with our characters or amongst each other (see *Marvel Zombies*, 2005–'06).
- **Technological zombies:** Some zombies defy the gooey, coagulated stereotype for cybernetic origins that critique the pervasiveness of technology in our lives. A classic instance can be found in *Star Trek*'s Borg (who also updated the hive-mind concept sometimes seen in earlier zombie depictions). This is especially obvious in the alien antagonists' first appearances as a relentless, unstoppable, all-consuming, and all-absorbing force that cannot be reasoned with. In fiction, Stephen King's *Cell* (2006), in which mobile phones wipe user's minds and transform them into aggressive, destructive zombie-like killers, is a good example. Arguably (mis)information can also cause zombification, with far-right media transforming many people into violent, mindless, foaming-at-the-mouth zombies in the early twenty-first century. Though, if they ever noticed it, I'm sure they'd think it was caused by 5G!

- **Funny zombies:** Who said the undead can't be witty? While the majority of zombie narratives are Horror, the figure has been around so long that it now engenders open parody. *Shaun of the Dead* (dir. Edgar Wright, 2004) opens with a protagonist who doesn't even realise he's surrounded by the undead: a definite comment on our disconnectedness and a premonition of life with smartphones and social media! In 2009, zombies invaded Regency England's novel of manners *Pride and Prejudice* (Jane Austen, 1813) via Seth Grahame-Smith's *Pride and Prejudice and Zombies*—itself arguably an act of literary zombification!—subsequently followed by the film of the same name in 2016 (dir. Burr Steers). The film *Warm Bodies* (dir. Jonathan Levine, 2013) features a sentient zombie as the heroine's love interest (yes, a Zom Rom Com!), though he starts out more on the zombie side than the human-ish side. And on the heels of that came television's *iZombie* (2015–'19), about a zombie woman working in a morgue so she has easy access to food; the iZombies however, aren't your shambling undead but humans with special dietary needs (each episode shows us at least one recipe… brain eggrolls, anyone?).

Things That are Cool About Zombies

The zombie represents any number of anxieties or fears on our part. It's a relentlessly versatile metaphor, evolving over time as our apprehensions change. On the surface these are stories of biological or historical ruptures but, on a deeper layer, they're about fears of enslavement, about rampant consumerism or contagious diseases, or about our internal struggles to accept, often during some calamity's aftermath, that the world we knew is gone. Zombie stories, in many ways, are socio-cultural coping mechanisms.

Protect Your Brain Case!

- **Causes:** There's no single cause of zombification; thus, fittingly, zombies have no respect for genre boundaries, slipping between Horror, SF, and Fantasy with ease. In Fantasy they can be the result of magical or other supernatural sources. In SF they can be the result of a bioengineered virus, alien pathogen, or reanimating technology run amok. The cause, in many ways, matters so little that many writers just handwave it away without explanation. That said, having a notion of the cause will benefit you as a writer because it'll affect your story's genre conventions. The rules of your storyworld will impact how your characters combat the zombie threat. Fantasy zombies will typically be answered by Fantasy tropes (a wizard steps up), SF zombies by SF tropes (nuking the entire

site from orbit), and so on. Though, of course, the manner by which this provides consistency of imagery and tone is a general principle rather than a rule. Genre boundaries are fluid, and it's your story to tell.
- **Zombies as a metaphor for disease:** Leprosy, the Black Plague, Polio, AIDS, Ebola, COVID-19… communicable diseases have always struck fear in societies (and led to discrimination against those suffering from them). Zombies are a literal and ambulatory personification of that terror, often the result of viral infection, either from natural causes or via escaped military experimentation. The figure intersects with fiction about pandemics as, "like viruses, these creatures exist only for the purpose of feeding off the living and of proliferating".[10] The language and imagery of an epidemic spread is usually how zombie propagation is depicted, with initial rumours of a "sickness" followed by news reports of sporadic violence, widespread fear of "infection", and eventually by extremes of social collapse. As with many illnesses, physical contact is key to transmission.
- **Stages of infection:** While some zombie bites result in instantaneous transformations, a writer can use a "ticking clock" to delay and ratchet up tension. This works best if, early in the story, you establish a recognisable series of stages through which the infection progresses. Common indicators include headaches and high temperatures, confusion, spasms, or a greenish or reddish tint to the skin. If we see a clearly unwell character in a zombie story (especially if they're concealing their condition), we know something bad is going to happen! Alternatively, there's potential for misdirection here. Readers are so conditioned to expect this trope that writers can use it to throw suspicion off the actual infected character. Maybe the person with the high temperature just has the flu and the person really infected is still hiding among your characters….
- **Blood'n'guts:** Zombies, by definition, are visually (and sometimes aurally: *squish*) disgusting. As animated corpses, they fall into the uncanny valley: something both living and dead, something that looks human but very obviously is not (see **Body Horror** for more). However, their depiction lives or dies (mostly dies, let's be honest) on rich descriptive language. The readers of these stories often delight in grotesque descriptions of rotting flesh, half-open skulls, gangrenous limbs, and trailing entrails. Writhing masses of snarling zombies become grotesque hordes that, denuded of recognisable or individual human characteristics, become something alien and horrifying. Describe colours and textures and stench for an immersive experience.

---
10. Petretto, 2006, p. 23.

ACTIVITIES

Escape plan: You and four of your closest friends are in one of the most popular enclaves of the 1980s: a roller-skating rink. (This can actually be set in the '80s or be a fun "throw-back" disco night you attend at a restored local rink.) Somewhere in the middle of one of the "slow skate" numbers (likely something sappy by Lionel Richie!), zombies are suddenly everywhere! How will you and your friends escape?

Reconstruction: Stories set some time after the zombie apocalypse tend to feature attempts to restore civilisation and return to normality. These can either be local efforts or larger enterprises conducted on a government level, but they almost always fail (this is a gleefully pessimistic field of fiction!). For instance, one of the most interesting aspects of Colson Whitehead's 2011 novel *Zone One* (and perhaps one of the most relevant to what we saw in responses to the COVID-19 pandemic), is how it captured what Svetlana Boym, in *The Future of Nostalgia* (2001), called Restorative Nostalgia: in that case the government's attempts to reinstate life exactly as was before the zombie apocalypse. Nevertheless, such normality is almost always only temporary. The zombies always get in. It's now a year after the Great Skate-Rink Zombie War and you, with whatever friends and family survived, want to start to pick up the pieces. As the new leader of your neighbourhood or town, what initial plans will you begin to formulate, and what threats will you face (by people, the environment, or leftover zombies)?

SUBURBAN HORROR

When we think of Horror, we often immediately picture creepy Victorian haunted houses, but there's a tradition of Horror fiction set in our mundane world too, in the cookie-cutter suburbs of well-manicured lawns and neighbourhood-watch associations. While this world is about projecting a happy, stable, conventionally successful life, we all know that every family has its secrets. Suburban horror lets those secrets out of the box. Are you ready to move in?

A Short History of Suburban Horror

The setting for Horror stories has evolved as we have moved (generally speaking) from an agrarian society to an urban one and then to a *sub*urban one. The suburbs developed in the late nineteenth and early twentieth centuries because of improvements in transportation such as trains and roads that meant people didn't have to live in the city centre but could commute to work from the outside. At the same time, there was also the development of "garden cities" that philanthropists built in Britain (which inspired the same in other countries) for factory workers and other blue-collar city employees to live in and so experience more "healthy" lives.[1] The suburb as we know it today really exploded after World War II, when living in a single-family home with all the modern conveniences and a car in the driveway became the goal for millions. Where the city is frantic and full of people, and the countryside is wild and difficult to control, the suburb is about order and cleanliness, clear borders between houses, and populated with the ideal nuclear family of father, mother, and children.

So, what's so scary about that?

Well Horror, as we've said, is about a loss of control and the status quo being subverted or undermined, and a suburb is based on the idea of sameness and conformity because in sameness there is "safety". For example, houses in a suburban neighbourhood or planned community are often duplicates of each other or variations of a small set of designs all built at the same time. In some places the rules of a homeowners' association (HOA) will say what a front garden can and even must look like. The families in a neighbourhood are usually in a similar socio-economic position since the houses are usually priced within a certain range; because of this and because of location, the families will *mostly* be similar politically, religiously, and culturally. Finally, the kids all go to local schools (in America, the schools will be run by a

---

1. Editors of Encyclopaedia Britannica, 2012, n.p.

school board that directs what is taught and when), and students sit in rows learning the same things together.

Because it's usually a place of conformity—mostly for women but also for men—suburbia can be terrifying because its accompanying loss of autonomy and individuality is rightly frightening to some people. The original suburban horror novel is Ira Levin's *Stepford Wives* (1972) about a neighbourhood in which the husbands replace their wives with **Robots** that act like the "perfect woman". The horror there has a lot to do with not just the weirdness of being replaced by unthinking, body-perfect automatons that don't talk back and are always ready for sex, but also as a reflection of what was going on in the Western world from the 1960s through the 1980s: second-wave feminism. Women fighting for their own power over their own lives was very unsettling to many, mostly men but even some women. And Levin took it to its extreme, using the spectre of suburbia, where everything is supposed to be safe and exist in clear sunshine, where everything is controlled and ordered unlike the destabilised cities supposedly riddled with crime due to heaving populations, and, in the process, he uncovered what was really happening beneath the surface. In other cases, the newness of these communities themselves, their lack of connection to social or geographical history, can be the locus of terror; in *The House Next Door* by Anne Rivers Siddons (1978), a brand-new home in a suburban neighbourhood becomes the site of horrible events, completely upending the lives of the neighbours. Not only is no one in the house safe, but neither is anyone nearby.

While suburbia has projected an image of safety from the "urban jungle"—that imagery having a racist component to it—this is a veneer that is usually very thin. Thus, the subgenre is underpinned by anxiety related to the disconnect between the image of the place and its reality. Drug abuse and addiction, which many people believe is limited to cities, has risen in recent years in US suburbs.[2] Rape and sexual assault in American suburbs accounted for over one quarter of cases reported to The National Crime Victimization Survey in 2017.[3] In the UK, suburbs also have their share of problems that were once considered the plight of urban living and are "under attack from numerous fronts" because of a believed lack of government attention to the problems.[4] These anxieties about "urban blight" encroaching on suburban lives express themselves throughout this subgenre. Moreover, slasher films became popular from the late 1970s to the '90s (see **Splatterpunk** for more) and many of these films featured teenagers and young adults, the very people their parents moved to the suburbs to protect, as their protagonists and victims. *A Nightmare on Elm*

---

2. Patterson, 2022, n.p.
3. Casteel, Wolfe, and Nguyen, 2018, n.p.
4. Huq, 2020, n.p.

Street (dir. Wes Craven, 1984) and its sequels is set in Springwood, Ohio, an imagined suburban town in Middle America, but even there the children aren't safe: a psychopathic serial killer inhabits kids' dreams for revenge on their parents. *Scream* (dir. Wes Craven, 1996) is set in the fictional suburban town of Woodsboro, but the kids *aren't* all right: psychopathic serial-killer teenagers hunt their peers, even at one point killing a kid with an electric garage door, one of the major symbols of suburban life. More recently, the Marvel television show *WandaVision* (2021) brilliantly deconstructs not just the socio-economic aspects of suburbia but also its evolving depiction in popular culture (specifically sitcoms) throughout the last half century. Like *Scream*, the series uses suburban detail knowingly, something that brings us to consider the writing element of trope.

A Spotter's Guide: Popular Tropes in the Neighbourhood

A trope is a thing (yes, we know, it's very specific!) that's found across more than one story in a genre: that is, it can be a character, a setting, an object, an event, etc. Some tropes will automatically brand a story as belonging to a certain genre. Sometimes, like in *Scream*, which is also a spoof on Horror film tropes and its sequels, the characters know that they're living amongst the expected tropes; this doesn't happen that often, though, and we find examples of the latter in work such as *The Walking Dead* where nobody has ever heard of zombies despite the primary-world setting! Suburban horror includes tropes and elements found in other Horror stories that, when combined with the supposedly safe and "generic" setting of suburbia (read, "pure" or built in a place where there was nothing before), work to enhance the feelings of creeping uneasiness:

- **Unsettled or angry spirits:** In *Poltergeist* (dir. Tobe Hooper, 1982), a family move into a planned suburban community built by the real-estate-development company the father works for. Before they can truly settle in, all manner of weirdness ensues. Disruptive spirits kidnap the younger daughter via a portal in her closet and keep her hostage in an alternate plane; her mother can hear her screaming for help from inside the static on the television. At the end of the film, as the family escapes, the father realises that his company lied about the graveyard his house was built on: the construction crew only moved the headstones and not the bodies to cut corners and save money, upsetting the spirits of the dead.
    - A sub-trope is the **Native-American burial ground trope**: Stephen King's *Pet Sematary* (1983) sees its protagonist bury a dead cat—and then his dead child and dead wife—in a Native American

burial ground because there's something magical about the spot that resurrects the dead. He discovers, however, that people buried there come back *not quite themselves*, to the point of being murderous. This is a particularly delicate trope because of a lack of sensitivity to cultural practices and the possibility of it being a racist depiction (that Native Americans are vengeful, even when dead), which can harm the community it's depicting. In the case of the King novel, the alteration of the cat, child, and wife might indicate the Native American spirits are getting revenge on those who upset their resting places, giving them agency, but the use of this trope can be problematic. For more on cultural appropriation, see **Supernatural Horror**.

- **Brain transplants:** While in *The Stepford Wives* the women seem to have been brainwashed or had their brains transplanted into robots, in the film *Get Out* (dir. Jordan Peele, 2017), the transplants are real while totally incongruous to the upstate New York setting, suggesting how suburbia can "brainwash" its inhabitants.
- **Alien invasion:** In the SF/suburban horror comedy *The Watch* (dir. Akiva Schaffer, 2012), set in Glenview, Ohio (always Ohio for some reason!), a group of men team up to be the new neighbourhood watch to fight off an alien invasion. It's easy to see how this trope sits in the suburban-horror subgenre because of the fear of what is outside the suburb coming in uninvited.
- **Alternate dimension/universe:** Clearly connected to the fear of alien (outside) invasion is the fear of something unseen inhabiting your (safe) suburban space. In the first series of *Stranger Things* (2016–present), Will is taken into the Upside Down, an alternate dimension inhabited by terrifying monsters. Like in *Poltergeist*, he communicates with his mother via a mundane household item: in this case, Christmas lights. The supposedly safe world of Hawkins, Indiana (again with Middle America), exists thinly atop a virtual hell.
- **Vampires:** In Grady Hendrix's *The Southern Book Club's Guide to Slaying Vampires* (2020), a group of 1990s wives go head-to-head against a handsome, charming man who's moved to the neighbourhood; unfortunately, he turns out to be a vampire that's taking Black children. The novel uses suburban horror to investigate questions of race relations, bringing to light the systemic racism prevalent in American society as well as the misogynistic expectations that women at the time experienced, harkening back, again, to *The Stepford Wives*.
- **Psycho killers:** Qu'est que c'est? In *The Burbs* (dir. Joe Dante, 1989), a weird family moves into the neighbourhood; they turn out to be killers who did away with the previous owners so they could have the

house. In this Horror comedy, the killer family has a "foreign" name (the Klopeks) and are depicted as looking a bit odd, feeding into the suburban fear of "different" people moving in next door, threatening social/racial/religious/economic conformity.

Things That are Cool About Suburban Horror

Suburbia is a familiar place and a familiar concept to many of us whether we're older writers who moved our families to the suburbs decades ago or younger writers who are the second or third generation to grow up in the 'burbs. If we're from the suburbs, we know what it's like to live in a place where everyone is supposed to want to be the same thing; if we didn't grow up there, we might feel suspicious about a place where everyone wants to be alike. So, while we love good old gothic-y haunted houses and things that go bump in the night, think of the challenge of writing something that's truly scary in our regular half-messy houses full of dog hair and dirty dishes and laundry that never seems to end and bills that make you want to run away and live in a cave. Modern life is *boring* in lots of ways, so to take that and make it scary gives you permission to approach all the mundanity from a new perspective and to get all the BS out of your system in a whole new way.

When the Neighbourhood Watch Watches YOU

- **There's more than meets the eye:** Levin's book *The Stepford Wives* is a terrifying book for a reader afraid for her—or his—own autonomy in a society that wants to label us and put us in restrictive boxes. It was specifically satirising suburbia and the patriarchy's panic about feminism. So, consider what modern movement or concern you could use a suburban horror story to really investigate. The purpose of this is to consider the theme, that is what your story is *really* about.
- **Break out of the box:** The suburbs—hell, *life*—has moved on since the 1960s and '70s, when suburban horror started to take hold, and even in the '80s when so many films mentioned here were released. We've exposed the undercurrent of horror running beneath the clean-living the suburbs promise, so how can you make this examination of suburban life new again?

ACTIVITIES

Mapping Identities: Draw a map of the house or flat you live in. You might live in a place where the dwellings to your right and left (or above and below) are either identical or mirror images of your own, or they might be completely different. For the sake of this activity, let's pretend that they're the same. To tap into our fear of robot-like conformity, in your mind create a schedule for the people living in the houses or flats surrounding yours that matches your own schedule exactly and furnish the rooms exactly the same down to curtain colour and the placement of photograph frames on the mantel. Now, take your protagonist (for the purposes of this exercise, it's you) and have them wake up and start the day in the usual way, but with the growing sense that this isn't their home. Something is *off*. What clues are there that this isn't the right house? How will your protagonist know that something is wrong? And what will your protagonist do? Is the goal to get back to their own home, or to investigate why this other home is the exact same?

Howdy, Neighbour: You've moved from the city to a suburban neighbourhood complete with identical houses, tidy front yards/gardens, and an elementary school within walking distance. Everything seems safe and clean, but you begin to suspect that something weird is going on in the 'hood. Subvert the expectations and instead of you being the invader, you're the one uncovering the mystery. Choose one of the tropes listed above and see how you can create terrifying situations while commenting on suburban unease.

TECHNO HORROR

Lots of Horror draws on the past—old buildings, mysterious crypts, and so on—but techno horror finds its frights in circuit boards and screens, in creepypasta memes and demons climbing out of your television. Want to know more? Then don't forget to like and subscribe....

A Short History of Techno Horror

Technology is all around us. As human beings, it has been for thousands of years. Yet back in the time of textile machines and printing presses, most people readily understood how technology worked. The same cannot be said in a twenty-first century where, despite its ubiquity in our lives, a great many of us are unsure of exactly how things like, say, the Internet (let alone the clock in our oven!) actually function. Technology has thus taken on the kind of mysterious and occasionally threatening aura that previous centuries associated with arcane ritual or religious rite (seriously, tell us that you don't want to sacrifice something for the teenager who fixed your Wi-Fi router). These associations make technology a prime subject for Horror writing, yes, but this subgenre truly thrives because technology is the very definition of a double-edged sword. Sure, it has the power to bring us together with distant friends and co-workers but, conversely, the very accessibility that technology grants leaves us vulnerable to unwanted attention from trolls (the online kind rather than the under-the-bridge type) or even criminals (see **Cyberpunk**). Sometimes modern technology even seems to have a life of its own and is determined to spite us with a kind of goblin energy (you'll know this if you've ever owned a printer). You're probably used to thinking of tech-run-amok as an element of large stories, such as the many works of **Apocalyptic Fiction** in which it brings about the downfall of humanity, but, in terms of techno horror, it's usually the smaller, more intimate encounters with technology that are the most chilling.

While techno horror generally focuses on the here and now, or on the very near future, its origins lie in the middle of the twentieth century after World War II and with the huge transformative potential of the so-called Atomic Age. This was a period of optimism and progress, especially in the West and in the United States. It was an era in which older technology was being updated or abandoned completely; modern appliances such as refrigerators and televisions became more affordable for the middle and working classes, cars were getting bigger and brighter (pink Cadillacs!), more and more people began to have telephones installed in their private homes, and advertising constantly blew the trumpets for technology as a force for good. But there was still apprehension about the direction in which society was headed, especially considering the onset of the Cold War and the accompanying possibility of nuclear annihilation. People feared that technology, heralded as a saviour, could also destroy the world if left unchecked.

While one might think that the natural setting for techno horror is in science labs or in space, some of it—most of it, in fact—is set very close to home. Ira Levin's novel *The Stepford Wives* (1972; explored in more depth in **Suburban Horror**) is early techno horror because technology/science is used to create "perfect" robotic spouses, illustrating the fear some had of a backlash against the second-wave feminism of the 1960s and '70s and the focus on securing the "nuclear family" as the most vital unit in society. Such upheaval continued in the 1980s, a time of continuing social change, with more women working outside the home and their kids often not having adult supervision after school (latchkey kids unite!). The 1980s also saw the rise of cable television and MTV, the AIDS epidemic (with the disease's associated social panic), and the continuing fear of nuclear war between increasingly networked superpowers. Along with this came new home-based technology such as VHS players, camcorders, microwaves, the Sony Walkman, and the earliest of mobile phones. Suddenly, instead of dodging the "gatekeepers" at the cinema or concert ticket booth, you could now watch the most violent and sex-filled films or listen to certain newer, more aggressive genres of music in the privacy of your own home without depending on broadcast channels (and without anyone overhearing, in the case of the Walkman). This unsettled some elements of society who were afraid of the sex and violence in films and music being more accessible to children or other sensitive viewers. Some people took the fear of new technology invading the home and changing our lives to extremes. In the US in 1984 a group of women with political ties formed the PMRC (Parents Music Resource Center) that pushed for a music-labelling system similar to film ratings, insisting that parents should have more of a say in controlling the sale of albums containing what they deemed "objectionable" lyrics or themes (containing references to violence, sex, drugs, or the occult; wow these groups really had a thing for the occult!).[1] A similar force could be found in the UK in Mary Whitehouse, president of the National Viewers and Listeners Association, who was active from the 1960s to the early '90s in trying to censor all manner of material from British television. The situation in the US with the PMRC, and to an extent in the UK with Mary Whitehouse, was closely related to the "Satanic Panic" of the early 1980s, in which whole sections of the population bought into conspiracy theories about demonic worship and saw danger to their children in every shadow.[2]

---

1. Schonfeld, 2015, n.p.
2. Yuhas, 2021, n.p.

Spotters Guide: Video Nasties

It's no surprise that techno horror of the 1980s in particular crosses vengeful spirits (something we thought we were too modern for!) with technology. These themes, usually tied to domestic tech, recur throughout this subgenre:

- **Television:** TV sets offer us a window into the outside world but, also, a portal through which external forces can enter. Classic examples of this include the films *Poltergeist* (dir. Tobe Hooper, 1982), in which a little girl gets sucked from her new suburban house (with all the mod-cons!) into another realm and can only be heard via the static-filled television; and especially *Videodrome* (dir. David Cronenberg, 1983), about a television producer who discovers a show (broadcasted via an illegal satellite dish, another example of technology forcing its way into homes) that shows snuff films in a commentary on the fear that violent, uncensored, straight-to-video entertainment was desensitising people to violence at the time.
- **Murderous and/or transformative robots:** Less profound than *Videodrome* but somehow just as culturally significant (!) was 1986's *Chopping Mall* (dir. Jim Wynorsk), a techno-horror teen-slasher flick in which high-security shopping-mall robots turn murderous against a group of adolescent store employees. Other notable works of robo-techno horror from the 1980s saw characters literally consumed by technology. An extreme example is the Japanese **Cyberpunk/Body Horror**/techno-horror mashup *Tetsuo: The Iron Man* (dir. Shinya Tsukamoto, 1989); this low-budget cult classic follows a Tokyo salaryman's grotesque transformation into a horrifying being overcome by metal parts, as well as his conflict with a tormentor known as the Metal Fetishist (played by the director). To achieve the protagonist's horrifying on-screen transformation, parts from—once again—old televisions and other common technologies were taped onto the actor's skin.[3] At the end, with The Iron Man and the Metal Fetishist having fused together into a perverse new gestalt mass (think a two-faced mobile junkyard shaped like a giant penis), the character(s) vow to transform the whole world into metal. It's a raw and brutal watch, definitely not for family movie night!
- **VCR/VHS players:** Less visually shocking (so more mainstream) but still potent examples of techno horror acknowledge the subgenre's deep roots and manage to straddle the line between creative work and reality. One recent example of a narrative preying on our discomfort with video technology is *Ring* (dir. Hideo Nakata,1998), based on a 1991 novel by

---

3. Mes and Sharp, 2005, n.p.

Koji Suzuki (and later adapted for English-speaking audiences as *The Ring*; dir. Gore Verbinski, 2002). The story, which involves a videotape that will lead to the viewer's death within a week, is probably best known for the deeply unsettling imagery of a faceless cursed girl crawling out of a television set. Suzuki's original novel is an example of what is called Japanese Horror (or simply J-Horror). J-horror features ghosts and spirits, much like Western horror, but grew out of the country's "fascination with technology and the familiarity that comes with it as a method of subversion"; it intersects with techno horror by how "various spirits emerge from and are often directly tied to household technology, thus introducing an everyday fear into something as simple as static on TV".[4]

- **Home computers:** This brings us to the appearance of the home computer, the source of so much anxiety for users trying to get to grips with operating systems, but also prime material for Horror writers. John McNeil's *Little Brother* (1983) imagines an early computer toy as a means of mind control that turns children into killing machines; *The Shadow Man* by Stephen Gresham (1986) combines a computer playmate, an 8-year-old boy, his witch mother, and a demon (yes, it's rather a lot!); and the film *Ghost in the Machine* (dir. Rachel Talalay, 1993) is about a serial killer whose consciousness is accidentally transferred into the electrical grid (a microwave and a hair dryer attack!) and who seeks his victims according to a scanned page from an address book he finds in a computer system (hey, no one ever promised it would make much sense). Various 1990s shows such as *The X-Files* (1993–2002) and *Buffy the Vampire Slayer* (1997–2003) also dallied with cursed or haunted computers, to varying effect (early examples were usually very cheesy).

- **Cell phones, video games, and online shopping:** Of course, even back in the early 1990s we had no idea that one day technology would so quickly connect us all, all the time, and create such havoc in our lives while simultaneously making it easier to shop, talk to distant relatives, and date. As tech continued to get better, smaller, and relatively cheaper throughout the early 2000s, Horror writers found further outlets for their scares. In *Cell* by Stephen King (2006) a signal broadcast over cell phones turns the population into mindless killers; the message here—that cell phones distract us and turn us into **Zombies**—isn't subtle! Meanwhile, in 2007's *Heart-Shaped Box* by King's son Joe Hill, an ageing rock star buys a ghost from an internet auction site (spirits via eBay!). And, finally, there are video games themselves, the focus of so much parental ire and fear: they've inspired films such as *Choose or Die* (dir. Toby Meakins, 2002) and *Stay Alive* (dir. John Frizzell, 2006) about

---

4. Dowell, 2022, n.p.

the games killing their players. Fast forward to the present and tech has embedded itself into our lives in almost parasitic fashion. The Internet coils around the globe like an invisible behemoth whose tentacles reach into our homes and imaginations. We've given up control of huge swaths of our civilisation to cat memes and social-media companies. Consider, for instance, the platforms that allowed us to work and study online during the COVID-19 years. The film *Host* (dir. Rob Savage, 2020) builds a classic Horror story onto the importance that online Zoom calls and "hangouts" were to all of us during the lockdowns: a group of friends hold an online séance and accidentally bring forth a malevolent spirit that kills them off, one by one. Certainly sounds like every online meeting we've ever had!

Things That are Cool About Techno Horror

We're surrounded by technology all the time. Even when we go outside, we usually have a cell phone with us that constantly pings GPS or maps, so writers now have a lot more to work with than a writer in the 1950s, for example. We've also seen the result of this obsession in dreadful news stories about people who cause car crashes because they're distracted by texting or who fall off cliffs when trying to get the perfect selfie (this is why selfie-sticks are banned at many Japanese railway stations!). We've basically forgotten how to live without our tech, from can openers to laptops. As a result, your readers are going to be familiar with the tech you use in your stories, which means you can avoid the task of explaining Science Fictional technology that doesn't yet exist; on the other hand, the invention of the cell phone means that suspense is difficult to build when a protagonist can just ring up or text a friend to warn them to watch out for the werewolf on the loose! Readers are also going to be familiar with society's anxiety about how we interact with technology (just read any daily newspaper—online, of course!—to see that). We either use it too much and it's taking over our lives, or we need more of it to have better lives (cue the mobs of people who camp out overnight to get the newest version of a certain brand of phone or video game console). Such anxiety turns to horror very easily, making techno horror a subgenre that is timely and current and one that will readily speak to your audience.

Read the Instruction Manual

- **Logic:** Yes, you're writing SFF/H, so of course you have licence to make things up, but some of the television shows and novels noted above are deemed silly or illogical because they didn't get the tech right. This doesn't mean you have to be a scientist or engineer, but you do have to think about your audience and remember that they know how to use a cell phone. You'll have to consider user logic as well as machine logic for the story logic to work.

- **Dating your material:** Tech changes, adapts, improves, and moves on. For instance, we generally don't have VHS machines in our homes anymore—many of us don't even have DVD players anymore!—so using one in a story you write now means either setting your story in the 1980s or having present-time characters note that it's an old machine that's rarely used.

ACTIVITIES

Haunted cells: Your cell phone is inhabited by the ghost of one of the people who helped make it. We know, though we don't always acknowledge, that a lot of our technology is made under not-so-great conditions in far-off countries (we touch on this a bit in **Steampunk**). Some books and films, such as *Poltergeist*, use the premise that modern life has been built on the graves of people from cultures that weren't respected, and their spirits are angry and want revenge (see **Suburban Horror**). Remember that SFF/H contains themes that are timely and important, and that's true for this story prompt, too: in the West, we know that our consumer habits are having a negative effect on the natural world and on other cultures. So, where did your phone come from? How might the fabrication process for the phone have affected the natural world or people living elsewhere? What might that spirit do for revenge?

Creepypasta: The most prominent home for cheap scares these days is the Internet. "Creepypasta" is the term used for short, highly memorable stories and images that spread across social media and through email (kind of like modern chain letters). They often include stories or accounts of murders or paranormal events and characters meant to unsettle readers (The Slender Man is perhaps the best known of these). Cursed video games or websites are also common. For this activity, take one of your horror ideas or stories and condense it down into a few shareable paragraphs. Perhaps it's about strange goings on about town, or lights in the sky, or eerie utterances in the dark. See if you can find some clipart online to illustrate the tale. Then post it to your social-media platform of choice and see what kinds of responses you receive. Use these as the basis of an expanded (or even a meta) version of the original post.

SPLATTERPUNK

Not for the squeamish or for the reader who values subtlety, here's a subgenre of graphic, often eroticised violence that utilises shock value and stomach-churning imagery to generate emotional responses. Some say this is writing entirely without literary merit, others insist it's a potent form of social commentary. This is *hard*core Horror. This is Splatterpunk.

A Short History of Splatterpunk

Though proto-splatterpunk existed for some time (two of the clearest examples being James Herbert's 1975 novel *The Rats*, and Michael Shea's 1980 story 'The Autopsy'), the subgenre first became an identifiable movement in the mid-1980s. The critic Xavier Aldana Reyes takes 1984 as its official starting point because this coincided with both the publication of the first of Clive Barker's seminal horror series the *Books of Blood* (1984–'85) and the establishment of the video-recordings rating system in the UK as "a reaction to the moral panic generated by the 'video nasties' scandals of 1982 and 1983".[1] Taking a lead from gory, so-called "splatter films", the subgenre's name is generally attributed to author David J. Schow at the 1986 World Fantasy Convention. He later recalled how this happened:

> I made up the term to describe hyperintensive horror—the Clive Barker "there are no limits" variety—[back] when it mattered. If Stephen King is comparable to McDonald's, then Splatterpunk—in its day—was akin to certain varieties of gnarly mushroom, the kind that could open new doors of perception, or, in noncompatible metabolisms, just make you puke.[2]

Schow's "in its day" is important, as he later expressed the belief that splatterpunk was less a subgenre and more an era, generally taken to be the second half of the 1980s.

Certainly, splatterpunk in those years was defined by visceral writing that lingered on, even fetishised, sickening or upsetting description, often of the human body, and so it's closely related to **Body Horror**. The violent transgressions so often merely suggested in **Gothic Horror** (or indeed even in the works of Horror masters such as Anne Rice and Stephen King) are here detailed with an excruciating and steady focus that many may find abhorrent (and, for that matter, should come with content warnings for readers). Nevertheless, the influence of splatterpunk in general, and Barker

---

1. Reyes, 2014, p. 16.
2. McCammon, n.d., n.p.

in particular, on the Horror scene at the time was profound. Though the settings remained familiar—dungeons, suburbia, etc.—the meat of the stories began to turn on highly explicit depictions of unspeakable acts such as murder, abuse, and sexual violations. The general tone of the subgenre has been likened to "uncut fever nightmares from the depths of a twisted psyche—unedited, raw, and powerful".[3]

Given its subject matter, it's perhaps no surprise that splatterpunk has been largely a male-led phenomenon. Prominent authors in the movement include John Skipp and Craig Spector, who often write and edit together. Skipp and Spector's work includes the bestselling **Vampire** novel *The Light at the End* (1986), in which an undead graffiti artist bloodily terrorises New York City; the superpowered vigilante novel *The Cleanup* (1987); and many short stories. The authors' approach to the subgenre typically mixes exceptionally dark humour with outrageous violence. At its best, their work causes reflective readers to question their own responses to the material and ask *why* they're enjoying such loathsome scenarios. Meanwhile Edward Lee typifies both the subgenre's aberrant depiction of sex as well as its practitioners' high level of output (Lee frequently produces two or three novels in a year). Both these pulp tendencies, generally viewed with suspicion by the literary establishment, are also the hallmark of Richard Laymon, an American writer perhaps better known in the UK. His work often includes graphic instances of rape, incest, paedophilia, and serial murder. See *The Cellar* (1980), *The Woods are Dark* (1981), and *Flesh* (1987), the latter nominated for the Bram Stoker Award and featuring an alien parasite that, in an almost meta comment on the subgenre, rewards its hosts' most violent and depraved desires with waves of pleasure. A similar blurring of the divide between pain and pleasure is evident in Barker's own World Fantasy Award-nominated novella *The Hellbound Heart* (1986). The story follows a jaded sadomasochist who, in search of fresh sensual experiences, unlocks a puzzle-box that transports him to a Hell dimension of eternal torture inhabited by beings directly inspired by the author's visits to BDSM clubs. The novella was quickly adapted into the film *Hellraiser* (dir. Clive Barker, 1987), which itself provided an object lesson in splatterpunk's reception by being deemed both "the greatest horror film made in Britain" (*Melody Maker*)[4] and an example of the "bankruptcy of imagination" (Roger Ebert).[5]

Two significant short-fiction anthologies brought the early splatterpunk period to its bloody conclusion: the Skipp and Spector edited **Zombie** splatterpunk collection *The Book of the Dead* (1989) and the Paul M. Sammon edited *Splatterpunks: Extreme Horror* (1990). Each book's

---
3. Person, n.d., n.p.
4. Kane, 2015, p. 51.
5. Ebert, 1987, n.p.

introduction attempts to define the subgenre's shape, though, crucially, not its limits. They attempted to shift understandings of splatterpunk beyond reactionary disgust at its contents and, instead, to provide an artistic basis for its existence. Reading splatterpunk, according to Skipp and Spector, is a multilevel experience:

> The first level [is] the ground floor of being. It's fear as a matter of simple biology: the flesh, surrendering to the laws of physics [...] The second level takes place on the stripped-naked faces of the people to whom this horror is occurring [...] The third level [is] the level of gestalt, of fusion and reintegration. At this point, you can no longer detach; the unknown has become tangible and all too real, beyond cheapening on the one hand or denial on the other. You can see the wet hole and the charred stump, yes; but beyond that—and in vital, visceral conjunction—you can know how it feels to be part of it.[6]

Women and women-identifying authors saw wider success in the subgenre throughout the 1990s (though earlier figures such as Roberta Lannes, whose 'Goodbye, Dark Love', 1986, was often mentioned as an early splatterpunk story, have since disavowed the genre as one intended to "disgust and gratify a reader's lowest self-needs").[7] Notable authors include Melanie Tem (*Blood Moon*, 1992), Kathe Koja (*The Cipher*, 1991, and *Skin*, 1993), Lucy Taylor (*The Safety of Unknown Cities*, 1995), and Nancy Kilpatrick (the Darker Passions series written as Aramantha Knight, begun in 1995). Alongside these, Poppy Z. Brite, a pseudonym of Billy Martin, produced several novels featuring openly bisexual and gay protagonists (their most successful work includes *Lost Souls*, 1992, and especially *Exquisite Corpse*, 1996). Splatterpunk also began to soak into mainstream writing during this period; examples include writers grouped under the banner of "Transgressive Fiction" such as Bret Easton Ellis (*American Psycho*, 1991), Ryu Murakami (*Piercing*, 1994), and Chuck Palahniuk (*Fight Club*, 1996), many of which have been adapted for cinema to varying levels of success and public outcry.

A Spotter's Guide: Blood Splatter Analysis

- **No limits:** Splatterpunk authors tend to recognise neither conventional decency nor social/cultural taboos. They seek to shock. As Sammon puts it, "like surrealism before it, Splatterpunk [is] a specific revolt against an artistic establishment—in our case, the traditional, meekly suggestive horror story".[8] Splatterpunk characters, if perhaps not their protagonists, tend to revel in their own deviancy. The subject matter of

---

6. Skipp and Spector, 1989, p. 8.
7. Tucker, 1991, p. 13.
8. Tucker, 1991, p. 13.

such stories is thus predictably off-putting (something that holds back its commercial appeal). Nevertheless, the subgenre at its most effective is not merely just horrific act after horrific act but, instead, depicts the impact of these upon its characters.

- **Sexual violence:** Where the gothic generally, and vampires in particular, portray romanticised versions of their protagonists' repressed sexual desires, splatterpunk is more brutal, and has in the past become outright misogynistic. This is often the moment where the material crosses the line of acceptability. Rape and rape revenge stories (with victims of all genders and gender identities) are not uncommon in this subgenre. They make for uncomfortable reading, especially because sexual violence is typically used as a plot point or a shorthand means of establishing an antagonist or a setting's awfulness. Be careful if you're writing this material, and please remember that sexual violence is a very real trauma for many people. While this kind of imagery was a mainstay of splatterpunk in the 1980s, do ask yourself whether it's truly necessary in your story.
- **Grotesque imagery:** Splatterpunk is a subgenre of excess, one that author William F. Nolan called "the Vomit Bag School of Horror, whether on screen or on the printed page—books and stories and films featuring gore for gore's sake, designed strictly for the purpose of grossing out an audience".[9] Bodily mutilation, excrement-eating babies, vagina-dentata stories, and religious accoutrements deployed as instruments of physical abuse with evangelical fervour are all examples of the form. At its most heightened, this is "artful and bold," but at its most pedestrian it can devolve into sadistic so-called torture porn.[10] On one hand, readers expect grotesque violence, but on the other hand there's the need for imagery to have meaning, even symbolism. You, as an author, must decide how you wish to balance these.
- **Exposition:** The typical style of splatterpunk is, in many ways, *without* obvious style. The subgenre favours a kind of forensic clarity to its prose with exposition that tends toward comprehensive description and explanation instead of clever or, Hell forbid, even beautiful turns of phrase. This cold, even nihilistic writing describes exactly what's happening without much in the way of decorative window dressing. These stories place you in their scenes as if they were happening right in front of you.
- **Punk:** We discuss how subgenres such as **Solarpunk** and **Cyberpunk** derive part of their philosophy from the anti-authoritarian punk energy in music. Splatterpunk adopts a similar, though perhaps more narrowly focused perspective. It's "an aggressively grubby underground

---

9. Skipp and Spector, 1989, p. 8.
10. Tucker, 1991, p. 13.

movement," one that Sammon describes as "erupting though" the "vicious Conservatism of Ronald Reagan and Margaret Thatcher".[11] Yet it's anti-establishment in response not just to social or political restrictions but also to the tone and style of what it deemed "quiet horror", a sense of the genre having become safe and conventional and, worse, no longer frightening in the years leading up to the 1980s. Splatterpunk writers wished to take off-limits subjects and use them to generate terror in their readers. As author Jeff Burk put it, "Sorry to break it to everyone, but ghosts and werewolves aren't real. Rapists, serial killers, terrorists, sex slavery, and random acts of cruelty are real. The thought of being stalked by a vampire does not linger in the back of my brain in the same way as what could happen when walking alone in the middle of the night".[12]

Things That are Cool About Splatterpunk

There's an argument to be made that art shouldn't be sanitised. It should hold a mirror up to the worst, most heinous excesses of society. Whether you believe that or not, or even how far you're willing to take it, is an authorial choice. Your milage will obviously vary with splatterpunk, but it's difficult to deny that, in the hands of its most aware proponents, it shines a harsh light on the normalisation of violence in our societies. As Horror author John Shirley explains, "I feel confident that even my darkest writing, at its most grotesque, is not salacious; that it is a kind of meaningful protest, a wakeup call—that it at least aspires to be art".[13]

Blood, Gore, and Bits of Sick

- **Transgression:** The readership for splatterpunk, while zealous, is nonetheless quite small. Not every reader or editor is going to be comfortable with this material (in fact, many outright state their disinterest). Make sure you read the submission guidelines for magazines or publishers to see if they exclude depictions of extreme violence, sexual and otherwise, and do investigate the small presses that specialise in this subgenre. This is all about marketing your work to the appropriate venues and audiences.
- **Reality:** No one can deny that our world is full of meaningless violence and horror. Splatterpunk attempts to process this fact by concentrating on bodily revulsion, torture, and scenes of nauseating horror. It compels

---

11. Tucker, 1991, p. 13.
12. Burk, 2014, n.p.
13. Shirley, 2011, n.p.

the reader or viewer into appallingly intimate contact with the most irredeemable of acts. This is, at best, not done out of mere adolescent sensationalism but, instead, to bring us face-to-face with the darkness inherent in the human psyche. It's what Skipp and Spector, in their artistic justification of the form, called "meat meeting mind, with the soul as screaming omniscient witness".[14]

- **Metaphor:** Despite its focus on outrageous excess, there's great potential in splatterpunk for metaphorical or allegorical discussion of real-world inspiration. These can be as straightforward as the notion that "New York City is Hell" (Skipp and Spector's *The Light at the End*) or as nuanced (for splatterpunk, at least) as Ray Garton's *Live Girls* (1987), which portrays vampires as Times Square sex workers and so provided a timely metaphor for the AIDS epidemic. Thus, while that novel still fulfils the expectations of the subgenre's reader, it also provides a deeper and—dare we say it—more literary meaning.
- **Cautionary tales:** Splatterpunk stories can also serve as warnings. They use shock value as a vehicle to articulate issues of grave concern. This is true on both the individual level, such as the subgenre's late 1980s concentration on the perpetrators of street crime, murder, and rape, but also on a wider level in the preponderance of splatterpunk stories, such as Jay Russell's 'City of Angels' (1990), taking place in post-nuclear-apocalypse futures. The "obscene detail" that splatterpunk affords to such end-of-the-world scenarios can be a means "to inspire outrage against such weapons".[15]
- **Anti-horror:** Splatterpunk is, in many ways, an example of what Barker's biographer Douglas Winter has termed "anti-horror", which is fiction that explores the real horror underlying everyday life. Anti-horror, he says, "rejects the Manichaean simplicity of God and Devil, good and evil, pushing the reader into a realm of ambiguity, forcing us to confront the real world".[16] This is visible in the subgenre's emphasis on terrors that could conceivably take place not because of vampires or demonic Hellbeasts, but because of complex intersecting social, economic, or psychological circumstances. The real Horror, splatterpunk says, has been inside us all along.

---

14. Skipp and Spector, 1989, p. 8.
15. Tucker, 1991, p. 13.
16. Winter, 2002, p. 191.

ACTIVITIES:

Moderating horror: You're a social-media moderator for a relatively popular web site that has user forums as well as a live-feed capability. You witness a horrific act live streamed on your platform. Once you shut down the connection, you're compelled to investigate. Was this real? Staged? Why was your site targeted? Who—and where—is the victim? And who— and where—is the perpetrator? Describe what you find.

Flip the script: Take a well-known film, something from the family or rom-com genres, and see how you can turn it bloody. These genres conform to formulaic structures and expected tropes, so how can you turn that on its head while still including a comment (remember theme!) on any of a number of modern concerns?

COSMIC HORROR

Cosmic horror straddles the lines between Science Fiction, Fantasy, and traditional Horror. It marks the boundary between the known and unknown with stories told on the cusp of a terrifying vastness. Its antagonists impose a withering toll on human psychic spaces, and their mere existence drives human beings insane. If you want to know them, you must stare into the abyss with us….

A Short History of Cosmic Horror

Cosmic horror depicts "a universe essentially horrible and hostile to humankind".[1] The author most associated with its creation is Rhode Island's H.P. Lovecraft (1890–1937), though we would be remiss if we didn't note that he was a well-known racist, something which obviously taints his legacy.[2] Lovecraft maintained that "the oldest and strongest emotion of mankind is fear, and the oldest and strongest kind of fear is fear of the unknown".[3] He's best known for his "Cthulhu Mythos", a series of horror stories that defined cosmic horror by drawing heavily from SF imagery and ideas and so, in many ways, rendering it the pulpiest of subgenres. The Cthulhu Mythos is built upon a foundation of trans-dimensional aliens known as "Great Old Ones" interfering "with human cultural and physiological Evolution" over the course of millennia.[4] It demarcates cosmic horror as an amoral space of existential dread in which reality as we know exists as merely a thin veneer of rationality and sanity, one beyond which vast and powerful beings lie waiting to return. These beings are often worshiped by "bizarre, atavistic cults, with members crude and grotesque in appearance," figures who readily serve as secondary antagonists for our characters.[5]

Unusually for a subgenre, the majority of the foundational texts are the work of a single author. Lovecraft's most influential stories include 'The Call of Cthulhu' (1928), which links together three narratives about cults, half-sunken islands, and a doomed expedition in search of the titular (perhaps tentacular?) squid-faced extraterrestrial; 'The Dunwich Horror'

---

1. Stableford and Clute, 2022, n.p.
2. For more on Lovecraft's racism, and how it has impacted SFF/H writing, see Nnedi Okorafor's 2011 blog post 'Lovecraft's racism & The World Fantasy Award statuette, with comments from China Miéville', Available at: http://nnedi.blogspot.com/2011/12/lovecrafts-racism-world-fantasy-award.html (Accessed 31 August 2022).
3. Lovecraft, 1927, p. 23.
4. Stableford and Clute, 2022, n.p.
5. Mariani, 2014, n.p.

(1929), in which a hideous young man and his grandfather hide something deeply unnatural in a New England farmhouse; the novella *At the Mountains of Madness* (1936), in which an Antarctic expedition encounters evidence of extraterrestrial beings; and the 1936 novella *The Shadow Over Innsmouth*, which follows a student exploring a largely abandoned town devastated by grotesque fish people and their followers. Evident in all these stories are the subgenre's two key themes: the meaninglessness of human existence and the fragility of human sanity. Because this is nihilistic, even fatalistic fiction, human beings are little more than playthings to cosmic antagonists (see also Clive Barker's **Splatterpunk** novella *The Hellbound Heart*, 1986). These are stories in which the achievements of our civilisation are literally nothing in a vast and uncaring universe. To discover this is the ultimate Copernican (perhaps Cthulhuican?) decentring of human importance. It literally drives characters in this subgenre to insanity (and, yet, in their madness, such tales suggest that this is an appropriate response to our existence).

The original cosmic horror stories by Lovecraft introduce a loose pantheon of Great Old Ones with such colourful names and identities as Ammutseba, Devourer of Stars; the mutagenic, foul-smelling cloud known as The Colour; Gog-Hoor, Eater of the Insane; the coiled, writhing tentacle mass Kassogtha, Bride and Sister of Cthulhu; the larva-like exile Nycrama, The Zombifying Essence; as well as Other or Outer Gods such as Yog-Sothoth, an all-knowing conglomeration of glowing spheres. Yet the Cthulhu Mythos has long since evolved into a popular playground for other writers (at times including the likes of Alan Moore, Joanna Russ, Neil Gaiman, and Elizabeth Bear) and has arguably achieved the status of a shared fictional universe. Many authors have expanded on Lovecraft's original cast of immense and indifferent deities. In particular, the American publisher and author August Derleth (1909–'71) did much to formalise the Mythos (the so-called "Elder Gods", for example, are his creation) though, in the process, he introduced strains of Christian thought, structure, and occasional optimism at odds with Lovecraft's original intentions. Though, of course, it should be noted the "essence of the mythos lies not in a pantheon of imaginary deities [...] but rather in a certain convincing cosmic attitude".[6] This is to say that you, as the writer, can (and perhaps should!) approach cosmic horror with your own monstrous deities and not be tied to those of the original Mythos; your work will satisfy the subgenre's reader as long as it evokes cosmic horror's "premise that common human laws and interests and emotions have no validity or significance in the vast cosmos-at-large".[7]

Cosmic horror continued to find a ready audience throughout the twentieth century. On television, anthology shows such as *The Twilight*

---

6. Joshi, 1995, pp. 165–166.
7. Fisher, 2016, p. 16.

Zone (1959–'64) and *The Outer Limits* (1963–'65) regularly drew on its themes and atmospheres to create unforgettable stories. Meanwhile, big-screen examples include the SF film *Event Horizon* (dir. Paul W.S. Anderson, 1997), in which an experimental spacecraft unleashes a malevolent force through a rift in the space-time continuum, and postmodern satire *The Cabin in the Woods* (dir. Drew Goddard, 2011), which mixes and matches many Horror tropes but, ultimately, revolves around a cult sacrificing people to enormous "Ancient Ones" sleeping beneath the Earth.

Back with prose fiction, American short-story writer and anthologist Thomas Ligotti is considered "one of the finest contemporary cosmic horror writers".[8] Ligotti's narrators are "part-time students, drifters, and curious nobodies" in an evolution of Lovecraft's stodgy Victorian professors; moreover, they don't "fear the subversion of human knowledge and existence; they long for it".[9] His post-Lovecraftian fiction from the early 1990s in particular presents phantasmagorical and "grotesque dreamscapes brimming with alien fauna, misshapen beasts, and human appendages".[10] In that way, Ligotti exemplifies how cosmic horror's distinct sense of awe and hopelessness crosses over with so-called "Weird" Fiction (see also the work of Jeff VanderMeer, particularly his Nebula Award-winning *Annihilation*, 2014) as the two subgenres share an interest in destabilising our protagonists' reality (indeed, "Weird" is how Lovecraft himself categorised his work). Two prominent examples from 2016 bring cosmic horror full circle by using it to explore racism and xenophobia in the United States: *The Ballad of Black Tom* by Victor LaValle revisits Lovecraft's story 'The Horror at Red Hook' (1925) from an African-American perspective; meanwhile, Matt Ruff's *Lovecraft Country* (and the 2020 television series) depicts the Jim Crow era as experienced through the eyes of a Black SF fan. More recently again, though similarly riffing on the subgenre's origins (in this case Lovecraft's 'The Whisperer in Darkness', 1931), Caitlin R. Kiernan's *Agents of Dreamland* (2017) mixes surrealism and **Body Horror** with a story of a fungus-obsessed doomsday cult and something unknowable lurking in deep space.

A Spotter's Guide: Shapeless Congeries of Protoplasmic Bubbles

- **Main character:** Cosmic horror protagonists tend to be individuals who are isolated, either geographically or socially, something that leaves them vulnerable to the subgenre's creeping psychosis. They're often a(n initially) rational academic, scholar, or studious type who devotes

---

8. Mariani, 2014, n.p.
9. Mariani, 2014, n.p.
10. Mariani, 2014, n.p.

considerable time to researching "sinister prehistories involving god-like species that existed before mankind" (something that in turn allows you the opportunity to create epistolary elements by incorporating faux-historical documents into your writing).[11] It's not unusual for the backbone of a cosmic-horror tale to be a protagonist's search for answers beyond their understanding (and neither, let us tell you, is it uncommon for real-life academics to go mad when they realise that their life's work has been futile!).

- **Setting:** Such stories are often set in places that ping our innate sense of "wrongness", such as intricate labyrinths in the Antarctic mountains or collapsed cities on the ruins of a shattered planet (as in Grant Morrison and Chris Burnham's comic *Nameless*, 2015). VanderMeer's *Annihilation*, for example, is set in a quarantined domain known as Area X, a place that resists knowability, where "normal certainties are inverted".[12] Another classic example is Lovecraft's own "nightmare corpse-city of R'lyeh," a place of "mud, ooze, and weedy Cyclopean masonry which can be nothing less than the tangible substance of Earth's supreme terror".[13] All "attempts to theorise and 'think'" these settings "are pitifully inadequate" for they are "weird in a way that transcends concepts of natural or unnatural".[14]

- **Vagueness of description:** Throughout this book we've discussed the power of sensory detail and specificity in creating convincing fiction. In the case of cosmic horror, however, a certain vagueness is actually beneficial! Specifically, this applies to the antagonists and their realms or seats of power as they tend to evoke an inherent unknowability. The eldritch beings' appearance occasionally distorts reality itself, which renders precise description impossible. Cosmic horror is thus unique in terms of how it derives its impact from "the gap between objects and the power of language to describe them".[15] Remember though, it's usually better to depict these as elusive, fragmentary impressions and as confusion or uncertainty on the part of your protagonist (perhaps as part of their psychic collapse) than to resort to something like a character saying, "It was indescribable!" That tends to come off a little lazy.

- **Character motivation:** Cosmic-horror antagonists are frequently locked out of our reality, be it by their own actions or by some kind of resistance or alliance against them in the deep past. They'll often be "sleeping" or in some other form of hibernation. Many stories revolve

---

11. Mariani, 2014, n.p.
12. Morton 2013, p. 5.
13. Lovecraft, 1928, n.p.
14. Tompkins, 2014, n.p.
15. Harman, 2012, p. 10.

around efforts—by human worshipers or by misguided scientists—to free or wake them. The question of inevitability (will these "gods" rise no matter what?) is really a measure of how closely the author wishes to hew to this subgenre's defining pessimism.
- **"Cosmic" style:** In terms of style, OG cosmic-horror stories are characterised by "faux-archaisms", "adjectival overload", and a "distanced, documentarian approach to the narrative".[16] Nowadays, though some writers still favour a prose "that distends by gradual degrees from quasi-clinical passages into strained heights", readability and literary flair are more in vogue.[17] Whatever you choose, the crucial thing is that this subgenre creates a feeling of distress via sensations of strangeness and *wrongness*.

Things That are Cool About Cosmic Horror

It's always a challenge to write about the terror of the incomprehensible. A challenge, too, to write about characters losing their minds (as such, cosmic horror shares some characteristics with **Psychological Horror**). But, more than that, this is a *trippy* subgenre to write! It eschews an excess of goriness for a fear of knowledge of the outside universe (and here we might note that Lovecraft only rarely left his very White Rhode Island). This outside "breaks through in encounters with anomalous entities from the deep past, in altered states of consciousness, [and] in bizarre twists in the structure of time".[18] In this way cosmic horror offers an alternative to traditional fantasy stories about an *escape* into another world. They are, instead, the ultimate intrusion narratives.

How to Think About the Unthinkable

Comic-horror antagonists are unfathomable to mere humans. They've existed for eons and live on a level far beyond us, yet, once our characters notice them, they're impossible to ignore. The philosopher Timothy Morton has developed a useful concept for thinking about just these kinds of entities "that are massively distributed in time and space relative to humans".[19] He calls these "hyperobjects" and, fittingly, holds them (metaphorically!) responsible "for the end of the world".[20] Their characteristics can serve as a quick checklist when writing cosmic horror:

---
16. Thornton, 2017 n.p.
17. Stableford and Clute, 2022, n.p.
18. Fisher, 2016, p. 16.
19. Morton, 2010, p. 1.
20. Morton, 2013, p. 2.

- **You can't escape them:** Cosmic horror antagonists "are viscous, which means that they 'stick' to beings that are involved with them".[21] Yet, for writers, this isn't just the innate sliminess and gooiness of beings drawn largely from the imagery of cephalopods (Google image search is your friend here!). The entities in these stories infect imaginations as easily as bodies; they're the evil that stares back out of the infinite abyss and the madness that comes in its wake. Once our characters become aware of the cosmic horrors just out of sight, they can never again be free of them.
- **You can't understand them:** They're "nonlocal" and so "any 'local manifestation' of a hyperobject is not directly the hyperobject".[22] What this means, in other somewhat mangled words, is that the tentacle is not the territory. Our character may experience the influence or appearance of the cosmic horror on our plane of existence, but they can never fully conceive or understand them. They can see the outbreaks of mania across the world catalysed by knowledge of something inhuman, but the grotesque beings behind it remain elusive; they can see a history of worship through scattered statues and manuscripts in museums and libraries, but they cannot fully grasp the belief system at play.
- **You can't set your watch by them:** Hyperobjects "involve profoundly different temporalities than the human-scale ones we are used to".[23] This is easily applied to Cosmic antagonists as they have typically endured for measureless eons of deep time. They exist and operate on timescales that dwarf human action and lifespan. In some cases, they even distort time (and space) itself, with various cosmic-horror beings, like some hyperobjects, generating "spacetime vortices, due to general relativity".[24] Their very presence warps reality around them and, as such, the temporal and physical geometry of the settings in these tales is often described in non-Euclidean terms (see M.C. Escher's artwork or the final sections of 'The Call of Cthulhu' for good examples).
- **You can't always see (all of) them:** These entities "occupy a high-dimensional phase space that results in their being invisible to humans for stretches of time".[25] We can see this in how entities such as The Great Old Ones phase in and out of our reality and so in and out of our awareness and comprehension. They're often locked away in literal alternate dimensions. As such, our protagonists can't entirely experience them either sensually within the storyworld—mind out of

---

21. Morton, 2013, p. 1.
22. Morton, 2013, p. 1 and 64.
23. Morton, 2013, p. 1.
24. Morton, 2013, p. 1.
25. Morton, 2013, p. 1.

the gutter, please; this means in terms of the characters' *senses*—or aesthetically in terms of their depiction within the narrative (consider this a writing challenge!). When interacting with malevolent cosmic gods, our characters ever only "see brief patches" of these gigantic entitles as they "intersect" with the world.[26]

- **You can't predict where they'll be:** Finally, "they exhibit their effects interobjectively; that is, they can be detected in a space that consists of interrelationships between aesthetic properties of objects".[27] A good example of this is the rampage of the invisible entity towards the end of 'The Dunwich Horror'. The townsfolk (until the very end) can't see that creature at all. They can only know it through its impact on the things around it, through the destruction that it causes to the objects it interacts with. This is because beings from cosmic horror are "hyper"—meaning over, beyond, or above measure—compared to human protagonists. They emerge from a sometimes figurative, sometimes literal "abyss" of/in/under spacetime, but they can and do interact with objects on our plane.[28] It is by these interactions that our protagonists come to know them.

---

26. Morton, 2013, p. 71.
27. Morton, 2013, p. 1.
28. Morton, 2013, p. 81.

ACTIVITIES

Academic research: Write a story about a scholar who has discovered a manuscript about a mysterious cult. Your character becomes obsessed with tracking down additional evidence of this group's practices and deity of choice. They begin to become alienated from their family and friends as they explore, for instance, libraries, archaeological sites, and so on until they discover a hidden city in a distant and difficult-to-reach location. What do they find within? And will it drive them mad? This activity may be a good opportunity to practice epistolary writing—that is, fiction in the form of letters between people—or other textual interventions such as fictional academic papers.

Humans are the cosmic horror: Humanity's insignificance is a core aspect of cosmic horror, but let's flip the table on this: write a story from the perspective of, say, an ant or a butterfly or any other small creature from whose perspective *we* are the hyperobject-like Great Old Ones. The idea here is to practice capturing the sense of awe and fear that occurs when encountering a ginormous and incomprehensible being that wanders in and out of your reality without even really noticing you.

CONCLUDING THOUGHTS

Like the Nick Fury post-credits scene at the end of a Marvel movie, we have one last thing to say. Fury used to talk about a group of extraordinary people who could fight the battles that others never could. He was talking about heroes, but he might as well have been talking about writers: about people like you who stand up for varied perspectives and positions, people who make us laugh and cry, and people help us process the challenges of our lives.

That may seem too big a claim for stories about spaceships or witches, but writers like you are the alchemists of modern life. You take images, ideas, philosophies—the basic elements of writing—and combine them to create new heroes and villains, new worlds and creatures. The stories you tell with these elements help readers make better sense of the reality around them or even of their own internal struggles. Sure, what we do as writers might sometimes seem supernatural, but that's only because storytelling, as Arthur C. Clarke once put it, is such a sufficiently advanced technology that it appears to be magic.[1] A mastery of it is, as we hope we have demonstrated in this book, the result of time and attention and practice and observation.

But mastery of writing also comes with responsibilities. To pick up the pen or wield the keyboard of a writer is to commit to righting wrongs. These can be small acts of heroism that give voices to those who have none, or more ambitious efforts that take a stand on issues that might affect thousands of people. You may say that not every story is didactically "about" issues such as these, and you would be correct, but every story—whether by direct address or by omission—takes a position on the world it is depicting. Know that even the smallest acts of inclusion or acknowledgment in your work will matter.

Because the most important thing is that a writer—a hero—never punches down. As writers, our words carry real weight. They should not mock the vulnerable or perpetuate inequalities. They should seek, even in the darkest of stories, to offer readers something more than mere hopelessness. Which is to say that the genres we work in—Science Fiction, Fantasy, and Horror—have an unrivalled ability to reach deep into the bright shining core of who we are as human beings. They offer us a rich imaginative and visual vocabulary to articulate the seemingly mundane in a multitude of ways that unveil the magic and wonder of our lives. Even the stories you write that you might think are too silly, or too weird or even a little bit twisted, have readers who are waiting for them. So embrace these subgenres and tropes.

Remember that you're a hero.

Know that you're a writer.

---

1. Clarke, 1962.

AUTHORS' BIOGRAPHIES

Tiffani Angus holds a PhD in creative writing and spent over a decade teaching writing and publishing at universities in the US and UK with a special emphasis on SFF/H writing. Her debut novel, *Threading the Labyrinth*, was a finalist for the British Science Fiction Association and British Fantasy Society awards for Best Novel. A Clarion 2009 graduate, she's published fantasy, science fiction, horror, and even erotica short stories. Currently a freelance writer and editor, she's also the co-director of the Underhill Academy, which provides online creative writing and publishing courses for SFF/H writers. She lives in Bury St Edmunds with her partner. You can find her at www.tiffani-angus.com.

Val Nolan holds a PhD in contemporary literature and has taught university level literature and creative practice for over a decade. He is the author of *Neil Jordan: Works for the Page* (UCC Press, 2022) as well as academic articles in *Science Fiction Studies, Foundation, Journal of Graphic Novels and Comic Books, Review of Contemporary Fiction, Irish University Review, Irish Studies Review,* and *Dictionary of Literary Biography*. A Clarion graduate (2009), his own fiction has appeared in *Year's Best Science Fiction, Best of British Science Fiction, Interzone, Unidentified Funny Objects*, and the 'Futures' page of *Nature*. His story 'The Irish Astronaut' was shortlisted for the Theodore Sturgeon Award. He is currently a lecturer in genre fiction and creative writing at Aberystwyth University in Wales.

REFERENCES

@AlexandraErin, (2022) Twitter. Available at: https://twitter.com/AlexandraErin/status/1573667589011787778 (Accessed: 30 September 2022).

@ErinLSnyder. (2022) Twitter. Available at: https://twitter.com/ErinLSnyder/status/1573668677215719424 (Accessed: 30 September 2022).

@EvanNichols. (2022) Twitter. Available at: https://twitter.com/EvanNichols/status/1573056839235039232 (Accessed: 30 September 2022).

@InvaderXan. (2018) 'Solarpunk and Art Nouveau'. *Solarpunk Druid*. Available at: https://Solarpunkdruid.com/Solarpunk-article/Solarpunk-and-art-nouveau/ (Accessed: 6 September 2022).

@last_fandaniel. (2022) Twitter. Available at: https://twitter.com/last_fandaniel/status/1574894986553958411 (Accessed: 20 September 2022).

@OfSymbols. (2022) Twitter. Available at: https://twitter.com/OfSymbols/status/1573505902380032017 (Accessed: 30 September 2022).

Abercrombie, J. (2010) 'The New Sword and Sorcery'. Available at: https://www.joeabercrombie.com (Accessed: 15 February 2022).

Adu-Gyamfi, Y. (2016) '"Thou shalt not suffer a witch to live" (Exod 22:18) and Contemporary Akan Christian Belief and Practice: A Translational and Hermeneutical Problem'. *Old Testament Essays*. Available at: https://www.researchgate.net/publication/302872407_Thou_shalt_not_suffer_a_witch_to_live_Exod_2218_and_contemporary_Akan_Christian_belief_and_practice_A_translational_and_hermeneutical_problem/fulltext/5734f07708ae298602df055c/Thou-shalt-not-suffer-a-witch-to-live-Exod-2218-and-contemporary-Akan-Christian-belief-and-practice-A-translational-and-hermeneutical-problem.pdf (Accessed: 20 July 2022).

Amazon.com. (N.D.) 'Content Guidelines for Books', in: Author, Publisher and Vendor Guides, Available at: https://www.amazon.com/gp/help/customer/display.html?nodeId=15015801&language=en_US&ref=efph_home_cont_200164670 (Accessed: March 1, 2022).

Angus, T. (2017) 'Where Are the Tampons? The Estrangement of Women's Bodies in Apocalyptic and Post-Apocalyptic Fiction'. Presented at WorldCon 75, Helsinki, Finland.

Ashley, M. (1997) 'Perrault, Charles', in Clute, J. and Grant, J. (eds.), *The Encyclopedia of Fantasy*, Available at: https://sf-encyclopedia.com/entry/perrault_charles (Accessed: 8 Feb 2022).

Asimov, I. (1950) *I, Robot*. New York: Gnome Press.

Asselin, S. (2019) 'Margret Cavendish', in Levy, M.M. and Mendlesohn, F. (eds.), *Aliens in Popular Culture*. Greenwood: Santa Barbara, CA, 2019, pp. 74–75.

Atwood, M. (2011) 'Margaret Atwood: the road to Ustopia', *The Guardian*, Available at: https://www.theguardian.com/books/2011/oct/14/margaret-atwood-road-to-ustopia (Accessed: 19 July 2022)

Avery, D., Dir. (2014) *One-Minute Time Machine*, Available at: https://www.youtube.com/watch?v=vBkBS4O3yvY (Accessed: 1 July 2022).

Bailey, L. (2022) 'Now Is the Time for Arnold Schwarzenegger to Make King Conan', *MovieWeb*, Available at: https://movieweb.com/now-is-the-time-arnold-schwarzenegger-king-conan/ (Accessed: 27 September 2022).

Balasopoulos, A. (2006) 'Anti-Utopia and Dystopia: Rethinking the Generic Field', Available at: https://www.academia.edu/1008203/_Anti_Utopia_and_Dystopia_Rethinking_the_Generic_Field_ (Accessed: 5 Sep 2022)

Banton, M.P. (2021) 'The Development of Professional Policing in England', *Britannica*, Available at: https://www.britannica.com/topic/police/The-development-of-professional-policing-in-England (Accessed 28 July 2022).

Bellis, M. (2019) 'History of Airships and Balloons', *ThoughtCo*, Available at: https://www.thoughtco.com/history-of-airships-and-balloons-1991241#:~:text=Ferdinand%20Zeppelin%201838%2D1917,in%20Germany%2C%20carrying%20five%20passengers (Accessed: 19 July 2022).

Benford, G. (1986/87) 'Effing the Ineffable: An Essay', *Foundation* #38 (Winter), p. 23.

Benford, G. (2019) 'Introduction', in Levy, M.M. and Mendlesohn, F. (eds.), *Aliens in Popular Culture*. Westport, CT: Greenwood, p. xiv.

Blish, J. (N.D.) '"Call a rabbit a smeerp"', *Turkey City Lexicon*, Available at: https://fritzfreiheit.com/wiki/Turkey_City_Lexicon (Accessed: 27 August 2022).

Bloom, C. (1998) *Gothic Horror: A Reader's Guide from Poe to King and Beyond*. London: Macmillan.

Boym, S. (2001) *The Future of Nostalgia*. New York: Basic Books.

Bradshaw, P. (2017) 'George A Romero: the zombie master whose ideas infected American cinema', *The Guardian*, Available at: https://www.theguardian.com/film/2017/jul/17/george-a-romero-director-night-of-the-living-dead-zombies (Accessed: 2 Aug 2022).

Brain, J. (N.D.) 'Historia Regum Britanniae', *Historic UK*, Available at: https://www.historic-uk.com/HistoryUK/HistoryofEngland/Historia-Regum-Britanniae/ (Accessed 13 Aug 2022).

Bregman, R. (2017) *Utopia for Realists*. London: Bloomsbury.

British Library, The. (2022) 'Beowulf', Available at: https://www.bl.uk/works/beowulf (Accessed: 13 Aug 2022.)

British Library, The (N.D.) 'King James VI and I's Demonology, 1597', Available at: https://www.bl.uk/collection-items/king-james-vi-and-is-demonology-1597 (Accessed: 20 July 2022).

Britt, K.W. (2020) 'Papermaking', *Britannica*, Available at: https://www.britannica.com/technology/papermaking (Accessed: 29 July 2022).

Brodeur, J.P., Walsh, W.F., Whetstone, T., Banton, M.P., and Kelling, G.L. (2021) 'police', *Encyclopaedia Britannica*, Available at: https://www.britannica.com/topic/police (Accessed: 29 July 2022).

Brooks, K.D. (2016) 'The Multiple Pasts, Presents, and Futures of Nnedi Okorafor's Literary Nigeria', *Los Angeles Review of Books*, Available at: https://lareviewofbooks.org/article/the-multiple-pasts-presents-and-futures-of-nnedi-okorafors-literary-nigeria/ (Accessed: 7 February 2022).

Bullard, T.E. (1989) 'UFO Abduction Reports: The Supernatural Kidnap Narrative Returns in Technological Guise', *The Journal of American Folklore*, 102 (404), pp. 147–170.

Buranyi, S. (2017) 'Rise of the racist robots – how AI is learning all our worst impulses', *The Guardian*, Available at: https://www.theguardian.com/inequality/2017/aug/08/rise-of-the-racist-robots-how-ai-is-learning-all-our-worst-impulses (Accessed: 19 July 2022).

Burk, J. (2014) 'You Sick Fuck, or Why I Love Extreme Horror', Available at: https://jeffburk.wordpress.com/2014/01/28/you-sick-fuck-or-why-i-love-extreme-horror/ (Accessed: 16 August 2022).

Butler, A.M. (2012). *Solar Flares: Science Fiction in the 1970s*. Liverpool: Liverpool University Press.

Caroti, S. (2011) *The Generation Starship in Science Fiction*. Jefferson NC: McFarland.

Cassells Household Guide. (c. 1880s) Vol 3, Death in the Household (1) (2) (3) (4). Available at: https://www.victorianlondon.org/cassells/cassells-35.htm (Accessed: 7 Aug 2022).

Cassese, E.C. (2017) 'George Romero's zombies will make Americans reflect on racial violence long after his death', *The Conversation*, Available at: https://theconversation.com/george-romeros-zombies-will-make-americans-reflect-on-racial-violence-long-after-his-death-81583 (Accessed: 2 Aug 2022).

Casteel, K., Wolfe, J. and Nguyen, M. (2018) 'What We Know About Victims of Sexual Assault in America', Available at: https://projects.fivethirtyeight.com/sexual-assault-victims/ (Accessed: 4 Aug 2022).

Centers for Disease Control and Prevention (CDC) (U.S.), Office of Public Health Preparedness and Response (2011) 'Preparedness 101; zombie pandemic', Available at: https://stacks.cdc.gov/view/cdc/6023 (Accessed :19 July 2022).

Chambers, B. (2021) in 'If the Aliens Lay Eggs, how does that Affect Architecture?: Sci-fi Writers on how they Build their Worlds', *The Guardian*, Available at: https://www.theguardian.com/books/2021/jan/05/if-the-aliens-lay-eggs-how-does-that-affect-architecture-sci-fi-writers-on-how-they-build-their-worlds (Accessed: 8 February 2022).

Cherry, K. (2022) 'A Historical Timeline of Modern Psychology', Available at: https://www.verywellmind.com/timeline-of-modern-psychology-2795599#:~:text=The%20Birth%20of%20Modern%20Psychology&text=Still%20others%20suggest%20that%20modern,as%20it%20still%20does%20today (Accessed: 5 Aug 2022).

Clarke, A.C. (1962) *Profiles of the Future; an Inquiry into the Limits of the Possible*. London: Gollancz.

Clarke, I.F. (1979) *The Pattern of Expectation, 1644–2001*. New York: Basic Books.

Climo, L. (2019) 'A Note from the Collections: Midwives and Healers in the European Witch Trials', *International Museum of Surgical Science*, Available at: https://imss.org/2019/12/18/a-note-from-the-collections-midwives-and-healers-in-the-european-witch-trials/ (Accessed: 20 July 2022).

Clute, J. (1997) 'Polidori, John'. in Clute, J. and Grant, J. (eds.), *The Encyclopedia of Fantasy*, Available at: https://sf-encyclopedia.com/entry/polidori_john (Accessed: 7 August 2022).

Clute, J. (1997) 'Taproot Texts'. in Clute, J. and Grant, J. (eds.), *The Encyclopedia of Fantasy*, Available at: https://sf-encyclopedia.com/entry/taproot_texts (Accessed: 8 Feb 2022).

Cole, S. (2017) 'Dracula Makes the Rules: Visionary Author Bram Stoker Born 170 Years Ago Today!' *Nightmare on Film Street*, Available at: https://nofspodcast.com/dracula-makes-rules-visionary-author-bram-stoker-born-170-years-ago-today (Accessed: 7 Aug 2022).

Crispin, A.C. (1989) 'Andre Norton: Notes from the Witch World', *Starlog Magazine* (147), pp. 54–57, Available at: https://archive.org/details/starlog_magazine-147/page/n53/mode/1up (Accessed: 8 Aug 2022).

Dagnall, N. and Drinkwater, K. (2018) 'The science of superstition – and why people believe in the unbelievable', *The Conversation*, Available at: https://theconversation.com/the-science-of-superstition-and-why-people-believe-in-the-unbelievable-97043 (Accessed: Aug 3 2022).

Davis, M. (2018) Personal website, Available at: https://www.miltonjdavis.com/who-i-am (Accessed: 9 Aug 2022).

Davison-Vecchione, D. (2021) 'Dystopia and Social Theory', *Ideology Theory Practice*, Available at: https://www.ideology-theory-practice.org/blog/dystopia-and-social-theory#_edn13 (Accessed: 28 March 2022).

Del Monte, L.A. (2013) 'Do Time Travel Paradoxes Negate the Possibility of Time Travel?' Available at: https://louisdelmonte.com/dotime-travel-paradoxes-negate/ (Accessed: 16 Aug 2022).

Del Rincón Yohn, M. (2021) 'J.R.R. Tolkien's Sub-Creation Theory: Literary Creativity as Participation in the Divine Creation', *Church, Communication and Culture*, 6(1), pp. 17–33.

Diodati, M. (2020) 'The Space Problem of Time Travel', *Medium*, Available at: https://medium.com/amazing-science/the-space-problem-of-time-travel-93b873264b98 (Accessed: 1 Aug 2022).

Doughan, D., MBE. (2021) 'J.R.R. Tolkien: A Biographical Sketch', *The Tolkien Society*, Available at: https://www.tolkiensociety.org/author/biography/ (Accessed: 2 Aug 2022).

Dowell, D.R. (2022) 'What Makes Japanese Horror Movies So Uniquely Frightening?' *GameRant*, Available at: https://gamerant.com/japanese-horror-movies-uniquely-frightening/ (Accessed: 19 July 2022).

Doyle, C.C., Shapiro, F.R., and Mieder, W. (eds.) (2012) *The Dictionary of Modern Proverbs*. New Haven, CT: Yale University Press, pp. 76–77.

Dozois, G. (ed.) (2017) *The Book of Swords*. London: Harper Voyager.

Ebert, R. (1987) 'Hellraiser', Available at: https://www.rogerebert.com/reviews/hellraiser-1987 (Accessed: 27 September 2022).

Eaton, S. (2021) 'Witches and the Devil in Early Modern Visual Cultures: Constructions of the Demonic Other', *Midland Historical Review*, Available at: http://www.midlandshistoricalreview.com/witches-and-the-devil-in-early-modern-visual-cultures-constructions-of-the-demonic-other/ (Accessed: 20 July 2022).

Eddy, C. (2019) 'Marlon James Talks Superheroes, the Joy of Fantasy, and His Stunning New Book *Black Leopard, Red Wolf*', Available at: https://gizmodo.com/marlon-james-talks-superheroes-the-joy-of-fantasy-and-1832275142 (Accessed: 24 September 2022).

Editors of *Encyclopaedia Britannica*, The. (2012) 'garden city', *Encyclopaedia Britannica*, Available at: https://www.britannica.com/topic/garden-city-urban-planning (Accessed: 4 August 2022).

Editors of *Encyclopaedia Britannica*, The. (2021) 'King Arthur', *Encyclopaedia Britannica*, Available at: https://www.britannica.com/topic/King-Arthur (Accessed: 13 August 2022).

Editors of *Encyclopaedia Britannica*, The. (2022) 'cyberpunk', *Encyclopaedia Britannica*, Available at: https://www.britannica.com/art/cyberpunk (Accessed: 28 September 2022).

Emery, D. (2021) 'Was This Victorian-Era Contraption Meant to Keep Vampires in Their Graves?' Available at: https://www.snopes.com/fact-check/victorian-grave-cage-mortsafe/ (Accessed: 2 Aug 2022).

Evans, M. (2009) *The Imagination of Evil: Detective Fiction and the Modern World*. London: Continuum.

Fisher, M. (2016) *The Weird and the Eerie (Beyond the Unheimlich)*. London: Repeater Books. [accessed both via Kindle and via paper book]

Fisher, M. (2018) *Flatline Constructs: Gothic Materialism and Cybernetic Theory-Fiction*. New York: Exmilitary Press.

Flynn, A. (2014) 'Solarpunk: Notes Toward a Manifesto', *Hieroglyph*, Available at: https://hieroglyph.asu.edu/2014/09/solarpunk-notes-toward-a-manifesto (Accessed: 6 September 2022).

Fornaro, M., Clementi, M. and Fornaro, P. (2009) 'Medicine and psychiatry in Western culture: Ancient Greek myths and modern prejudices', *Annals of General Psychiatry*, Available at: https://annals-general-psychiatry.biomedcentral.com/articles/10.1186/1744-859X-8-21 (Accessed: 5 Aug 2022).

Freiheit, F. (N.D.) 'Fat Writing', *Turkey City Lexicon*, Available at: https://fritzfreiheit.com/wiki/Turkey_City_Lexicon (Accessed: 27 August 2022).

Fultz, J.R. (2018) 'The Mud, The Blood and The Years: Why "Grimdark" is the New "Sword and Sorcery", *Grimdark Magazine*, Available at: https://www.grimdarkmagazine.com/grimdark-is-the-new-sword-and-sorcery (Accessed: 29 September 2022).

FuneralBasics.org. (N.D.) '8 Intriguing Funeral Customs from the Victorian Era', Available at: https://www.funeralbasics.org/8-intriguing-funeral-customs-victorian-era/ (Accessed: 2 Aug 2022).

Games Workshop Limited. (N.D.) Available at: https://warhammer40000.com/ (Accessed: 1 July 2022).

Gleick, J. (2019) *Time Travel: A History*. London: 4th Estate.

Goicoechea, M. (2020) 'Bruce Sterling: Schismatrix Plus (Case Study)', in McFarlane, A., Murphy, G.J., Schmeink, L. (eds.), *The Routledge Companion to Cyberpunk Culture*. London: Routledge, pp. 24–31.

Goodare, J. (2019) 'A royal obsession with black magic started Europe's most brutal witch hunts', *National Geographic*, Available at: https://www.nationalgeographic.co.uk/history-and-civilisation/2019/10/royal-obsession-black-magic-started-europes-most-brutal-witch#:~:text=In%20the%201590s%2C%20King%20James,torture%20and%20death%20of%20thousands.&text=Burning%20witches%20alive%20was%20common,before%20their%20bodies%20were%20burned (Accessed: 20 July 2022).

Grossman, L. (2009) *The Magicians*. New York: Viking.

Haddad, D. (N.D.) 'An Interview with Cemetery Research Expert Joy Neighbors', *Family Tree Magazine*, Available at: https://familytreemagazine.com/cemeteries/cemetery-superstitions-little-known-facts-and-genealogy-secrets/ (Accessed 3 Aug 2022).

Hamilton, J. (2017) 'Explainer: "Solarpunk", or How to be an Optimistic Radical', *The Conversation*, Available at: https://theconversation.com/explainer-Solarpunk-or-how-to-be-an-optimistic-radical-80275 (Accessed: 22 July 2022).

Hampton, G.J. (2015) *Imagining Slaves and Robots in Literature, Film, and Popular Culture: Reinventing Yesterday's Slave with Tomorrow's Robot*. Lanham, MD: Lexington Books.

Hansard Commons (12 March 1868). Vol. 190. Available at: https://api.parliament.uk/historic-hansard/commons/1868/mar/12/adjourned-debate#S3V0190P0_18680312_HOC_54 (Accessed: 23 June 2022).

Harman, G. (2012) *Weird Realism: Lovecraft and Philosophy*. Winchester: Zero Books.

Hassett-Walker, C. (2021) 'How You Start is How You Finish? The Slave Patrol and Jim Crow Origins of Policing', *American Bar Association*, Available at: https://www.americanbar.org/groups/crsj/publications/human_rights_magazine_home/civil-rights-reimagining-policing/how-you-start-is-how-you-finish/ (Accessed 28 July 2022).

History.com Editors. (2020) 'First detective story is published', *History*, Available at: https://www.history.com/this-day-in-history/first-detective-story-is-published#:~:text=Edgar%20Allan%20Poe's%20story%2C%20%22The,series%20of%20murders%20in%20Paris (Accessed: 29 July 2022).

Hobbes, T. (1839-1845) *English Works*, in Molesworth, W. (ed.) (i. 85) Quoted in Gleick, J. (2019) *Time Travel: A History*. London: 4th Estate.

Horror Writers Association. (2012) Available at: https://horror.org/2011-bram-stoker-award-winners-and-vampire-novel-of-the-century-award-winner (Accessed: 7 Aug 2022).

Hunt, A., et al. (2022) 'Robots Enact Malignant Stereotypes', *FAccT '22: 2022 ACM Conference on Fairness, Accountability, and Transparency*, pp. 743–756.

Huq, R. (2020) 'How British politics forgot the suburbs – and why they should come first for reinvestment', *The New Statesman*, Available at: https://www.newstatesman.com/politics/uk-politics/2020/02/how-british-politics-forgot-suburbs-and-why-they-should-come-first-reinvestment (Accessed 4 Aug 2022).

Hurley, K. (2013) 'We Have Always Fought: Challenging the Women, Cattle and Slaves Narrative', *A Dribble of Ink*, Available at: https://aidanmoher.com/blog/featured-article/2013/05/we-have-always-fought-challenging-the-women-cattle-and-slaves-narrative-by-kameron-hurley/ (Accessed: 25 Oct 2022).

Hurley, K. (N.D.) 'Worldbreaker Saga', Available at: https://www.kameronhurley.com/worldbreaker-saga/ (Accessed: 6 Aug 2022).

Isto, R. (2019) 'How Dumb Are Big Dumb Objects? OOO, Science Fiction, and Scale', *Open Philosophy*, #2, p. 554.

Jackson, R. (1981) *Fantasy: The Literature of Subversion*. Oxford: Routledge.

James, E. (1999) 'Per ardua ad astra: Authorial Choice and the Narrative of Interstellar Travel', in Elsner, J. and Rubies, J-P. (eds.), *Voyages and Visions: Towards a cultural history of Travel*. London: Reaktion Books, pp. 252–271.

James, L. (2019) 'The Nine Types of Vampires and What They Represent', *Unwinnable*, Available at: https://unwinnable.com/2019/04/21/the-nine-types-of-vampires-and-what-they-represent/ (Accessed: 7 August 2022).

Jameson, F. (1973) 'Generic Discontinuities in SF: Brian Aldiss' Starship'. Science Fiction Studies, 1(2), pp. 57–68.

Jameson, F. (1991) *Postmodernism, or the Cultural Logic of Late Capitalism*. Durham, NC: Duke University Press, pp. 331–340.

Jenkins, S. and Taylor, P. (1984) 'Wolf at the Door'. *Monthly Film Bulletin*, pp. 264–65. Reprinted in Zucker, C. (2013) *Neil Jordan: Interviews*. Jackson, MS: University Press of Mississippi, p. 49.

Johnstone, M. (2019) 'Ursula K. Le Guin', in Levy, M.M. and Mendlesohn, F. (eds.), *Aliens in Popular Culture*. Santa Barbara: Greenwood, CA, pp. 158–159.

Jong, D. (2019) 'Civilization and Its (Dys)contents: Savagery, Technological Progress and Capitalism in Industrial and Information Dystopias', *Intersect*, 12(3), pp. 1–23.

Jordan, J.M. (2019) 'The Czech Play That Gave Us the Word "Robot"', *MIT Press Reader*, Available at: https://thereader.mitpress.mit.edu/origin-word-robot-rur/ (Accessed: 23 September 2022).

Jordison, S. (2011) 'Back to the Hugos: *The Forever War* by Joe Haldeman', *The Guardian*, Available at: https://www.theguardian.com/books/booksblog/2011/apr/14/back-to-the-hugos-joe-haldeman (Accessed: 7 July 2022).

Joshi, S.T. (1995) *Miscellaneous Writings*. Sauk City, WI: Arkham House, pp. 165–166.

Joyce, J. *Ulysses*. (excerpt) Available at: https://archive.org/stream/MollyBloomMonologEnd/MollyBloomMonologhyEnd_djvu.txt (Accessed: 28 July 2022).

Kane, P. (2015) *The Hellraiser Films and Their Legacy*. Jefferson, NC: McFarland.

Kaveney, R. (1981) 'Science Fiction in the 1970s: Some Dominant Themes and Personalities', *Foundation*, #22, pp. 5–34.

Ketterer, D. (1989) 'Margaret Atwood's *The Handmaid's Tale*: A Contextual Dystopia', *Science Fiction Studies*, 16(2), pp. 209–217.

Killheffer, R.K.J., Stableford, B.M. and Langford, D. (2022) 'Aliens' in Clute, J. and Langford, D. (eds.), *The Encyclopedia of Science Fiction*, Available at: https://sf-encyclopedia.com/entry/aliens (Accessed: 8 February 2022).

King, S. (2006) *Danse Macabre*. London: Hodder. Kindle Edition.

Kirkus. (2018) *The Grey Bastards*, Available at: https://www.kirkusreviews.com/book-reviews/jonathan-french/grey-bastards/ (Accessed: 6 Aug 2022.).

La Bossiere, C. R. (1974) 'Review: "The Scarlet Empire": Two Visions in One', *Science Fiction Studies*, 1(4), pp. 290–292.

Lacina, L. (2020) 'How Betty and Barney Hill's Alien Abduction Story Defined the Genre', *History*, Available at: https://www.history.com/news/first-alien-abduction-account-barney-betty-hill (Accessed: 9 May 2022).

Laman, D. (2021) 'The Enduring Appeal of Body Horror', *Collider*, Available at: https://collider.com/why-body-horror-is-good/ (Accessed: 13 Aug 2022).

Lamhourne, R., Shallis, M., and Shortland, M. (1990) *Close Encounters? Science and Science Fiction*. Bristol and New York: Adam Hilger.

Langford, D. (2022) 'Zombies' in Clute, J. and Langford, D. (eds.), *The Encyclopedia of Science Fiction*, Available at: https://sf-encyclopedia.com/entry/zombies (Accessed: 4 August 2022).

Langford, D. and Nicholls, P. (2021) 'Macrostructures' in Clute, J. and Langford, D. (eds.), *The Encyclopedia of Science Fiction*, Available at: https://sf-encyclopedia.com/entry/macrostructures (Accessed: 7 Sept. 2022).

Latham, R. (2020) 'Literary Precursors', in McFarlane, A., Murphy, G.J., and Schmeink, L. (eds.), *The Routledge Companion to Cyberpunk Culture*. London: Routledge, pp. 7–14.

Lauri, M. (2013) 'Utopias in the Islamic Middle Ages: Ibn Ṭufayl and Ibn al-Nafīs', *Utopian Studies*, 24(1), pp. 23–40.

Lauro, S.J. (2015) *The Transatlantic Zombie: Slavery, Rebellion, and Living Death*. New Brunswick: Rutgers University Press.

Le Guin, U.K. (1979) 'The Child and the Shadow' in Wood, S. (ed.), *The Language of the Night: Essays on Science Fiction and Fantasy*. New York: Perigee, pp. 59–71.

Le Guin, U.K. (1979) 'Escape Routes' in Wood, S. (ed.), *The Language of the Night: Essays on Science Fiction and Fantasy*. New York: Perigee, pp. 201–206.

Le Guin, U.K. (2017) 'Ursula K. Le Guin Explains How to Build a New Kind of Utopia', *Electric Lit*, Available at: https://electricliterature.com/ursula-k-le-guin-explains-how-to-build-a-new-kind-of-utopia-15c7b07e95fc (Accessed: 28 March 2022).

Le Guin, U.K. (2017) 'Utopiyin, Utopiyang'. *No Time to Spare: Thinking About What Matters*. New York: Houghton Mifflin Harcourt, p.85.

Lem, S. (1984) *Microworlds*. Boston: Houghton Mifflin Harcourt.

Lewis, A.H. (1896) 'Further Facts in the the case of the Labour Record of Mark Hanna, the Republican Party's Manager', Owensboro Daily Record, Oct. 16 1896, p. 2.

Li, G. (2013) '"New Year's Dream": A Chinese Anarcho-cosmopolitan Utopia', *Utopian Studies*, 24(1), pp. 89–104.

Lindsay, D. (1920) *A Voyage to Arcturus*. London: Methuen & Co. Ltd.

Lloyd, A.J. (2007) 'Education, Literacy and the Reading Public', *British Library Newspapers*, Detroit: Gale. Available at: https://www.gale.com/binaries/content/assets/gale-us-en/primary-sources/intl-gps/intl-gps-essays/full-ghn-contextual-essays/ghn_essay_bln_lloyd3_website.pdf (Accessed: 29 July 2022).

Lovecraft, H.P. (1927) 'Supernatural Horror in Literature', *The Recluse*, No. 1, pp. 23–59. Found online at: https://www.hplovecraft.com/writings/texts/essays/shil.aspx (Accessed: 26 September 2022).

Lovecraft, H.P. (1928) 'The Call of Cthulhu', *Weird Tales* 11(2), pp. 159–178, 287. Found online at: https://www.hplovecraft.com/writings/texts/fiction/cc.aspx (Accessed: 26 September 2022).

Luckhurst, R. (2014) The Victorian Supernatural', *British Library*, Available at: https://www.bl.uk/romantics-and-victorians/articles/the-victorian-supernatural#:~:text=Spiritualism%20in%20literature,the%20histrionics%20of%20the%20Gothic (Accessed: 20 July 2022).
Lupton, J.H. (ed.) (1895) *The Utopia of Sir Thomas More*. Oxford.

Mackay, C. (2021; 1852) *Extraordinary Popular Delusions and the Madness of Crowds*, Available at: https://www.gutenberg.org/files/24518/24518-h/24518-h.htm#witch (Accessed: 20 July 2022).

Malerman, J. (2014) *Bird Box*. London: Harper Voyager.

Malmgren, C.D. (1993) 'Self and Other in SF: Alien Encounters', *Science Fiction Studies*, 20(1), pp. 15–33.

March-Russell, P. (2020) 'Urban fantasy novels: why they matter and which ones to read first', *The Conversation*, Available at: https://theconversation.com/urban-fantasy-novels-why-they-matter-and-which-ones-to-read-first-137942#:~:text=The%20history%20of%20urban%20fantasy,of%20Bleak%20House%20(1853) (Accessed: July 18, 2022).

Mariani, M. (2014) 'Terror Incognita: The Paradoxical History of Cosmic Horror, from Lovecraft to Ligotti', *LA Review of Books*, Available at: https://lareviewofbooks.org/article/terror-incognita-paradoxical-history-cosmic-horror-lovecraft-ligotti/ (Accessed: 2 September 2022).

Mariani, M. (2015) 'The Tragic, Forgotten History of Zombies', *The Atlantic*, Available at: https://www.theatlantic.com/entertainment/archive/2015/10/how-america-erased-the-tragic-history-of-the-zombie/412264/ (Accessed: 2 Aug 2022).

Markley, R. (2019) *Kim Stanley Robinson*. University of Illinois Press: Chicago.

Mayor, A. (2019) 'Robots guarded Buddha's Relics in a Legend of Ancient India', *The Conversation*, Available at: https://theconversation.com/robots-guarded-buddhas-relics-in-a-legend-of-ancient-india-110078 (Accessed: 23 September 2022).

McCammon, R. (ed.) (N.D.) *The Splatterpunk Files*, Available at: http://www.robertmccammon.com/splatterpunks/index.html (Accessed: 14 August 2022).

McFarlane, A. (2022) *Cyberpunk Culture and Psychology: Seeing through the Mirrorshades*. London: Routledge.

McFarlane, A., Murphy, G.J., and Schmeink, L. (eds.) (2020) *The Routledge Companion to Cyberpunk Culture*. London: Routledge.

Mendlesohn, F. (2003) 'Introduction: Reading Science Fiction', in James. E. and Mendlesohn, F. (eds.), *The Cambridge Companion to Science Fiction*. Cambridge: CUP, p. 1–2.

Mes, T. and Sharp, J. (2005) *The Midnight Eye Guide to New Japanese Film*. Berkeley, California: Stone Bridge Press.

Miller, J. (2014) '5 Bizarre Paradoxes of Time Travel Explained', *Astronomy Trek*, Available at: https://www.astronomytrek.com/5-bizarre-paradoxes-of-time-travel-explained/ (Accessed: 15 Aug 2022).

Miller, T.S. (2014) '*Lagoon* by Nnedi Okorafor', *Strange Horizons*, (30), Available at: http://strangehorizons.com/non-fiction/reviews/lagoon-by-nnedi-okorafor/ (Accessed 7 February 2022).

Moore, A. (2012) 'The Round Table at Winchester', *Hampshire History*, Available at: https://www.hampshire-history.com/the-round-table-winchester/ (Accessed 13 Aug 2022).

Mortimer, I. (2013) *The Time Traveller's Guide to Elizabethan England*. London: Vintage Books.

Morton, T. (2010) *The Ecological Thought*. Cambridge, Mass.: Harvard University Press.

Morton, T. (2013) *Hyperobjects: Philosophy and Ecology after the End of the World*. Minneapolis: University of Minnesota Press.

Morton, T. (2022) *Spacecraft*. London: Bloomsbury.

Moylan, T. (2014) *Demand the Impossible*. Oxford: Peter Lang.

Moylan, T. (2000) *Scraps of the Untainted Sky*. London: Routledge.

Murphy, B.M. (2013) *The Rural Gothic in American Popular Culture: Backwoods Horror and Terror in the Wilderness*. Basingstoke: Palgrave Macmillan.

Nagel, T. 'What is it Like to be a Bat?', The Philosophical Review, 83:4 (Oct. 1974), pp. 435–450.

Neal, M. (2014) 'Preparing for extraterrestrial contact', *Risk Management*, 16(2), pp. 63–87.

Nevins, J. (2008) 'Introduction: The 19th-Century Roots of Steampunk' in VanderMeer, A. and VanderMeer, J. (eds.), *Steampunk*. San Francisco: Tachyon, pp. 3–12.

Newman, L.H. (2014) 'Less Than 40 Percent of Web Traffic Comes from Humans', *Slate*, Available at: https://slate.com/technology/2014/02/humans-make-up-only-40-percent-of-web-traffic-the-rest-is-from-bots.html" https://slate.com/technology/2014/02/humans-make-up-only-40-percent-of-web-traffic-the-rest-is-from-bots.html (Accessed: 25 Oct 2022).

Newman, L.S. and Baumeister, R.F. (1996) 'Toward an Explanation of the UFO Abduction Phenomenon: Hypnotic Elaboration, Extraterrestrial Sadomasochism, and Spurious Memories', *Psychological Inquiry*, 7(2), pp. 99–126.

Nicholls, P. (2021) 'Sword and Sorcery', in Clute, J. and Langford, D. (eds.), *The Encyclopedia of Science Fiction*. London, Available at: https://sf-encyclopedia.com/entry/sword_and_sorcery (Accessed: 3 May 2022).

Nicholls, P. and Clute, J. (2021) 'Gothic SF'. in Clute, J. and Langford, D. (eds.), *The Encyclopedia of Science Fiction*. Available at: https://sf-encyclopedia.com/entry/gothic_sf (Accessed: 11 August 2022).

Nicholls, P. and Langford, D (2022) 'Steampunk' in Clute, J. and Langford, D. (eds.), *The Encyclopedia of Science Fiction*, Available at: https://sf-encyclopedia.com/entry/steampunk (Accessed: 27 July 2022).

Niven, L. (1987) 'The Alien in Our Minds', in Slusser, G.E. and Rabkin, E.S. (eds.) *Aliens: The Anthropology of Science Fiction*. Carbondale: Southern Illinois University.

Nolan, V. (2015) 'Utopia is a Way of Saying We Could Do Better: Iain M. Banks and Kim Stanley Robinson in Conversation', *Foundation: The International Review of Science Fiction*, #119, pp. 65–76.

Okorafor, N. (2014) *Lagoon*. London: Hodder and Stoughton.

Online Etymology Dictionary (N.D.) 'Witch', Available at: https://www.etymonline.com/search?q=witch&utm_campaign=sd&utm_medium=serp&utm_source=ds_search (Accessed: 20 July 2022).

Orwell, G. (1949; 1983) *1984*. New York: Penguin Books.

Owl Lady (2016) 'Centauri Dreams: Proxima Centauri & the Imagination', *The Owl Lady's Blog*, Available at: https://owlladysblog.blogspot.com/2016/01/centauri-dreams-proxima-centauri.html (Accessed: 17 June 2022).

Patterson, E. (2022) 'Heroin Crisis in the Suburbs Instead of the Streets', Available at: https://rehabs.com/heroin-streets-to-suburbs/ (Accessed: 4 Aug 2022).

Peck, M. (2012) 'Aircraft Carriers in Space', *Foreign Policy*, Available at: https://foreignpolicy.com/2012/09/28/aircraft-carriers-in-space/ (Accessed: 7 July 2022).

Person, L. (1998) 'Notes Toward a Postcyberpunk Manifesto', *Nova Express*, 4. pp. 11–12

Person, L. (N.D.) 'The Splatterpunks: The Young Turks at Horror's Cutting Edge', *The Splatterpunk Files*, Available at: https://www.robertmccammon.com/splatterpunks/splatter-2.html (Accessed: 14 August 2022).

Petretto, C. (2006) 'Attack of the Living Dead Virus: The Metaphor of Contagious Disease in Zombie Movies', *Journal of the Fantastic in the Arts*, 17(1), pp. 21–32.

Project Gutenberg. (2021) *Beowulf: An Anglo-Saxon Epic Poem*, Translated from The Heyne-Socin Text by Lesslie Hall (1892), https://www.gutenberg.org/files/16328/16328-h/16328-h.htm#III (Accessed: 13 Aug 2022).

Rabkin, E.S. (1977) 'Conflation of Genres and Myths in David Lindsay's *A Voyage to Arcturus*', *The Journal of Narrative Technique*, 7(2), pp. 149–155.

Regalado, M. (2019) '9 nightmarish things in *The Handmaid*'s Tale inspired by history', Available at: https://www.insider.com/handmaids-tale-based-on-real-world-origins-history-events-2019-8 (Accessed: 28 March 2022).

Reyes, X.A. (2014) *Body Gothic: Corporeal Transgression in Contemporary Literature and Horror Film*. Cardiff: University of Wales Press.

Rieder, J. (1982) 'Embracing the Alien: Science Fiction in Mass Culture', *Science Fiction Studies*, 9(1), pp. 26–37.

Roberts, A. (2014) *Get Started in: Writing Science Fiction and Fantasy*. London: Hachette UK.

Roberts, A. (2015) '*Aurora* by Kim Stanley Robinson review – "the best generation starship novel I have ever read"', *The Guardian*, Available at: https://www.theguardian.com/books/2015/jul/08/aurora-kim-stanley-robinson-review-science-fiction (Accessed: 11 September 2022).

Robinson, K.M. (2022) 'Sociopath v. Psychopath: What's the Difference?' Available at: https://www.webmd.com/mental-health/features/sociopath-psychopath-difference (Accessed: 5 Aug 2022).

Roddenberry, G. and Coon, G.L. (1968) 'Bread and Circuses'. *Star Trek*.

Romance Writers of America. (N.D.) 'Romance Trailblazers', Available at: https://www.rwa.org/Online/Awards/RITA/romance_trailblazers.aspx (Accessed: 7 March 2022).

Roush, W. (2020) *Extraterrestrials*. Cambridge, Massachusetts: MIT Press.

Ruggeri, A. (2016) How Bedlam became London's most iconic symbol', *BBC Culture*, Available at: https://www.bbc.com/culture/article/20161213-how-bedlam-became-a-palace-for-lunatics (Accessed: 5 Aug 2022).

Ryman, G. (2015) Panel: 'Arcadia or Armageddon? An exploration of utopian and dystopian futures'. At Nine Worlds GeekFest, 7-9 August. London.

San Miguel, M.F. (2018) 'Appropriated Bodies', *Atlantis*, 40(2), pp. 27–44.

Sargent, L.T. (1994) 'The Three Faces of Utopianism Revisited', *Utopian Studies*, 5(1), pp. 1–37.

Saulter, S. (2015) Panel: 'Arcadia or Armageddon? An exploration of utopian and dystopian futures'. At Nine Worlds GeekFest, 7-9 August. London.

Sawyer, A. (2011) 'The Science Fiction Short Story', in Cox, Alisa (ed.), *Teaching the Short Story*. London: Palgrave, p. 96–116.

Scharmen, F. (2015) 'What Is a Big Dumb Object?', *Journal of Architectural Education*, 69(2), pp. 178–186.

Schonfeld, Z. (2015) 'Parental Advisory Forever: An Oral History of the PMRC's War on Dirty Lyrics', *Newsweek*, Available at: https://www.newsweek.com/2015/10/09/oral-history-tipper-gores-war-explicit-rock-lyrics-dee-snider-373103.html (Accessed: 19 July 2022).

Shirley, J. (2011) 'Splatterpunk Utopia: In Defense of Violent Entertainment', Available at: https://gizmodo.com/splatterpunk-utopia-in-defense-of-violent-entertainmen-5828246 (Accessed: 15 August 2022).

Shurin, J. (2015) 'New Releases: *The Goblin Emperor* by Katherine Addison', *Pornokitsch*, Available at: https://www.pornokitsch.com/2015/01/new-releases-the-goblin-emperor-by-katherine-addison.html (Accessed: 24 September 2022).

Skipp, J. and Spector, C. (1989) 'On Going Too Far, or Flesh-Eating Fiction: New Hope for the Future' in Skipp, J. and Spector, C. (eds), *Book of the Dead*. London and New York: Bantam Books, p. 10.

Slusser, G.E. and Rabkin, E.S. (1987) 'Introduction: The Anthropology of the Alien' in Slusser, G.E. and Rabkin, E.S. (eds.), *Aliens: The Anthropology of Science Fiction*. Carbondale: Southern Illinois University, pp. vii–xxi.

Smith, A. and Hughes, W. (eds.) (2013) *EcoGothic*. Manchester: Manchester University Press.

Smith, Nadine (2021) 'How Body Horror Movies Helped Me Process Gender Dysphoria', *Them*, Available at: https://www.them.us/story/body-horror-gender-dysphoria-essay (Accessed: 13 Aug 2022).

Smith, Noah (2018) Available at: https://twitter.com/Noahpinion/status/1002598573316247552 (Accessed: 25 July 2022).

Sonofbaldwin (2015) 'Humanity Not Included: DC's Cyborg and the Mechanization of the Black Body', *The Middle Spaces*, Available at: https://themiddlespaces.com/2015/03/31/humanity-not-included/ (Accessed: 19 July 2022).

Spark, A.S. (2019) 'Grimdark and Nihilism', *Grimdark Magazine*, Available at: https://www.grimdarkmagazine.com/grimdark-and-nihilism/ (Accessed: 6 Aug 2022).

Spiers, M.C.B. (2021) *Encountering the Sovereign Other: Indigenous Science Fiction*. Lansing: Michigan State University Press.

SPIN staff (2019) 'William Gibson: Our 1988 Interview', Available at: https://www.spin.com/2019/08/william-gibson-mona-lisa-overdrive-neuromancer-december-1988-interview-new-romancer/ (Accessed: 29 July 2022).

Springett, J. (2017) 'Solarpunk: A Reference Guide', Available at: https://medium.com/Solarpunks/Solarpunk-a-reference-guide-8bcf18871965 (Accessed: 22 July 2022).

Stableford, B.M. (2021) 'Dystopias'. in Clute, J. and Langford, D. (eds.), *The Encyclopedia of Science Fiction*, Available at: https://sf-encyclopedia.com/entry/dystopias (Accessed: 22 June 2022).

Stableford, B.M. and Clute, J. (2022) 'Lovecraft, H P'. in Clute, J. and Langford, D. (eds.), *The Encyclopedia of Science Fiction*, Available at: https://sf-encyclopedia.com/entry/lovecraft_h_p (Accessed: 31 August 2022).

Stableford, B.M. and Langford, D. (2022) 'Military SF'. in Clute, J. and Langford, D. (eds.), *The Encyclopedia of Science Fiction*, Available at: https://sf-encyclopedia.com/entry/military_sf (Accessed: 19 July 2022).

Stableford, B.M. and Langford, D. (2022) 'Utopias'. in Clute, J. and Langford, D. (eds.), *The Encyclopedia of Science Fiction*, Available at: https://sf-encyclopedia.com/entry/utopias (Accessed: 19 July 2022).

Stableford, B.M., Langford, D. and Clute, J. (2022) 'Robots'. in Clute, J. and Langford, D. (eds.), *The Encyclopedia of Science Fiction*, Available at: https://sf-encyclopedia.com/entry/robots (Accessed: 19 July 2022).

Stapledon, O. (1999; 1937) *Star Maker*. London: Gateway.

Stefanie. (2021) '19 Books Like Outlander: Scottish Time Travel Books For People Who Like Outlander', Available at: https://greatbritishbookclub.com/19-books-like-outlander-scottish-time-travel-books-for-people-who-like-outlander/ (Accessed 2 March 2022).

Steinberg, D. (dir.) (1998) 'The One with Phoebe's Uterus'. *Friends*. Season 4, Episode 11.

Sterling, B. (1986) 'Preface', *Mirrorshades: The Cyberpunk Anthology*. Westminster, Maryland: Arbor House.

Strother, A. (2019) 'James Tiptree Jr', in Levy, M.M. and Mendlesohn, F. (eds.), *Aliens in Popular Culture*. Santa Barbara, CA: Greenwood, pp. 273–274.

Suvin, D. (1992) *Positions and Presuppositions in Science Fiction*. Kent: Kent State University Press.

'Swordsmen and Sorcerers' Guild of America (SAGA)'. (2010) *Academic Dictionaries and Encyclopedias, Wikimedia Foundation*, Available at: https://en-academic.com/dic.nsf/enwiki/1857647 (Accessed: 8 Aug 2022).

Temple, E. (2017) 'Margaret Atwood on What It's Like To Watch Her Own Dystopia Come True', Available at: https://lithub.com/margaret-atwood-on-what-its-like-to-watch-her-own-dystopia-come-true/ (Accessed: 28 March 2022).

Tharoor, I. (2015) 'How *Game of Thrones* drew on the Wars of the Roses', *The Guardian*, Available at: https://www.theguardian.com/books/2015/may/29/game-of-thrones-war-of-roses-hbo (Accessed: 25 July 2022).

Thomas, G. W. (2020) 'A Brief History of Sword & Sorcery', *Dark Worlds Quarterly*, Available at: https://darkworldsquarterly.gwthomas.org/a-brief-history-of-sword-sorcery/ (Accessed: 9 Aug 2022).

Thornton, J. (2017) '*Agents of Dreamland* by Caitlín R. Kiernan', *The Fantasy Hive*, Available at: https://fantasy-hive.co.uk/2017/12/agents-of-dreamland-by-caitlin-r-kiernan/ (Accessed: 2 September 2022).

Tolkien, J.R.R. (1988) 'On Fairy-Stories'. *Tree and Leaf*. London: Harper Collins, pp. 1–82.

Tompkins, D. (2014) 'Weird Ecology: On The Southern Reach Trilogy', *Los Angeles Review of Books*, Available at: https://lareviewofbooks.org/article/weird-ecology-southern-reach-trilogy (Accessed: 10 October 2020).

Tranter, K. (2007) '"Frakking Toasters" and Jurisprudences of Technology: The Exception, the Subject and Techné in *Battlestar Galactica*', *Law and Literature*, 19(1), pp. 45–75.

Truffin, S.R. (2008) *Schoolhouse Gothic: Haunted Hallways and Predatory Pedagogues in Late Twentieth-Century American Literature and Scholarship*. Cambridge: Cambridge Scholars Publishing.

Tucker, K. (24 Marchbloom 1991) 'The Splatterpunk Trend, and Welcome to It', *The New York Times*, p. 13.

VanderMeer, J. (2018) *Wonderbook: The Illustrated Guide to Creating Imaginative Fiction, Revised & Expanded*. New York: Abrams Image.

Vann, M.R., MPH. (2014) 'The 10 Worst Mental Health Treatments in History', *Everyday Health*, Available at: https://www.everydayhealth.com/pictures/worst-mental-health-treatments-history/ (Accessed: 5 Aug 2022).

Vredenburgh, F. (2014) 'Review of *Griots: Sisters of the Spear*', in Davis, M.J. and Saunders, C.R. (eds.), Blackgate, Available at: https://www.blackgate.com/2014/01/14/griots-sisters-of-the-spear-edited-by-milton-j-davis-and-charles-r-saunders/ (Accessed: 9 Aug 2022).

Warner, M. (2014) *Once Upon a Time: A short history of fairy tale*. Oxford University Press.

Wells, H.G. (2022) *The Time Machine*, Available at: https://www.gutenberg.org/files/35/35-h/35-h.htm (Accessed: 16 Aug 2022).

Westfahl, G. (2005) 'Aliens in Space', in Westfahl, G. (ed.), *The Greenwood Encyclopedia of Science Fiction and Fantasy: Themes, Works, and Wonders*, Vol. 1. Westport, Conn.: Greenwood Press, pp. 14–16.

Wheale, N. (1995) *The Postmodern Arts: An Introductory Reader*. London: Routledge.

White, C.J. (2021) '5 Modern Cyberpunk Stories', Available at: https://www.tor.com/2021/03/26/5-modern-cyberpunk-stories/ (Accessed: 30 July 2022).

Williams, R. (1978) 'Utopia and Science Fiction', *Science Fiction Studies*, 5(3), pp. 203–214.

Winter, D.E. (2002) *Clive Barker: The Dark Fantastic*. London: HarperCollins.

Wisker, G. (2015) 'Disturbances, Disorder, Destruction, Disease: Horror Fiction Today'. In Berberich, C. (ed.) *The Bloomsbury Introduction to Popular Fiction*. London: Bloomsbury, pp. 129–146.

Wolf, M.J.P. (2012) *Building Imaginary Worlds: The Theory and History of Subcreation*. New York: Routledge.

Wolfe, G.K. (2012) *Evaporating Genres: Essays on Fantastic Literature*. Middletown, CT: Wesleyan University Press.

Yuhas, A. (2021) 'It's Time to Revisit the Satanic Panic', *The New York Times*, Available at: https://www.nytimes.com/2021/03/31/us/satanic-panic.html (Accessed: 19 July 2022).

Zipes, J. (1992) *Breaking the Spell: Radical Theories of Folk and Fairy Tales*. New York: Routledge.

Zipes, J. (1991) *Fairy Tales and the Art of Subversion: The Classical Genre for Children and the Process of Civilization*. New York: Routledge.

Zipes, J. ed. (2014). 'Introduction: Rediscovering the Original Tales of the Brothers Grimm'. *The Original Folk & Fairy Tales of the Brothers Grimm: The Complete First Edition*. by Grimm, Jacob and Wilhelm. Zipes, J. trans. Princeton and Oxford: Princeton University Press, pp. xix–xliii